ISLAM
AMONG
THE SPIRES
An Oxford Reverie

Kenneth Cragg

Kenneth Cragg.
14. viii. 04

By the same author

Readings in the Qur'an, 1st ed. 1988, 2nd ed. 1999

With God in Human Trust: Christian Faith and Contemporary Humanism, 1999

The Weight in the Word: Prophethood: Biblical and Quranic, 1999
(These from Sussex Academic Press)

The Event of the Qur'an: Islam in its Scripture,
1st ed. 1971, 2nd ed. 1994

City of Wrong. A Friday in Jerusalem, trans. from Muhammad Kamil
Husain's *Qaryah Zalimah*, 1994
(From Oneworld Publications, Oxford)

ISLAM
AMONG
THE SPIRES
An Oxford Reverie

Kenneth Cragg

MELISENDE
London

Islam among the Spires
by Kenneth Cragg

ISBN 1 901764 18 4

First published 2000 by
Melisende
39 Chelmsford Road
London E18 2PW
Tel. +44 (0)20 84989768
Fax +44 (0)20 85042558
E mail: melisende@cwcom.net
www.melisende.cwc.net

Editor: Leonard Harrow

Printed at the St Edmundsbury Press, England

FOREWORD

It was fifteen years ago that the Centre for Islamic Studies was established in Oxford. Whilst not being part of the University of Oxford, it falls into the rather curious category of institutions in Oxford which are described as 'Other institutions not belonging to the University but having some association with it'. The Centre's presence in Oxford has not been without controversy, predominantly in connection with its quest for a permanent home. That matter, however, is now resolved and to the spires of Oxford will be added a new tower, if not a minaret.

So much for the institutional, but what of the intellectual? How are we to view this manifestation of Islam in Oxford's midst? What Kenneth Cragg does in this book is to address a range of issues which may be perceived to have a Christian, an Islamic and a secular perspective; and he does this through an Oxford optic. Mapping the path to the challenges of monotheistic religions today are Matthew Arnold and his 'Gipsy'; but in the process we learn much of the place of Arabic, and thus of Islamic writings, in Oxford from the early 17th century onwards. This story owes much to Edward Pococke, a towering figure through much of that troubled century in Oxford—the 'pioneer of Oxford Arabic'. Indeed, it is only over the past 100 years or so that the study of Arabic and Islam regained momentum from Pococke's time through, as the author outlines, the work of Margoliouth and Gibb and, more recently, in terms of politics and state, that of Hourani.

Having established Oxford's historical links with Islamic studies, Kenneth Cragg then takes the work and ideas of a number of distinguished Oxford 'figures'—for example, Cardinal Newman, John Ruskin, Thomas Valpy French (a 19th-century rector of St Ebbe's), J R R Tolkien, Philip Larkin, Iris Murdoch—and through their ideas addresses a range of difficult and challenging issues in relation to Islam. These are best encapsulated in the question: 'What has Oxford to offer to Islam?'; but they cover such issues as the need within a university context to be open to the challenges of all knowledge, the impact of Western thought on

Islam in an ever-more globalised world, how in that world to engage with the current debates on gender and sexuality, the confrontation (for both Christianity and Islam) with the secularism of today, and the challenges for absolutism.

Kenneth Cragg here evidences a rare ability to weave together the history of Islamic and Arabic study in Oxford and the perspectives of eminent Oxonians, with the current challenges for the interface of Christianity and Islam. This work confirms the view expressed to me recently that the author is 'the outstanding Christian scholar in Britain of contemporary Islamic faith'.

Peter North
22 June 2000

PREFACE

'On the morning of the 23rd I left the observatory. I have never seen Oxford since, excepting its spires, as they are seen from the railway.' Readers familiar with John Henry Newman remember these farewelling words in his *Apologia pro Vita Sua*. The spires are still there but today's traveller is more likely to see from the railway an Institute of Business Studies. The sad Newman was not interested in the arrival platform though—as he wrote—he had earlier thought of 'the snapdragon growing on the walls opposite my freshman's rooms ... as the emblem of my own perpetual residence even unto death in my University.'

Spires are more perpetual symbols of permanence than 'causes', while for students 'residence' is very transitory. Little wonder, then, that the poet, Matthew Arnold, should opt like Newman for 'the spires' when he mused of 'lost causes'. His now famous words have become almost a synonym for the university. He saw the spires to better advantage, from the hills above Cumnor and the Hinkseys in the dream of his 'scholar gypsy' who had also 'left the University.'

Those departing have never deterred those arriving. The turn of a millennium sees a minaret negotiating to stand 'among the spires', on behalf of the Oxford Centre for Islamic Studies which was founded in 1985 and has been fruitfully operating from large premises in George Street in the City Centre. It has the approval of the University's Hebdomadal Council which is committed to the fullest practical co-operation with the aims of the Centre.

These are to encourage world-wide links between scholars and institutions towards a more informed awareness of Islam, its past, present and future. Saluting the University's own long tradition of the study of Islam, it seeks to promote a trans-disciplinary scholarship and research while offering teaching in languages and Islamic thought at every level, some of its Fellows holding also College Fellowships to this end. It proposes Junior and Visiting scholarships for research in Islamics as well as studentships at various levels, and programmes of lectures, conferences and publications.

The design for its permanent location on ground provided by Magdalen College has been under prolonged discussion with Oxford City Council and its sub-committees, with a view to adequate accommodation for students and offices, with the appropriate amenities—prayer-hall, lecture halls, library and tower. These are architecturally Islamic in their design and decor while meant to belong harmoniously with the Oxford tradition of stone and spire, in full collegiate style. Its *Journal of Islamic Studies* is already in flow.

Islam is no new arrival in the University. It was centuries ahead of the railway when pilgrims of learning came down on foot over Shotover and sought out long forgotten hospices, like White Hall or Stapledon Hall lying beneath successor Colleges, or repaired to priories and monastic houses, like those now buried under Westgate Centre. But an Islam, as it were, 'under its own management' is a new phenomenon deserving a welcome from the old.

Accordingly, the purpose of 'Islam among the Spires' in these pages is to have the sundry themes of academic Islam today cluster around an array of Oxford personalities whose mind and story readily focus the issues the Centre must confront. It is no part of this book to determine the intellectual pattern of the Centre's *raison d'être*. Only the Centre has that task as the onus of its presence. Yet it may be possible from outside to muse—no more—on what it might be. Hence the sub-title 'An Oxford Reverie'. So much of what appertains to the OCIS has been broached in other idiom by a medley of Oxonians across the years. What is academic freedom? What 'the idea of a University'? How should definitive faith, with a sacrosanct Scripture, relate to the widening universe of knowledge? What of contemporary feminism and the dogmas that long excluded or baited it—here in Oxford and in the long tradition of a patriarchal Islam?

Or how does religion handle irreversible and ubiquitous technology? How might it arrest—in duly valid terms which are not those of assertive dogma—the current pride of science and the tide of mechanisms that flow unbidden into society, sexuality and mind-set? No less urgent—how may religious faith hear and heed the latent, or raucous, agnosticism, the insistent secularity, of culture today? In and through all these—what of the converse of religions both inside their trusted sanctuaries and in the open market of a University? How do they address the tensions within their own houses between schools of thought and the passions of intellectual protectionism in conflict with the uncoercing, uncoerced will to understand and gently to commend?

The questions multiply. They have long been brooding under the spires. The chapters that follow belong with their legend and may perhaps give it a conversing voice responsive to the new dimension of an Islamic presence. *Dominus illuminatio mea* Oxford chose long ago to shape its mind and destiny. For many it has become more enigmatic than once it was. The Muslim's Qur'an knows it well enough, if without that *mea* in the cry *Deus illuminatio est* (Surah 24.35). Perhaps the heart of our reverie now is *illuminatio nostra* as both our assurance and our aspiration—unless, like Thomas Hardy's peasant menfolk, we play dice by the light of glow-worms.

Kenneth Cragg
Oxford
June, 2000

I am indebted to Sir Peter North, CBE, QC, DCL, FBA, Vice-Chancellor of the University from 1993 to 1997, and Principal of Jesus College since 1984, for his kind Foreword to *Islam among the Spires*, and to Leonard Harrow, editor of Melisende, for his patient editorial care and expertise.

'The state of being engaged in musing.'

Oxford English Dictionary 'Reverie'.

'The spire cranes.'

Dylan Thomas

'In whose blent air all our compulsions meet,
Are recognised and robed as destinies.'

Philip Larkin, 'Church Going'.

'I thought you would cost no more than money.'

William Golding, 'The Spire'.

'Universal sympathies cannot make a man inconsistent.'

Elizabeth—to Robert—Browning.

'Is there so small a range
In the present strength of manhood
That the high imagination cannot freely fly?'

John Keats

The *Sunnah*, interpreting that of the Prophet himself, is co-extensive with
the 'Consensus' of the Muslim Community—essentially an ever expanding
process ... The real genius of the Tradition—to show how these may be
made operative again ... the necessary prerogative of creating and recreat-
ing the content.'

Fazlur Rahman

'Men gave thee nothing but this happy quest ...
And still the haunt beloved a virtue yields.'

Matthew Arnold

CONTENTS

Chapter 1

THE DREAMING OF THE SPIRES

i

For the poet of the famous sentiment we must know his to have been disturbed slumbers. The memorable lines about 'the dreaming spires' came from a notable son of the place. There are even surer reasons for having the Arnold of the poetry preside over this Chapter's introit to the issues turning on the present 'official' arrival of Islam in Oxford.[1]

Matthew Arnold is as good a mentor as any for the duties of religion in the contemporary scene. He spoke from within a Victorian agnosticism which breathed a strange dejection, a febrile melancholy, over the instincts of worship and the confidence of dogma. It is one which, in the changed terms of a millennial turn of history's calendar, still persists; and one which, broadly, Islam is yet to engage, reluctant as Islam has always shown itself for rigorous doubt of itself or a readiness for things tragic and conjectural.[2]

First we have to ponder what Arnold intended by his celebrated words. They belong with two poems, 'The Scholar Gipsy' and 'Thyrsis', in which he sang of wanderings across Oxford's western hills, through the villages of Cumnor and the Hinkseys and the meadows of Bablockhythe. He took from Joseph Glanvill, of Exeter and Lincoln Colleges (1636-80), the legend of a student who forsook his university out of disillusion or frustration to brood among the hills and commune with nature. The youth became a symbol of mystery, a wry comment on the pretensions of the donnish world and a story fit to carry the veiled

---

[1] 'Official' that is, in the form of an endowed enterprise under the formal patronage of the university and with an approved physical location and academic tenure. Islam, as we must see in other chapters, has long been a presence in the university with roots in the Middle Ages.

[2] It has often been noted that there have been few deep sceptics, few tragic figures in Islam, committed as Islam has been to 'great victory' and 'evident success', and equipped with a Scripture 'in which there is no dubiety' (Surah 2.2). The Shi'ah are the exception—see Chapter 7 and Chapter 2, note 38.

mystery of Arnold's own self-commentary as a 'failed' poet.[3] The hints and queries enshrined in 'The Scholar Gipsy' were a vehicle well suited, some twelve years later, for a threnody, 'Thyrsis', which Arnold wrote following the death of his friend and fellow denizen of those hills, Arthur Hugh Clough (1819-61).[4] It is well to be alert to the musings whence his cryptic praise of Oxford flowed.

> And that sweet city with her dreaming spires,
> She needs not June for beauty's heightening.
> Lovely all times she lies, lovely tonight.[5]

'The winter eve was warm'—hence the note about 'not needing June.' Are there those who would now murmur a gloss:

> She needs not mosque for beauty's heightening?

Elsewhere in the Preface to his *Essays in Criticism*, at around the time of 'Thyrsis', Arnold enlarged on that beauty in a mood of rapture.

> 'Beautiful city! So venerable, so lovely, so unravaged by the fierce intellectual light of our century, so serene! ... adorable dreamer whose heart has been so romantic, whispering from her lovers the last enchantments of the Middle Age ... home of lost causes and forsaken beliefs.'[6]

Are we to conclude that he was admiring a medieval relic with a benign—and thereby a culpable if prized—immunity from the turmoil of the real world, so far from 'the naked shingles' of lost faith he had memorably painted in his 'Dover Beach', that other threnody for lost religion?

---

[3] Cf. 'That inner fracture or fault in Arnold's will to continue as a poet was caused by his revolt against intuition and his belief in a more rational outlook.' Park Honan, *Matthew Arnold: A Life*, London, 1981, p. 279.

[4] Thyrsis was a shepherd in Virgil's *Eclogues*. The poem so named refers back to 'The Scholar Gipsy' and its pastoral, dirge-like quality has been read as marking the waning of Arnold's poetic muse. Yet, with its 'mist and hum of the majestic Oxus' in the East, it has little to say of Clough's work and quality, for all the ardour round his memory of him as Arnold's 'acolyte'.

[5] Matthew Arnold, *The Poems*, ed. Kenneth Allott, London, 1965, 'Thyrsis', p. 499.

[6] Matthew Arnold, *Lectures and Essays in Criticism*, ed. R H Super, Ann Arbor, 1962, Preface, p. 290.

Arnold's poetry loved to be exclamatory. 'So serene!'—'adorable dreamer!' It seems odd that he could have visualised his Oxford oblivious of 'fierce intellectual light'. Had it not been well nigh convulsed by John Henry Newman's defection to Rome and the sharp controversies around it? Or was it that Arnold saw these as out 'of our century', an irrelevance that only confirmed how far gone in dreams his Oxford was? If he was indulging a deep emotion, he was also deep in irony.

It follows that a lively register of Oxford's loveliness cannot stay with the romance without allowing the unease, nor savour the wistfulness and take no count of the yearning. In the spirit of a Matthew Arnold there can be no place for triumphalism in Islam's instalment into Oxford but only for the high seriousness, the search for integrity which, in prose and verse alike, Arnold commended to all education and to theists most of all. That perspective is the reason why we start with him, as a beautiful building is due to be added to the Oxford skyline.

It requires that we explore the point of 'The Scholar Gipsy'. If the 'gipsy' word derives from Egypt, is the poet implying some kind of esoteric search, with English insularity earning his rebuke?[7] His émigré from academia was 'youthful' making his exit the more noteworthy. Yet Arnold thought his friend Clough 'too quick a despairer'. He was himself a lingering one. A certain languid weariness marks the two poems, moving nevertheless with a rare ardour. What is the mystic 'elm tree' they search for in its 'gone-ness'? They keep the spires in sight and 'the line of festal light in Christ Church Hall', but their quest is in the glades and meadows. There are obvious hints of Milton's Lycidas, of Keats and Shelley, while the shade of Wordsworth broods over all.[8] For 'strong is the infection of our mortal strife.' Perhaps Arnold is musing Virgil-like, around the meaning of experience. As Tennyson wrote of Ulysses

---

[7] See *Letters—1848-1888*, London, 1895, ed. G W E Russell, Vol. 1 (1865 written), p. 359. He deplored his country's 'want of knowing how the world is going and must go and of preparing herself accordingly.' 'The English were living as if Muslims, Hindus never existed and lacked any school of Eastern cultures despite having large (political) eastern interests.' Arnold seems to have been unaware of Max Müller (1823-1900) who settled in Oxford in 1848 whose editing of *Sacred Books of the East*, from 1876 went far to remedy the situation at least academically.

[8] The English critic, Quiller-Couch called Arnold 'Wordsworth's Widow'—an unhappy gibe, though the kinship is clear enough.

There is a secret in his breast
Which will never let him rest.[9]

In that very mood Arnold himself was later to write:

Over the whole *Aeneid* there rests an ineffable melancholy:
not a rigid, a moody gloom like the melancholy of Lucretius:
no, a sweet, touching sadness, but still a sadness, a melancholy
which is at once a source of charm in the poem.[10]

One is drawn to the same verdict about the poems of Matthew
Arnold. Charm itself might be their all, the joy and thrill of words their
only *raison d'être*. So any reader might feel in the loveliness in the flow
of 'The Scholar Gipsy'

'As some grave Tyrian trader ...
... snatched his rudder, and shook out more sail,
And day and night held on indignantly
O'er the blue Midland waters, with the gale
Betwixt the Syrtes and soft Sicily,
To where the Atlantic raves
Outside the western straits, and unbent sails
There, where down cloudy cliffs, through sheets of foam,
Shy traffickers, the dark Iberians come:
And on the beach undid his corded bales.[11]

But for what meaning are we entranced? Who is this 'Palestinian',
sighting hostile Greeks and urging his vessel strenuously westward with
a cargo that stays 'unbaled' to us? On one count we do not need to ask.
Yet Arnold was the last poet to stay word-content. He had 'a something
in the breast' to which 'light words bring no rest.' For

There rises an unspeakable desire
After the knowledge of our buried life.[12]

---

[9]   Alfred Lord Tennyson, *Poems and Plays,* Oxford, 1965, 'Ulysses', p. 89, lines 245-6. Arnold
      echoes the theme in 'The Buried Life': 'There's a something in this heart, To which thy light
      words bring no rest,' *op. cit.*, p. 273.

[10] See Lionel Trilling, *Matthew Arnold*, London, 1939, p. 165 and 389.

[11] *The Poems, loc. cit.* 'In Utrumque Paratus', p. 56, lines 37-40.

[12] *Ibid.*, 'The Buried Life', p. 273, lines 47-8.

There is a no less rich lyricism in Islamic poetry—not least among the Persians. For Islamic languages lend themselves to rhetoric and rhythm. But, as we must examine in Chapter 8, they have only rarely registered the depth of self-interrogation Matthew Arnold epitomises. His dreams were troubled ones. His verse almost dried up while he turned his energies to the prose of literary criticism and the heavy business of inspecting the nation's schools. He felt he had failed to achieve the one poem of which he was capable. He lived under the aura of his father, Thomas Arnold (1795-1842), renowned headmaster of Rugby School, and under the fear of a comparably early death. Everything about him made him a fit mentor of the duties housed within religious architecture.

ii

It was not that—to borrow from the later Nietzsche of another place— he somehow thought his 'spires' 'the tombs and monuments of God'. His catechism of them was much more subtle. Were they, perhaps, the presiding genius of academic illusions, purveyors of lost securities, or perpetuators of effete enchantments? Were they neglecting a due moral activism in only pretending to be 'somewhere to grow wise in'? A later contemporary, W B Yeats (1865-1939), might think to 'sail to Byzantium' and have 'the sages standing in God's holy fire' 'be the singing masters of his soul.'[13] But were 'singing masters' the soul's truest need? Arnold's *Culture and Religion* would explore the problem—but perhaps they were only themselves a part of it.

These scrutinies of sincerity in the mind of Matthew Arnold derived from entire immersion in the tutelage of Oxford, just as the self-awareness of Muslims must stem from. the complete resources of their long tradition. Universities, west or east, north or south, can admit no conspiracies of silence. The more they think to inter-fertilise—as we explore in Chapter 3—the more must this be so.

Arnold was a Scholar at Balliol College in 1840 and five years later became a Fellow of Oriel College. During his student years he had listened at St Mary's to John Henry Newman (1801-1890)—of whose intellectual significance more in Chapter 3 and who received Clough into the Roman Church. Thomas Arnold became Regius Professor of

---

[13] W B Yeats, *Collected Poems*, London, 1953, Stanza iii, p. 217.

History while continuing as headmaster at Rugby. Matthew himself was Oxford's Professor of Poetry through two five-year periods, between 1857 and 67. Among his successors at Balliol was Gerard Manley Hopkins (1844-89), a figure well qualified to symbolise the mental toils of Victorian Christianity, while A C Swinburne (1839-1909) challenged accepted standards of faith and conduct in swinging rhythms that had Oxford students parading in them round the city streets. Balliol College would soon reach the peak of its philosophical eminence, with the redoubtable Benjamin Jowett (1817-94) its Master and T H Green, Tutor in Philosophy (1836-82).

Such was the ferment in the nurture that made him the poet he attained to be, with all the while behind him and above him the awesome summons of his father's fame, the summons to discipline and duty. His own title of 'Professor', he said, made him uneasy. Yet 'assume the singing robe' he would, in a will somehow to recruit the western Thames valley as a kind of Grasmere from which to visualise those 'dreaming spires' and draw their academic doubtfulness into a purely aesthetic charm. What indeed was the relation of beauty to truth, of truth to beauty? The poetic charm of Oxford was one with the tryst of loyalties.

There is little to show that Matthew Arnold was acutely alive to Islam. He adapted *Shahnameh's* 'Sohrab and Rustum' in 1853, via Alexander Burnes, who had travelled in Persia during Arnold's childhood, but only to afford a kind of Homer-like study in courage and fate, rather as Shelley had entitled a French-style uprising in the name of liberty 'The Revolt of Islam'. There was also 'The Sick King of Bokhara' where locale mattered little. Remarks in *Essays in Criticism* on a Persian Passion Play we can note anon. His was a different kind of mental yearning from the sensual hedonism of Edward Fitzgerald's *Rubaiyat of Umar Khayyam* (1859). If we are letting Arnold's 'spires' take us into the juncture of Oxford and Islam it can only be in their human terms, for lack of explicit converse between the writer and the Islamic East. Arnold's resources came from Hellenism and the testing legacy of his father's Christianity with its arousal of robust debate in pulpit and pew.

Even so, a non-theologian Arnold can help us monitor the mind and heart of religions and then relate the themes to Islam in preparation for the more explicitly doctrinal concerns of Chapters 8 and 9. Poetry and prose alike, on his part, take us to the liabilities of radical monotheism, Islamic or other, and to the grounds of religious assurance. Stemming from these are its negotiation with culture and its whole responsibility to society both in its own dominant territory and beyond. 'In the sea of life enisled', as Arnold put it—following John Donne—he was addressing more than Oxford in the lines

> Chief dreamer, own thy dream.
> Thy brother world stirs at thy feet unknown,
> Who with a monarch's hath no brother's part,
> Yet doth thine inmost soul with yearning teem.

or with 'The New Sirius'

> ... opinion trembles,
> Judgement shifts, convictions go,
> Life dries up, the heart dissembles—
> Only what we feel we know.[14]

iii

By 'the monarch's part'—seen here as ignoring its brotherly counterpart in lively social conscience—Arnold intends the old Biblical conception of human 'dominion', endowing humankind with an authority over nature, by dint of how nature lavishly enables it. This his Victorian generation proudly enjoyed in the gathering achievements of the industrial sciences and skills, grandly exhibited under the Prince Consort's eager patronage in the great Crystal Palace Exhibition of 1851. It is the irony of all human creaturehood that the context which calls us to the sacred leaves us the option to be thanklessly secular.

The Qur'an is no stranger to this truth. It affirms the human entrustment with the good earth and all its fertile powers. It enjoins perpetual gratitude at the realisation of the human privilege. The obligation to *Zakat* enshrines the social relevance of private wealth, the responsibility of property and income to take 'a brother's part' in the daily scene. The significant contentions between the Semitic faiths in no way diminish this common truth: they only exist because of it. The Qur'an gives no

---

[14] *Poems, loc. cit.,* 'The New Sirius', 38, lines 81-84 and 'In Utrumque Paratus', p. 56, lines 37-40. 'The dreamer' here is humankind, wielding the kingship over nature in techniques of science while evading the social duties of which Arnold cried in 'Dover Beach': 'Ah, love, let us be true to one another ...' The 'trust' to man of the natural order is a salient theme in the Qur'an (cf. Surah 2.30f). See Chapter 9, below.

warrant to its Muslims to academicize their pursuit of its meanings in studious neglect of poverty or injustice, violence or deprivation across its wide dispersion. It needs no Matthew Arnold to tell it so: to sense his kinship would be one way of sharing the spires.

At once another note in his poetry takes on Islamic point. It has to do with the frustrations of prophet-messengers—those mentors sent to summon human creaturehood to the dignity it exercises and, by urgent reminder, to halt its oft forgetfulness. There are striking, if unwitting, accents of the Qur'an in Arnold's poem: 'The Lord's Messengers'. He may well have had in mind the cult of 'heroism' explored in Thomas Carlyle's famous lectures, exalting the destiny of men of power and vision, among whom Carlyle had included Muhammad.[15] Even the conclusion to the poem has an authentic ring for the Islamic mind.

> 'Thus saith the Lord to His own.
> See ye the world below?
> Warfare of man from his birth
> Too long let We them groan:
> Haste, arise ye and go.
> Carry My peace upon earth
>
> Gladly they rise at His call,
> Gladly obey His command.
> Gladly descend to the plain.
> Ah! How few of them all
> Those willing servants shall stand
> In the Master's presence again.
>
> Some in the tumult are lost,
> Baffled, bewildered, they stray,
> Some, as prisoners, draw breath,
> Some, unconquered, are crossed
> (Not yet half through the day)
> By a pitiless arrow of death.

---

[15] The now famous lectures (1840) helped to shape the popular repute of Thomas Carlyle as 'the sage of Chelsea.' His inclusion of Muhammad in 'The Hero as Prophet' used highly dismissive language about the Qur'an but pioneered a fitter appraisal of Muhammad's achievement—one which 20th century Muslim apologists have keenly saluted.

Hardly, hardly, shall one
Come with countenance bright
At the close of the day from the plain,
His Master's errand well done,
Safe through the smoke of the fight,
Back to his Master again.'[16]

    The New Testament parable of the messengers to the vineyard of insurrectionist husbandmen seems Arnold's inspiration here. Could he have known that the Qur'an, based on the same theme of divine 'messengers', had also said: 'Some of them you (Meccans) said were liars and some you put to death'? (Surah 2.87)

    The riddle of human obduracy, of divine unwantedness, is deep not only in Christian faith but in the heart of the Qur'an. For Arnold, in despairing mood, it seemed to spell the ultimate futility of religion as haunting disillusion darkening the human scene. Were life and culture and being itself no more than a diseased unrest? The question makes heavy common ground between all religions and provokes them into their deep temptation—either to respond with a sharpened dogmatism or to concede, as Arnold was prone to do, that faith is only selectively viable as a soulful poetry. In the latter event its dream-quality is the more confirmed.

    It is readily apparent that Islam historically has long been engaged with this issue of Allah's 'messengers' facing the hazards, the indifference, of their societies. It was writ large in the Meccan experience of Muhammad himself.

'When they have seen a chance of trading or amusement
they have gone off after it and left you (s.) standing there.
Say: "The things of God are better than amusement and
commerce."' (Surah 62.11)

    'Say' seems a futile bidding among the deaf. In that context the pagan Meccans did not merely forsake the Prophet's preaching pitch; they sensed his implicit threat to their vested interest in idolatry and pilgrimage and hardened their opposition to the point where Muhammad is described as 'vexing his very soul' over their enmity (18.6).

---

[16] *Op. cit.,* 'The Lord's Messengers', pp. 453-54.

It was out of this impasse of suffering and dismay that the Hijrah came about, the emigration to Medina in prospect of a sanctuary potential of becoming a power-base for the active vindication and establishment of the preached faith. Thus Islam drew its definitive story from the twin facts of Muhammad's vocal mission and its ultimate city-state achievement—the second originating its Hijri Calendar, the years and centuries from 622 AD. Something of the same experience that taught Christianity to understand the world of humankind as a crucifying place *vis-à-vis* the claim and love of God gave Islam, in its differing idiom, its *religio-regio* character. Both characterisations sprang from this central incidence of *antilogia* (as the New Testament calls it), the 'contradiction' that disowns the words and decries the lips of 'messengers' in divine 'sending'.[17] 'Dream' could be the right word to tell of academies if they ignore the realism prophetic adversity signifies. We will need to take the point further later. It was all there, antecedently, in the Hebraic tradition of Hosea, Isaiah and Jeremiah. It underlay the whole depiction of Messianic hope.

The contemporary world of religious concern, confessional and institutional, knows only too well its own version of hard-going in the unheeding world. Any university 'Centre for Islamic Studies' has for a basic liability the presentation of an authentic response to secular disinterest and ill-will. Arnold's 'the judgements shift, convictions go' has more inclusive bearing now. His generation coped confusedly with Charles Darwin, but Freud and Marx, the logical positivists and deconstructionists lay below the horizon. The general drift in the West from attention to wonder, to worship and to duty is more pervasive. The Victorians, for the most part, cared about their agnosticism and gave it a religious fervour in moral anxiety for the public consequences of their private questionings. The kind of residual reverence that characterised the forfeiture of ancestral piety in George Eliot or Thomas Carlyle is less evident now. That being 'out of earshot' Surah 62.11 lamented long ago in Mecca, as a Prophet's pained perplexity, is more chronic in what we might call the secular negligibility of God today.

There is much conjecture about how far this degree of secularity happens in the world of Islam. There are Muslims who suggest that their faith is immune from such inroads and stands exempt from the capitulation it perceives on the part of Christian apologists. However,

---

[17] 'The Epistle to the Hebrews', 12.3.

the sheer stridency of some of its exponents indicates how unsure of itself that thesis is. For misgivings are liable to drown themselves in fresh counter-assertiveness.

Islam, to be sure—like Zionist-minded Judaism—has large political sources of self-assurance that bolster religious expression both social and cultural. It has been pre-occupied for a whole half-century with new political autonomies in the wake of receding Western imperialism. In Pakistan it partitioned a sub-continent in its name and, so doing, generated a massive apologetic for its vindication, while elsewhere in Asia and Africa it has brought its genius to test, mapping itself—we might say—religiously and ideologically simply by placing itself again on the map in these contemporary terms. Impartial observers, surveying the scene, either in the sub-continent, or Saudi Arabia, or Algeria, or Indonesia, can hardly be sanguine with the evidences. Doubtless the hazards have been many, the odds heavy, but at least intellectuals within Islam must have some measure of an enormous self-interrogation. There is no adequate salvation or solution in politicisation alone. Indeed its incidence often only sharpens the demands and reloads the stakes.

While a 'Muslim secularity' might seem a contradiction in terms it has a widespread incidence even inside proper conformity. The way faith-sanctions obtain in Islam can both facilitate and obscure that situation. Avowed apostasy is anathema, but short of it one's formal adherence need not be in question. All faiths know this phenomenon of approximate belonging and partial believing.

There can be no doubt that the factors entailing secularity in the West operate on a world scale. Speed, trade, the information revolution, have made old immunities obsolete. Cultures can no longer isolate themselves, though the fact itself makes their psychic identity more tenacious. Muslims share comparably all the pressures and constraints of current technology and are liable to draw the same conclusions about a secular humanism 'on its own' in a cosmos of human loneliness, far from the old Islamic terms of omnipresent, omnicompetent, omniscient divinity 'close as the jugular vein.' The self-interrogation that presses on the private soul and the communal faith from the 'findings' of the sciences has no less a burden for the mind in the household of Islam. The slumbers that dream under spires are likely to be uneasy ones if they keep authentic waking hours.

Are religious faith and practice then like a failing academy a 'scholar gipsy' must leave, letting hallowed learning give way to mystical poetic search as the only relief from public fruitlessness and private grief? Where are 'the Lord's messengers' now? For whom do they still come? The Qur'an always taught that they had been a long, unfailing sequence from the time of fabled Enoch, with no people lacking its *ummi*, its 'native',[18] apostle? Why has the succession ceased? Given its alleged age-long urgency and comprehensive tribal incidence, why should our darkened place and time not enjoy its resumption? If, as the Qur'an teaches, its own finality is irrepeatable, what does that require of the trustees, the present heirs, of its vital uniqueness as 'the seal of prophethood'? What manner of exegetes ought *zawiyas* ('corners' in the mosque) and Islamic centres to be?

For their marketplaces, their city schools, their campuses, are liable, if not alert, to secular interrogation. So, too, are their novelists. Arnold's reverie in verse about the fate of Allah's 'messengers' finds— all unknowingly—a strange reverberation in the most celebrated of living Egyptian writers, Najib Mahfuz. In his *Awlad Haratina*, (English title: 'Children of Gebalawi') he sets in the thug-ridden quarters of a timeless Cairo, the stories—under disguised names—of three 'messengers' in sequence, Moses, Jesus and Muhammad. Though differing, in their quality and cast of mind, they all experience hostility and ambiguous 'success'. They face intimidation, each handling it in his own idiom. What they achieve is found to be short-lived. After their demise their followers fall out among themselves. Evil re-instates its power and, like a refrain, in every case things revert to what they always were.[19]

Elsewhere in a long flow of acute narrative power, Najib Mahfuz depicts what 'dreaming spires' may monumentally overlook—sordid biographies, social pathos, boredom, human lostness and private perplexity. In his different context this is no less a register than Arnold's poesy of the realities religious faith supposedly measures, fathoms and redeems. Contemporary writing, all in the same vein, can readily be found across all the lands of the mosque. A sense of betrayal over the inadequacy of responsive reckoning with this mood from within the custody of dogma

---

[18] A pivotal word used of Muhammad (in Surah 7.157-58). Often translated 'native' or 'illiterate' the likeliest meaning is 'from a people not (yet) scriptured.' The 'illiteracy'—it would seem— is not that of a complete inability to read or write but rather that Arabs were not (yet) people of their own Book. See further my *The Event of the Qur'an*, London, 1971, Oxford, 1994, p. 56 f. The Qur'an's prophets are of and to their own people, this being part of their credential.

[19] There are now numerous translations of the novels of Najib Mahfuz (born 1912). *Awlad Haratina* first appeared in English (trans. P Stewart) in 1981, with a subsequent revision, 1997. See also Rashed el-Enany, *Naguib Mahfuz: The Pursuit of Meaning*, London, 1993.

only contributes to its increase. Are we to conclude—as Arnold's lines and Arab writing join oddly to suggest—that we, in our humanness, are characters in a play its author has abandoned, leaving us to devise the plot as, distractedly, we may?[20]

iv

The intellectual obligations of religious authority in Islam may usefully be deferred to Chapters 3 and 8. They can be prefaced here by several related issues. Foremost among them is the distinction, within the theme of secularity, urgently to be made between a 'secular polity in the state' and thorough-going disavowal of the religious meaning of human life. Though they may inter-act, they by no means coincide. A secular polity argues the state's 'indifference' to the religious allegiance, if any, of the citizen/subject in respect of entire liberty of worship and conviction and the equal exercise of rights and duties within the law.

Such a polity, in contemporary terms, in no way necessitates disowning the historical identity (impossible anyway) of a continuing, tradition of majority faith, so long as it is not oppressive or legally advantaged over against minorities. This posture of operative 'neutrality' between religions in society *may* be used to argue that religious faith is pure optionality—an attitude all genuine conviction must deplore. But, rightly conceived and interpreted, it by no means underwrites that notion. On the contrary, it can be seen as the most ultimately 'religious' shape of religious society in its avowed care for the freedoms which alone can sustain authentic faith. It has the potential to invigorate majorities and minorities alike. It can honestly present itself as the essential form of *Shari'ah*, in the light of the Qur'an's own reading of faith-diversity even to the point of plural forms and liturgies.[21] As we must see shortly, it also has much to contribute to the psychic health of religious institutions,

---

[20] So 'Empedocles on Etna', Act ii. 'Baffled for ever and still thought and mind / will hurry us with them on their homeless march.' *Poems, op cit.*, p. 189, lines 358-9.

[21] In many passages the Qur'an declares the divine sanction of religious diversity (e.g. 5.48, 11.118, 16.93 and 42.8), if the key word *millah* has that sense. 2.148 and 5.48 could be read as even explicit sanction for differing rituals or liturgies. Some exegetes suggest that later abrogation may be assumed in such cases when Islam became more self-sufficient. The fact that no people lacked its 'prophet' might allow such a status to the Buddha or Plato, though authentic prophets all had the same message—that of the Qur'an. Mutual emulation of communities is commended in these verses.

whether 'established' or 'sectarian'—a matter of which Arnold thought his Oxford should be kept well aware.[22]

Understood in the juridical sense such secularity is a far cry from the sort that means and intends entire repudiation of divine 'messengers', seeing humans as 'on their own', their rendezvous of worship as no more than ' the tomb of God'. The response to this ultimate version of the ambiguous 'secular' on the part of 'people of faith' needs to be discerning. It is pointless merely to insist on divine Lordship as something that excluded human *khilafah* or entrustment. It would be futile merely to cry *Allahu akbar* without acknowledgement of His deputing of liabilities creaturely to us—these being the sure token of His greatness.

More philosophical aspects of this issue must come in chapters following. The case here returns us to what we noted earlier about humans as 'chief dreamers' being 'monarchs' in the good earth. To hold to a dogma of divine omnicompetence in absolute terms that disavow and disown the divine magnanimity evident in our creaturehood, its powers and responsibilities, is not to know how that competence presides. We can only be 'absolute for God' in being infinitely grateful with, and awesomely reverent about, our undoubted *amanah*, or 'entrustedness'.[23]

The God of the Bible and the Qur'an is no Greek-style tyrant, chaining a pretentious Prometheus to the rock out of jealousy about what he might do with the sun he willed to harness. Have we not done this, implementing beyond their first meanings the point of Surah 56.71: 'Do you see the (nuclear) fire you kindle?' Nor is He like the deities of pagan superstition—fickle, tedious and benevolent or malevolent by turns and nothing long. A right theism embraces the human autonomy in order rightly to read it in the wonder that hallows it and—only wisely so— worships the Almighty Giver. It tells the secular in ancient words: 'Be fruitful, multiply, have dominion via plough and wheel, via spade and flint and fire, via the implosive and explosive power you will uncover and harness in the shape that nature tells.'

---

[22] In *St Paul and Protestantism*, London, 1869, and elsewhere, he saw how sectarianism imprisoned its people in narrowness and induced an introverted self-importance as the psychic consequence of confined mental scope. See further Chapter 2.

[23] *Amanah* (Surahs 2.30f and 33.72, with 7.172) is a key-term in Islam as the 'trust' offered to and taken up by humankind in its creaturely *khilafah* over creation, the 'viceregency' we exercise. Some are minded to interpret the *amanah* as only, or also, the duties of religion and the chastity of women. The point is noted more fully in Chapters 6 and 9.

With all that mandate, however, it will urge what—because of it—is mandatory, of modesty and charity, of awe and fear, of dignity and liability, of thankfulness and righteous dealing. It might be said that we can only be intelligently theist in being also wisely humanist—for one and the same reason, namely the sure sovereignty of Allah. Chapter 9 returns to this ruling theme.

It is evident, in any event, that the findings and attainments of modern technology cannot be disinvented or unscrambled. Religious faiths, eastern or western, have to know them as irreversible and requiring to be reined in, inside their comprehension as enlarging obligation both social and economic. Laboratories must not be allowed to become a law unto themselves, nor the resulting structures of technology an autocracy of invention, with the maxim: 'Since we can we may.' This is the warning of Quranic theism in today's world. It can more wholesomely be heard and heeded if it stands only in the binding power of its own authenticity as the witness of its academies and the guiding light of its sciences. The vocation is eminently sharable across all human faiths. For they are all caught in the same destiny through time and place.

This, perhaps we may say, is akin to that *Labbaika* in the Meccan pilgrimage, with which the pilgrim announces himself as consciously 'present' before Allah. 'Here I am'—doubly here by ritual duty and by personal endeavour (for the word is in the dual though on one mouth). It is in that way a rite may tell—and transact—an attitude, a habit. Only so does the sacred know itself, not as an implacable adversary of the secular but as holding the secret of its welfare and its proper destiny. The wise theist both welcomes and warns techniques and wills their due—but perilously conditioned—prosperity. It is in both welcome and wisdom that theism—if it truly knows itself—greets and hallows the manifold works of human hands. Only so doing does it keep its own sanity, away from stridency and the arrogance of unyielding dogma.

There is thus a strange paradox in Matthew Arnold's poetic plea: 'Chief dreamer, own thy dream.' By 'own' he meant concede that dream is all it is. The meaning of the foregoing, however, is that we 'own' it for the hallowing vision it truly is, the due and liberating perception of the sacred in the secular, of the secular for the sacred. We have to take Arnold's proximate unfaith ('Sophocles heard it long ago') as illuminating the real measure of its opposite. He alerts us by the very fervour of his yearning, as when—in 'Dover Beach'—he wrote of 'the world that seems to lie before us like a land of dreams.' Then, we recall, he was returning from his honeymoon. Was it only for that reason he added: '... so various, so beautiful, so new'—the very terms that justify the theist, the Christian and the Muslim?

v

Christianity resolves the secular/sacred theme by the same accent on creation, creaturehood and 'dominion' we have seen in Islam. The common ground is important. It is deepened for Christian faith in the further perception of redemption, that is, of 'God in Christ'. The 'priesthood' flowing from this has too long been discounted, hardly ever seriously studied, among Muslims. It needs to figure in the purview of the Oxford Centre. Matthew Arnold, too, for his part missed it in bringing the Jesus of that 'God in Christ' into the embrace of his agnosticism.

> Now he is dead, far hence he lies
> In that lorn Syrian town
> And on his grave with shining eyes
> The Syrian stars look down.[24]

He was thus left to the poetry of a religious mysticism—(religion as the poetry of life)—and a noble moralism with no central sacrament.

When the New Testament spoke of us as 'kings and priests' there was an echo of the Hebraic theme of 'a holy nation' and 'a royal priesthood'—a transfer of adjectives whereby political nationhood was meant for 'consecration under God' and 'peoplehood' to understand itself as 'hallowed'. This concept gave Hebraic expression, in terms of Sinaitic law, to the universal human calling we have examined in *khilafah*, 'dominion'. In this reading of our human-ness all that is material, economic, political and social is a 'priesthood', a capacity for being known and accepted as 'under God'. In this way we are all 'priests' of our own personhood, our own sexuality, of all in which we express and fulfil ourselves.

Islam has shown much resistance to the 'priest'-word—by derivation a shortening of the Greek word, *presbyteros*, meaning an 'elder' in the Christian community. This basic sense of a personal 'priesthood' that 'consecrates' all its powers and impulses, its skills and purposes, to

---

[24] *Poems, op. cit.*, 'Obermann once more', p. 527, lines 173-76.

God, is the setting of the other dimension that derives from Christian understanding of the Passion of Jesus. The forgiving love which faith learns there and—in Christ—attributes to God, is the well-spring, when received in penitence, of our pardon and soul-peace. As such, its once-for-all 'happenedness' in history is recalled and celebrated in 'the bread and wine' of Holy Communion or Eucharist (the Thanksgiving), understood as ordained by Jesus for the Church. In turn, those 'elders' who preside over the Christian ritual are doing so in the name of all in a 'priesthood' which stands in the meaning of 'God in Christ', so perceived and received.

They do so under several interpretations of their office. For Christianity is no less diversified than Islam, in the variety of what it would call 'ecclesiology', which might be defined as 'all things reciprocal between community of faith and the faith of community'. Without the term *ecclesia* (which by origin means 'something corporate brought into being') Islam has its 'ecclesiology' in the role of *'ulama'*, the exegetes of the Qur'an, the *fuqaha'* and the muftis who handle the *Shari'ah*. Islam has its sacraments in prayer-prostration, fasting and pilgrimage—all personally transacted, but it is deeply 'ecclesial' in its own shape by dint of its genius *qua* law and the necessity, in law, for learned search and authoritarian reading. Hence the writ of the *madhahib*, or Schools, and the incidence of sects.

That there are deep psychic matters here in the area of religious practice and for confessional personnel we will have reason to probe in Chapter 8. Here the vital point is to know Christian 'priesthood' as belonging with the hallowing of all material things and witnessing to the sacred destiny of the secular. For 'the bread and wine' of Jesus' history are also the inclusive symbols of 'what we do with what there is,' namely plough and reap and tend and mill and prune and produce. Neither bread nor wine just happen. They can well symbolise an entire technology—all of which, as with them, we may lay upon 'a holy table'. Oxford can offer its Muslims an ample initiation here, if we will mutually abate prejudice and 'dream' beyond indifference.

If we are to entertain that hope, and not set it among already 'lost causes', it is well to return—before leaving him—to why this sensitive Oxford poet saw his 'spires' the way he did. We revert to Matthew Arnold's perception of 'failing messengers', his measure of the futility, seemingly, of religious mission 'in the Name of the Lord'. 'Do you think you can compel them to believe?' was the question addressed to Muhammad by Allah (Surah 10.99) It is noteworthy that the verse yields the noun in the oft-cited Surah 2.256: 'There is (ought to be) no compulsion in religion.'

What should prophets, what should eager believers, make of this human capacity for heedlessness, for disdain even of the divine word which surely *ought* to succeed? Fatalists—and not only in Islam—have had their answer and seen some divine decree contradicting divine legislation and truth, thereby implying divine inconsistency, with only a spectator or a tyrant in heavenly places. It seems a necessary part of a right theism to hold that God is master of His righteousness, neither wayward nor volatile, the will of His law being the law of His will.

We are back then with the mystery of unbelief, of a God-resistance in the human scene and self. The uncompelled quality of true faith must be linked with the realism of the human autonomy, the implication of which is that He will have His human purposes only as we readily make them our own. Belief, and all that flows from it of surrender and a right society, will not be under compulsion or duress. Only in being not so could it remain moral and genuine. The *islam* sought from us must be brought by us. Hence the urgency of prophets *to* us. Hence again the heedlessness that will pain and perplex them.

Every reader soon finds that the Qur'an itself is deep in this quandary. Had Mecca's humans been readily an audience there need have been no Hijrah from it. Had the Hijaz been all preaching-susceptible, there need have been no warfare to ensure establishment. The very command in Surah 96 to 'utter' *(iqra')* was at once countered by *kalla*, a most emphatic *antilogia* (as Greek would have it) from a local hearer: 'Nay! Never! Let it not be!' All is evidence of how radically far our human autonomy reaches.

There is need for more penetrating Islamic thought into this phenomenon of human neglect—and, more, defiance—of Allah. Christian tradition, as noted earlier, teaches us to read our world as a crucifying place. For the New Testament focuses it all into the drama of the Passion of Jesus. The forces in coalition to bring it about then expressed the capacity for wrongness of all humankind. Islam does not see it that way and prefers the hypothesis of a mysterious, vindicating rescue in which the intended evil climax was frustrated and Jesus not crucified.

That may satisfy Muslim scruples about divine and/or prophetic inviolability but leaves the fact of an evil intention, with all it symbolises about us, unresolved. Jesus remains one whom, because of his divine mission, some in his environment intended to kill. 'Intention' has always been crucial in Islamic law and ethics. All the issues about Jesus apart, the enmity all 'messengers' know is central to the panorama of the Qur'an. It is at the heart of the concepts of *kufr* and *zulm*, the repudiation of truth and the wrongfulness of society. That the reality of these runs deep is clear from the strong accent, in Muhammad's case, on 'success' being attained and being seen to be firmly in hand. Yet a truth or faith that seeks and claims its vindication in violent terms, must remain at odds with its own principle of uncompulsiveness. Success also is an ambiguous term.

Through all this runs the question as to what the sanctions of religious conviction should finally be—which is only the other side of the rule of uncompulsiveness. It may be argued that some measure of compulsion in the form, for example, of social pacification or necessary response to enmity physically wielded, is justified and can innocently engender belief. So Muslim tradition would hold. There is an occasion in Surah 49 where some 'arabs' came to a victorious Muhammad professing 'faith' who needed to be told that they had only 'submitted'.[25] No doubt 'submission' in physical terms in a power-situation could lead, with due education, into 'faith' spiritually confessed. So again Muslims can claim. There is no religion in history that has ever been consistently innocent of less than spiritual inducements.

Nevertheless, the quality of heart and soul allegiance will always remain the question, and with it this puzzle—so central to Matthew Arnold's melancholy—of religion frustrated in its own intentions, failing by the criteria it must bring to its own success. What this means for its 'officialdom', those who preside over its means and ends in rite, code, creed and culture, was never far from Arnold's mind. There are also the large questions all the foregoing sets for eschatology, that is, for any summation in history.

Everything doubtless impinges also on our experience of plurality and diversity intensifying over recent decades, turning interior loyalties into outward obligations. 'An Oxford Reverie' has much further to go. It is fair here to conclude that, being by its nature uncompelling, truth must stay on that very sufferance in the pattern of the Cross of Jesus and only

---

[25] Surah 49.14-18. It would seem that 'submission' *(islam)* was made to Muhammad 'as doing him a favour.' The continuing state of unfaith had to be exposed and dealt with. Something of the same confused situation lay behind the *riddah*, or 'taking back of submission' after the Prophet's death by people supposing that his passing absolved them of the nexus.

thereby know and tell itself in a world gathered to its mystery. Then the faith that finds it so will always be needed in the human scene and, by the same token, always present in it universally.

Meanwhile, how Oxford and the Bodleian came to the love and lore of Arabic—given how far Islam belongs with the language of its Qur'an—is where our story has first to go. Edward Pococke, Fellow of St John's College, whose name inaugurates it, may well have gone through the Hinkseys on the way to his retreat in the Rectory of Childrey during the Civil War and Commonwealth in the mid-17th century, but he was no 'scholar gipsy'. Erudite and assiduous, he lived among Semitic Scriptures, their texts and meanings.

Chapter 2

THE PLACE OF ARABIC:
FROM POCOCKE TO GIBB

i

There has always been something deeply reciprocal between the Arabic language and the Islamic Scripture. The Qur'an has pride of place in all study of syntax and vocabulary as the criterion of diction and euphony. Arabic, in turn, has the dignity of being the exclusive language of revelation in Islam, the indispensable vehicle of the sacred text. *Wahy*, as the experience of prophetic recipience, moved through no other speech.

The language might be said to have responded to that honour by proving the medium through which Islam itself was introduced and commended to the world at large. The arts of Arabic—grammar and recital—in the *tajwid* or 'beautifying' of the Qur'an on user's lip for hearer's ear mediated the claim and the meanings of Islam through the varied language cultures of its wide expansion. These might well baptise the faith idiosyncratically into their social idiom, Persian, Indian, Turkish, African or East Asian, but never superseding the Arabic of the Qur'an.

The attraction or the utility of Arabic in the different context of the West and of Christian Europe were no less vital factors in the fortunes of Islamic faith. Utility was important given the role of Arabic in the transmission to the West of Muslim sciences and arts. Meanwhile we need to measure the place of Arabic as ensuring—if we may so speak—the claims of Islam for academic reckoning in a haven of studies primarily linguistic and, indeed, Biblical. When at the turn of the 17th century, Oxford began to interest itself in the language it was still ill-at-ease with the prejudice that held 'imposture' to be the tag it should attach to 'Mahomet' and his 'pseudo-Koran'. It was largely thanks to a devotion to Arabic as a language that the long rejectionism meted out to Muslims could be either circumvented or diminished.

The outstanding Oxonian is this context was the admirable Edward Pococke, first of Corpus Christi College (1604-90). Were the Centre for Islamic Studies looking for honorary patrons from the Oxford story Pococke could well be the first to qualify. He was the pioneer of a long sequence of Arabic study in the university whereby the language set the faith of Islam in the frame where, Arabic apart, it would hardly have been, seeing that Divinity was so long satisfied with Christian limits,[1] even after the monumental labours of Max Müller and Monier Williams in presenting the texts and the tenets of Asian religions. It would be fair to say that factors deriving from the lure of Arabic kept Islam within the sights of Oxford scholars so that any new centre via Muslim initiative should know that its faith and culture have always been 'under the spires' since Oxford's fourth century.

ii

In his role as a pioneer of Oxford Arabic, the career of Edward Pococke illustrates all the main influences involved. He had early contacts with Holland where scholars like Erpenius standing in the Erasmus tradition of Renaissance learning were developing oriental studies. In these the fame of Gabriel Sionata and the prestige of the Maronite College in Rome kindled sympathies and queries, exercised by the perceptions western Christendom had of the situation of the Eastern Church.[2] These influences were reinforced, for scholars of the Reformed tradition, by the claims of Hebrew as central to Biblical lore. Arabic sheltered, as it were, under the wing of the Hebraic as did also Syriac. Pococke took up the study of all three after his initial encounter with the Greek and Latin classics. Indeed, when more than two and a half centuries later, a Faculty of Oriental Languages officially arrived in Oxford, its two divisions were named 'Semitic' and 'Indian.'

Arabic was thought useful for Biblical exegesis and the comparison of texts, a help—as William Laud had it—to 'the divine and

---

[1] See, for example: Henry Chadwick: *Frontiers of Theology*, Cambridge, 1981. He recognised that there were questions about the distinctiveness of Christianity, but 'the critical question was the relation of theology to religious faith and experience'. 'History and philosophy were the two frontiers the theologian needed to cross on either side of his work.'

[2] The Maronite College had been founded in Rome in 1584 and long remained a vital factor in relating the Arab/Greek Orient to Europe. Sionata, (d. 1648) was a powerful stimulus to western interests in Arabic via scholars in the Netherlands. There were interested parties in the Church of England even prior to Laud. Bishop Arthur Lake, of Bath and Wells, donated a Qur'an to New College in 1617, while Archbishop Bancroft sponsored, from Egypt, Yusuf ibn Abu Daqa (Josephus Abudaeners) in 1610 to teach Arabic.

infallible revelation by which the originals of Scripture were first written.'[3] However, the means by which its claims were implemented was the commercial activity of the Levant Trading Company in Ottoman territory. A sequence of clerical chaplains to the Company, mainly based at Aleppo, were deputed to collect Arabic texts during their sojourns whereby to furnish scholarship at home. Soon after becoming Archbishop of Canterbury in 1633, Laud secured from Charles I a Royal Letter requiring all returning ships to bring at least one manuscript in Arabic or Persian.[4]

It was via the patronage of Laud that Edward Pococke became so significant an Arabist. After ordination as a priest in 1629, he was appointed to Aleppo where, surviving the plague, he remained some five years, refining his language skills, garnering manuscripts, pondering the shape of Eastern Christendom and becoming perceptive of Islam. Laud, planning an Arabic Chair, brought him back to Oxford as its first incumbent. Laud's endowing of its hopes was among his 'Acts of Bounty' 'at least for his life-time' lest his estate might not suffice for longer. Still larger 'bounty' was bestowed in the large collection of Arabic and Islamic texts which Laud was instrumental in bringing to the Bodleian Library so that it became among the foremost treasure houses of resources for scholars.[5]

It was, however, primarily as Professor of Hebrew that Pococke made his long and politically troubled way through the century till his death in 1690. Arabic teaching—or better—research was limited to graduates and to vacations. Hebrew and Biblical interests predominated but slowly concerns with Islam found their modest place, enough to allow Pococke to develop perspectives on Islam that later found their way into George Sale's Preface to his version of the Qur'an and even to impress Edward Gibbon, the historian.

His career was beset by adversity during the period of the Civil War and the Commonwealth. He visited Laud in prison in the Tower and

---

[3] Cited from D Baker, ed. *Religious Motivation*, London, 1978, pp. 215-40. Cf. H Trevor-Roper, *Archbishop Laud, 1573-1645*, London, 1940, pp. 281-84.

[4] *Ibid.*, and for the Levant Company, chartered in 1591, see Alfred C Wood, *A History of the Levant Company*, New York, 1935, and: J B Pearson, *Biographical Sketches of Chaplains to the Levant Company, 1611-1706*, Cambridge, 1883.

[5] It could rival any other centre in Europe at a time when there was an unsatisfied hunger in a dearth of texts. Thomas Hyde, Pococke's successor, became Bodley's librarian in 1665. Other pioneers were William Bedell and Matthew Pasor, a resident German Arabist, John and Thomas Greaves, Thomas Corfield, Henry Jacob and John Bainbridge, the Savilian Professor of Astronomy.

rode out the stormy times as Rector of Childrey in Berkshire where he endeared himself to his rustic flock. The Restoration in 1660 brought him back to Christ Church and his Canonry and to a calmer fulfilment, during which time he wrote extensive Commentaries on Biblical prophets and translated sundry Islamic texts from Arabic to Latin, among them Al-Maydani's 'Proverbs of 'Ali' and *Mukhtasar fi-l-Duwal*, or 'Specimen Historiae Arabicum', of Bar Hebraeus.

His 18th century biographer, Leonard Twells, reluctant to forego prejudices which Pococke himself surmounted, tells how his hero 'read the Alcoran of that imposter Mahomet with great care and critical diligence ... combating the folly, the confusedness, and incoherency therein ...' He goes on, however, to explain how

> ... he had observed in many that professed his (Muhammad's) religion, much justice, candour and love and other excellent qualities which seemed to prepare them for the kingdom of God: and therefore he could not but persuade himself that, were the sacred doctrines of the Gospel duly proposed to them, not a few might open their eyes to discern the truth of it.[6]

Hence Pococke's diligence in translating into Arabic Hugo Grotius' *De Veritate Religionis Christianae* in 1660. He noted certain errors in it in a Preface for which he received Grotius' thanks. They had to do with alleged Biblical anticipations of Muhammad, later to become a stock theme of polemic, and with the legends of the Prophet about the dove on his shoulder inditing the Qur'an which, as malicious inventions, he omitted from his translation.

He rendered Ibn Tufayl's *Risalat Hayy Ibn Yaqzan* into Latin in 1671[7] as well as the English Liturgy into Arabic and from Arabic to Latin the 'Annals of Eutychius', Patriarch of Alexandria. His method as a translator was to get beyond literalism and be ready for idiomatic renderings that truly conveyed the meaning. He furnished his version of

---

[6] Leonard Twells, *Life of Edward Pococke*, London, 1816, p. 77.

[7] A famous narrative of 'Alert, the son of Awake,' written by Abu Bakr ibn Tufayl (c. 1110-85) about a youth in a desert who attained Islam without any formal education, as the due goal of natural reason, based on sense-perception and innate intelligence. When one named Asal reaches him with Islam in dogma and practice, he finds the two concur entirely, except that harsh aspects of the Qur'an disturb him and leave him perplexed.

Mukhtasar fi-l-Duwal and other works with extensive annotations drawn
for Al-Hariri's *Maqamat*, from Al-Ghazali, Al-Suyuti and Al-Shahrastani's
Kitab al-Milal wa-l-Nihal, many of which found their way later into
George Sale's Preface.

Pococke cared to dispel misconceptions of the *Jahiliyyah* or the
times before Islam, and wrote objectively about sects in Islam, and the
doctrine of 'the light of Muhammad'. He saw himself—in words cited
by Twells—as 'a bounden servant', at once an assiduous scholar and a
committed, patient believer.

iii

The quality of Edward Pococke as an initiator of Oxford Arabic may
well be savoured by reference to the unsavoury controversy evident in
two contemporaries, the one Humphrey Prideaux (1648-1724), the other
Henry Stubbe (1632-76), both of Christ Church, whose books set battle
lines in a very different temper of mind. Both had little or no Arabic skill.
Prideaux was a Lecturer in Hebrew and ultimately Dean of Norwich.
Stubbe was briefly Second Keeper of the Bodleian and spent some five
years as a physician in Jamaica. The one wrote of 'The True Nature of
the Imposture' (Islam via Mahomet), the other 'An Account of the Rise
and Progress of Mahometanism and a Vindication of him and of his
Religion from the Calumnies of the Christians'. Doubtless because of its
drift it was not published until 1911, but was well known in Restoration
times.

The two writers had two features in common, namely that any
vindication of Islam would involve sharp inter-Christian questionings
and that the critique of Islam would necessitate a Christian mind alert to
its own identity. The two persist to this day—if, hopefully, in better terms
than those of Prideaux's enmity and Stubbe's facile pen.

That any reckoning with Islam is involved in New Testament
scholarship has always been mandatory, if seldom fully undertaken.
Stubbe's 'vindication' of Islam, after the proper 'de-calumnising' of
Muhammad's marriages, of the nature of his inspiration and the expansion
of his religion, resolved itself into a 'unitarian' re-writing of the New
Testament and a disavowal of the Christian sacraments. The thesis was
that the early Church was a Jewish entity that could 'never have believed
Christ to be the natural *(sic)* Son of God by eternal generation or any

tenet depending thereon.' Nor could they have entertained the curious
notions of a 'Holy Spirit' and a divine 'Trinity', either of which would,
to them as Jews, have 'been a blasphemy'. Moreover, they had 'only lay
elders', nor was the name of priest then heard.[8] The Christian sacraments
which later developed were sheer paganism. After Constantine, everything
went awry in divisive 'paganisation'.

With this repudiation of the New Testament's *confessio*, the way
was open for Stubbe to write extensively on the religion of Abraham
fulfilled in Islam, the vocation of the Prophet and the story of Islam's
world-wide career, whereby

> Faith was no longer clogged with the necessity of believing
> a number of abstruse notions they cannot comprehend ...
> contrary to the dictates of reason and common sense,
> (together with) troublesome and expensive and superstitious
> ceremonies.

Stubbe credited Pilgrimage and the Fast to 'Mahomet's foresight'.
As for the *Jihad*, levying war in Arabia was to restore the old religion,
while, outside Arabia, any propagation by the sword was 'only as a
consequence of their victories'.[9] It was well, in some of his 'positives',
that Stubbe set Prideaux straight, but no authentic relation to Islam could
be based on such wholesale disembowelling of Christian Scripture and
doctrine. Had the faith ever held Jesus to be 'the *natural* Son of God'?
Had not faith in 'the Word made flesh' been simply continuous with the
ancient Jewish belief in 'divine agency', whereby 'messengers' had their
'sending' as divine 'doing' from within the divine 'being'? Was not Islam
similarly involved in the doing/being reality of Allah juxtaposed, in strange
sequence, in the *Shahadah* with 'Muhammad His Apostle'?

Stubbe's impatience with the sacraments of cleansing water and
commemorative 'bread and wine' could suggest his measure of sympathy
with Islam—so long censorious of both, but could hardly in that animus
bring the two faiths into intelligible discourse. In strenuously repudiating
Prideaux, Stubbe had done nothing to mediate the reality of the
significance Islam held for Christians, nor to expound 'God in Christ' as

---

[8] See on Henry Stubbe, P M Holt, *A 17th Century Defender of Islam*, London, 1972. All
    Stubbe's citations from Arabic authors were drawn from Latin translations. Passages cited
    here pp. 15 and 19.
[9] *Ibid.*, pp. 166, 180.

reciprocal to that significance. It would have been wiser to stay in the gentle scholarship of Pococke.

Their barren ineptness apart, and their relevance for future times beyond their own, there was another intriguing feature they possessed. It had to do with the Islamic relation as bearing on Christian ecclesiology and sects. Stubbe wrote an 'Apology for the Quakers'. He had a double-edged interest. Such 'private judgement' in things of faith could well rebuke the divisions among the doctrinaire before and long after Chalcedon. Had not Christian divisions been a chief line of dismay about Christendom in the Qur'an? Islam could well exemplify unity. Yet Islam had its own sects and the Quaker-style mind could admit of further fragmentation among the faithful, so perhaps there was case for a monolithic Church? But the impressive solidity of Islam, in eyes like Henry Stubbe's could also suggest that it might have some value to the cause of anti-papalism. Both before and during the Protestant Reformation in Europe, Islam attracted the attention of sectarians discoursing inside a contentious Christianity.

Pococke, it could be said, had no adequate successors, either in temper or competence, until late in the 19th century among Oxford Arabists. His immediate successor, Thomas Hyde (1636-1703) was primarily concerned with Persian. While the ample resources of the Bodleian which he and Laud had helped to gather continued to be envied and drew scholars to their wealth, Arabic was for long ancillary to the Regius Chair in Hebrew, while Islam still incurred the prejudices of Pococke's 18th century biographer.[10]

Around the turn of Pococke's century. the exiguous resources of Arabic under Laudian auspices were aided, though still only meagrely, by 'Lord Almoner's Professorships in Arabic', established by William III in 1700, to undertake teaching in the language for men intending careers overseas. Despite their title, these posts appear to have been less prestigious. They served to indicate the confusion as to the precise academic duties attaching to the care of Arabic, as between the lowlier teaching of grammar to undergraduates and the 'professing' of literary lore. The latter, in any event, had to take second place—or third when Persian competed—to the primary interests of Hebrew.

---

[10] On Pococke see also 'An Oxford Arabist,' in P M Holt, *Studies in the History of the Middle East*, London, 1973, pp. 1-25; on Prideaux and the debt of G Sale to Pococke, see ed. B Lewis and P M Holt, *Historians of the Middle East*, Oxford, 1962, pp. 290-302.

However, one Almoner holder, the worthy Jean Gagnier, during the third decade of the 18th century, produced a 2-volume *Vie de Mahomet* which marked the beginning of a will to wrestle with the Prophet in genuinely historical terms.[11] Though the Almoner 'Chair' persisted until 1913 as secondary to the Laudian, its contribution to Islamic studies remained modest in the extreme. Thomas Hunt (1738-48) held both Chairs together, while he worked on texts of 'Abd al-Latif al-Baghdadi, a scholar, physician and traveller, a contemporary of Salah al-Din by whom he was held in great regard. His narrative of plague in Cairo makes him a kind of Daniel Defoe of Islam.

After Hunt, there was a succession of undistinguished figures meriting Edward Gibbon's comment on how 'oriental studies have languished,' among them Richard Browne,[12] Henry Ford, Benjamin Brayney and Thomas Winstanley. The last named held the Laudian Chair in conjunction with the Camden Chair in Ancient History (1790-1823) where his main assets lay. It needs to be recalled that throughout the 18th century the Bodleian Library was steadily augmenting its Arabic treasures, its manuscripts and oriental books, and from time to time professors who doubled as librarians were liable to discourage would-be students in deference to their bookish tasks.

The pattern persisted through most of the 19th century. Richard Burton, for example, as a freshman in 1842, was turned away by the Laudian, Stephen Reay, who was Bodley's sub-librarian and much preoccupied. Reay's requirement was that the freshman seeking tuition should first ensure a group of six or more of like mind to attend a 'professorial' lecture. It would seem that the alternative resource, in the Almoner's Chair, had no great capacity, as Principal of Magdalen Hall, for undergraduate Arabic. So not until 1891 did Arabic gain place within the Oxford BA Honour School. Where there were authentic Arabic skills, as in the celebrated Edward B Pusey (1800-82), they belonged to minds engaged in the other disciplines of Hebrew and theology.

---

[11] Jean (or Thomas) Gagnier, *Vie de Mahomet*, 2 vols. 1731, Amsterdam. Gagnier also occupied himself with Abu-l-Fida, the Muslim geographer.

[12] Browne was appointed by Lord North, whether or not in the terms whereby a contemporary found preferment by preaching before the Prime Minister from the text, in Psalm 75.6: 'Promotion cometh neither from the cast, nor the west, nor yet from the south.' Gibbon himself at Magdalen, had been deflected from Arabic in 1753 despite his schoolboy interest, which he owed to Edward Pococke.

iv

The story of Oxonian Arabic and its bearing on the themes of Islam enters the 20th century with the name of David Samuel Margoliouth (1858-1940) who held the Laudian Chair from 1889 to 1937, when he was succeeded by a no less definitive figure in the person of Hamilton A R Gibb. The contribution of these two scholars, though much queried by recent Muslim critics, may fairly be said to have resumed the painstaking qualities of Edward Pococke in the very different idiom of their generations.

D S Margoliouth was of Jewish extraction. His father, Ezekiel, had served as a missionary. The son combined a wide Hebrew erudition with a prodigious industry in the field of Arabic literature and Islamic history. At twenty-three, he became a Fellow of New College and later held lectureships in India. He followed Pococke's example in a study of Commentary (Jephet) on the Book of Daniel in his first year in the Professorship. Before the turn of the century he had translated the Letters of the celebrated Muslim sceptic, Abu-l-'Ala al-Ma'ari, and published *Analecta Orientalia* (1888), *Chrestomathia Baidawania* (1894) and organised numerous manuscripts in the Bodleian Library, for whose interests he was assiduous for almost half a century. Later came his work on Yakut's *Dictionary of Learned Men* (between 1907 and 1927) and the *Eclipse of the Abbasid Caliphate* (completed in 1922) and in the last year of his life *Lectures on Arabic Historians* (1939).

The three works in which he gave to his Arabic Chair a significant bearing on Islamic study were *Mohammed and the Rise of Islam* (1906), *Mohammedanism* (1911) and *The Early Development of Mohammedanism* (1914). He was writing before western scholarship learned that only 'Islam' and not 'Mohammadanism' (or any variant spelling) is the valid noun.[13] Now, almost a century on, there is a certain datedness about his work. Yet the set of his mind, as concerned neither

---

[13] The error, now almost everywhere renounced, was a natural one, on the analogy of 'Christ' and 'Christianity'. Yet it is evident at once that—as the Qur'an demonstrates—only 'Islam' is the authentic name. Even the personal name 'Muhammad' occurs a mere four times in the Qur'an, the abstract noun never. Edward Said, however, in *Orientalism*, 1979, p. 280, is unfair to H A R Gibb when, in reference to Gibb's *Muhammadanism*, 1949, he writes: 'It is time to mention Gibb's preference for the word …' (p. 280). (Gibb was well aware of the issue and only allowed the 1949 title reluctantly, on the insistence of his OUP publishers who saw the book as a revision of Margoliouth's early title of that name.) Elsewhere Said refers frequently and castigatingly to Gibb's allegedly 'biased' usage of the term 'Islam', pp. 279f.

for panegyric nor for indictment, was deferential, though Muslim readers were doubtless dismayed by the parallel he drew with Joseph Smith and Mormonism in 'the employment of "revelations" as a political instrument'.[14]

That feature gives something of a 'tongue in the cheek' character to Margoliouth's presentation, as of one lacking the will, if not the ability, to think in genuine empathy with Muslims in their Islam. Reference, for example, to Mount Hira' in the *preparatio* of Muhammad is entirely lacking in *Mohammedanism* and bare in the extreme in *Mohammed and the Rise of Islam*.[15] He adopts a sardonic tone in pondering the vital issue of the Prophet's inner psyche in the incidence of vocation—where doubtless, there remains an enormous theme of integrity. Contemporary Muslims now would think it deserved more—and keener—from a biographer than

> He never compromised that high dignity by any of the humility, genuine or affected, which meets us in the speeches of those who preached a doctrine without political ambitions.

Margoliouth implies that 'the adoption of the role of Prophet' 'had the desire of personal distinction or ... rather for a place in the community whence he could enforce his ideas on the rest.'[16] A mythicization of Islam's origins in the interests of adulation is one thing: a failure to measure dimensions proper to its age-long status in believers' experience is another.

Perhaps we should conclude that, for all his erudition, Margoliouth at the turn of the 19th/20th centuries was still a partial prisoner to the assumptions of his day. He seems to have been obsessed with Arabia as 'a heat-belt' where 'a man's conscience was God's concern': he was 'a Moslem who professed Islam.' 'Those who can express no approval of (Mohammed's) moral qualities cannot refrain

---

[14] In the preface to *Mohammed and the Rise of Islam*, pp. vii-viii, also he referred to 'a long series of [biographies] which it is impossible to end, but in which it would be honourable to find a place' p. iii. The comparison with Joseph Smith recurs, p. 136.
   It is linked with the 'tablets' idea in *Mohammedanism*, p. 64.
[15] See p. 90. A different assessment of *tahannuth*. 'meditation, in the cave' may 'be found in my *Returning to Mount Hira', Islam in Contemporary Terms*, London. 1994, pp. 16-28.
[16] *Mohammed*, p. 82.

from admiring his intellectual ability.'[17] The narrative of the origins of a world-faith, due to take in the centuries, needs to know a proleptic element, allowing its long destiny to be imaginatively present in its genesis. For this, the learning of Margoliouth—in contrast, for example, to Louis Massignon—was unready in the bare matter-of-fact-ness of his treatment. It might be said in extenuation that the Muslim sources hardly encouraged him, seeing that the earliest 'Lives' of the Prophet are as problematic, in their embarrassing features, for contemporary Muslim exponents as for their western counterparts. However, the deep issue inside the *Shahadah,* namely the crucial association it makes between 'God and His messenger', needed more, and other, than:

> If men failed to agree with his second dogma, his own apostleship, he devised ingenious reasons for showing that they disagreed with him concerning the first dogma—the unity of God. Hence we are justified in supposing that the second was the dogma to which he attached the greater importance.[18]

The long tenure of Margoliouth gave way in 1937 to the Arabic régime of Hamilton A R Gibb—for, given the esteem and authority he garnered, régime it proved to be. The 1939-45 War years apart, when he was advising policy through the Royal Institute of International Affairs, he drew Oxford Arabic into a more lively and perceptive temper, with a steady emphasis on modern writing, without detriment to the traditional

---

[17] *Mohammedanism*, pp. 115-6. Was it this note that prompted Gibb to begin his own edition under the same title: 'The legend that Islam was born of the desert is taking a long time to die!'? The perfunctory comment about 'conscience' (p. 56) flies in the face of the careful distinction 'in Surah 49.14 between *islam* as bare allegiance and Islam as authentic faith. It also ignores the steady emphasis on *niyyah* or 'right intention' and on 'sincerity'—*ikhlas.* Also citing p. 60.

[18] *Mohammed and the Rise* etc, p.81. See also the discussion (pp. 215f). What is deeply puzzling in the phenomenon of prophethood as it bears on the persona is not explored in Margoliouth's terms: 'He (Muhammad) inherited the devotion and adulation which had hitherto been bestowed on the idols,' p. 216. It is a claim gratuitously offensive to the mind of Islam. 'He ere long became hedged in with a state that differed little from that which surrounded a god.'
On bearings, either to other, of those two parts of Islamic witness (two sentences coupled with no explanation as to how they inter-relate, i.e. a theological parataxis), see my *The Weight in the Word; Prophethood, Biblical and Quranic*, Brighton, 1999, Chap. 8, pp. 117-37, also Chapter 8, below, where the issue is crucial.

focus on 'things remote and medieval' with careful attention to developments in Arabic literature.

Born in Alexandria, Egypt, in 1895, where his parents lived, he retained his love of Egypt and renewed it with scholarly visits throughout his middle years. His thought, and much of his cast of mind about religion, were nourished in his Edinburgh schooling and his initiation into academic Semitics in the (then infant) School of Oriental Studies in London, where his mentors were Denison Ross and Thomas Arnold. He wrote initially on *The Arab Conquest of Central Asia* (1923) and later published translations, namely *The Travels of Ibn Battuta* (1929) and *The Damascus Chronicle of the Crusades* (1932), a translation of Ibn al-Qalanisi.

Invited, while still relatively young to participate in the Leiden *Encyclopaedia of Islam*, he took up the task with a zeal and competence that earned admiration from his colleagues.[19] When he arrived in Oxford in 1937 to occupy the Laudian Chair and a Fellowship at St John's College, he brought the fruits of that early apprenticeship from Cairo and London and, significantly for his later thinking around Islamic modernism, his lively acquaintance with the brothers Mustafa and 'Ali 'Abd al-Raziq, enliveners of Egyptian Islam.[20]

His tenancy of the Arabic Chair and the range of mind with which he occupied it were perhaps best attested by the logic of his departure from it in 1955—a decision which many greeted with surprise. When the Jewett Chair of Arabic became vacant at Harvard and he was consulted about candidates, he hinted that he might be one himself. He had grown frustrated by obstacles in Oxford then, to his hope of closer linkage between Arabic studies and other disciplines, especially history.[21]

---

[19] See the tribute paid by G Levi Della Vida in his 'Letter of Dedication' to *Arabic and Islamic Studies in Honor of H A R Gibb*, ed. George Makdisi, Leiden, 1965—a *Festschrift* presented to Gibb on his 70th birthday, to which fifty international scholars contributed. It referred to his 'all embracing concept of the study of Islam ... his firm and continuous consciousness of the fundamental unity of Islamic civilization', pp. xv f.

[20] Sir Thomas Arnold (1864-1930) author of *The Preaching of Islam*, London, 1920; *The Caliphate*, Oxford. 1924; and editor of *The Legacy or Islam*, Oxford, 1931 (with Alfred Guillaume). Mustafa 'Abd al-Raziq (1885-1947) was briefly 'Shaikh al-Azhar' and a student of Muhammad 'Abduh. 'Ali 'Abd al-Raziq (1888-1966)—a more forthright reformist— startled the mid twenties with his *Islam wa Usul al-Hukm* in the wake of the end of the caliphate (1924) with the thesis that it had never been 'essential to Islam' and could well be left unlamented.

[21] After his departure, and thanks to the Hayter Report of 1961, the situation at Oxford improved considerably in respect of inter-disciplinary studies. However, Gibb's point was clear in that his excellent successor, A F L Beeston, filled the Chair in terms that had more to do with language philology and lexicography. He held the Chair from 1955 until 1978.

He was drawn to the opening Harvard offered into the wider field of Middle Eastern politics and social ideas. That Oxford might ever be forsaken seemed to some a strange aberration. That Gibb should have chosen it was a measure of his breadth of sympathy, his interpretation of the nature of Arabic itself.[22]

His Oxford tenure saw a spate of literary activity amounting, in the words of Albert Hourani, to 'a coherent body of original thought in Islam'.[23] There was his 1949 complete overhaul of Margoliouth's *Mohammedanism*, contributions to *The Muslim World* and *The Journal of World History*, and his 1960 contribution on 'Arabiyya' in Vol. 1 of the (new) *Encyclopaedia of Islam*,[24] together with *Islamic Society and the West*.[25] Most fertile of all was his *Modern Trends in Islam*, based on lectures given in 1945 at the University of Chicago, in which he allowed himself a sort of *confessio fidei* around the vocation of scholarship with Arabic.[26]

It would be fair to say that in the person of H A R Gibb Oxford played a decisive role in the 'comprehension' of Islam in both senses of the word, namely an inclusive range of interest across Islamic unity with diversity, and a venture of perceptive interpretation to the mind of the West, both academic and cultural. In both ways his writings, with the prestige of his erudition, acted as a kind of catalyst to which Muslim scholars responded—some with the relish of emulation as to one whose sympathies and quality deserved their admiration, others with hostility

---

[22] Does this explain why Edward Said claims Gibb for 'an Orientalist' rather than an 'Arabist'—as, allegedly, with proof from Gibb himself? All in all, it makes an odd accusation, given the full extent of Gibb's concern with Arabic literature and his several translations. Edward Said, *Orientalism*, New York, 1978, p. 53. Said's quarrel—ultimately—is with Gibb's ambition for an inter-culture study beyond the cavils about entering on a career with a set vision of 'the Orient' (p. 263.). See below.

[23] Albert Hourani in *Proceedings of the British Academy*, Vol. lviii, 1972, pp. 493-521. Much of Hourani's own influence on Islamic studies in traceable to the esteem in which he held Gibb as his teacher and friend. See: Abdulaziz al-Sudairi: *A Vision of the Middle East: An Intellectual Biography of Albert Hourani*, London, 1999.

[24] *The Muslim World Quarterly*, Hartford, Vol. 38, 1948, pp. 17-28 and 113-123, and pp. 185-197, 280-291. And *Journal of World History*, Vol. l. No. l, Paris, 1953, pp. 39-62. These papers with others listed there, appeared in *Studies in the Civilization of Islam*, ed. S J Shaw and W R Polk, Princeton, 1962.

[25] H A R Gibb (with Harold Bowen): *Islamic Society and the West*, I *Islamic Society in the 18th Century*, Oxford, 1957.

[26] *Modern Trends in Islam*, Chicago, 1947, (though lectures in Chicago) was the 'peak' product of Gibb's Oxford years and the most focused shape of his scholarship as at once an academic and a religious vocation. See below.

resentful of the verdicts he presumed to reach, while still grudgingly aware of his competence.

There was no doubt of his intimate, personal rapport with Muslim 'liberal' thinking in Cairo and beyond, nor of the care he brought to the ambition for the broad sweep of analysis all his writings sought. Introducing the edited book of sundry papers in 1962, he wrote of

> ... a slowly maturing conviction that literature and history, being both expressions of a living society, cannot be studied in isolation from each other without distortion of the underlying reality.

insisting also that 'behind each generalization ... lies a considerable body of detailed study of the original sources.'[27]

The contrast with Margoliouth is everywhere evident in the capacity for the mind's identity with what it treats, while he is generations away from the prejudice of the age to which his patient predecessor, Edward Pococke, was in fee. He reaches for the kind of survey-inclusiveness attempted by his Oxford contemporary, Arnold Toynbee. His analysis of the initial progress of Islam within the tribes of Arabia, in the months before and after Muhammad's death, is a case in point. He saw 'three different levels'—that of total conversion out of full credence, that of formal allegiance to a new communal reality and the third among the tribesfolk whose adherence still required the proven sanction of power.[28] That order of things becomes the clue to what ensued in the developing caliphal politics of Islam under the Umayyads and beyond.

Similarly with his sense of what he liked to call the 'Islamic stamp' discerned in the collective temper of Tradition, its gathering and ethos well into the medieval period. He notes how

> The great biographical dictionaries of Orthodox scholars are concerned very little with their individuality as persons,

---

[27] *Arabic and Islamic Studies in Honor of H A R Gibb*, ed. George Makdisi, Leiden, 1965, Introduction.

[28] *Studies, op. cit.* p. 5. It is on this passage that Ziya al-Hasan Faruqi comments: 'It was beyond his comprehension to see Muhammad as a divinely inspired prophet' to whom tribesmen could respond in those terms. It was 'a materialistic view of Medinan policy,' and a clear index to prejudice. In *Orientalism: Islam and Islamists*, ed. Asaf Husain, Robert Olsen and Jamil Qureshi, Vermont, 1984, pp. 181-82. Surah 49.14 would seem to confirm Gibb's view. Cf. Chapter 1, note 25.

but only with their contributions to the transmission of the collective heritage.[29]

He stays alert to factors of sociology, of agriculture and the city, of shifting economic conditions and the ebb and flow of peoples, invading and invaded. The inroads of Turks and Mongols deeply fractured the old Arab ethos of Islam by a regionalising of language usage, but there was a strong counter-action in the ubiquity of the much travelling Sufi orders with their *tariqas,* disseminating common ideas. He notes in this context how the sharp individual emphasis of Sufi devotion in quest of the unitive state was nevertheless capable of developing, by this ubiquity, a degree of doctrinal formulation capable of intellectual negotiation with the philosophers.

In this way he could move, with finesse and vision, through the meticulous to the panoramic, from the local to the extensive. Al-Mawardi's 'Theory of the Caliphate', Ibn Khaldun's 'Political Theory', 'The Social Significance of the Shu'ubiya', and 'The Armies of Saladin', embodied both his applied scholarship and his personal enthusiasms. For he was a great admirer of Salah al-Din, analysing the numbers, equipment and racial origins of his soldiers in great detail. He saw in his Kurdish hero an exemplification of Islam by dint of a moral vision transcending the mere expulsion of the Crusaders and seeking to 'revive the political fabric of Islam, as a single united empire',[30] a man to whom history denied the full measure of his moral worth in political result. As for the great Ibn Khaldun, Gibb was concerned to rescue another 'hero' from the charge of some scholars that he had quite failed to show the way to 'reform' the religious institutions he so analytically described, arguing that in his famous *Muqaddimah*, Ibn Khaldun was essentially a scholar studying history and society, with a brief only to examine, explain and explore as phenomena. This aim he combined with a complete personal Islamic loyalty—one which he was not concerned to relate critically to the other task. This was, in no way, a neglect of faith but rather, a pursuit of logic towards an ultimate theory of the caliphate.[31]

---

[29] *Studies, op. cit.* p. 18.

[30] *Ibid.*, p. 100.

[31] *Ibid.*, pp. 171f. Gibb is taking issue with Erwin Rosenthal and Kamil Ayad in their handling of *Al-Muqaddimah*. Ibn Khaldun (1332-1406) was by birth a Tunisian. His study was to be a Prolegomena and pondered the factors contributing to civilizations. See Franz Rosenthal, *The Muqaddimah: An Introduction to History*, trans., 2 vols., New York, 1958, and Charles Issawi, *An Arab Philosophy of History*, London, 1950.

This leads Gibb to identify what must always remain the issue *par excellence* for institutional religion. He sees what has often been alleged to be Ibn Khaldun's 'pessimism' as stemming, not from a sociology *Al-Muqaddimah* has failed to address, but from a profound realism—in religious terms—about ever 'reconciling the ideal demands of the *Shari'ah* with the facts of history' as those 'facts' spring from human nature. Ibn Khaldun

> '... drives home the lesson, over and over again, that the course of history is what it is because of the infraction of the *Shari'ah* by the sin of pride, the sin of luxury, the sin of greed ... Since mankind will not follow the *Shari'ah* it is condemned to an empty and unending cycle of rise and fall.'[32]

Gibb here, by 'minding' Ibn Khaldun, reaches the heart of a religious realism, the pain of the 'if-only fallacy' that attends on all religious pretension—the panacea is there, if only 'it' were heeded.

Significant as all these tokens were of Gibb's industrious scholarship around Islamic themes, the central core has to do with his perception of the person of Muhammad and of the Qur'an. Its very grounding in the assumptions of his scholarship closed upon the ultimate question of whether what is *de fide* to its confessed adherents does, or does not, admit of being studied and assessed as a human phenomenon in its own right. May *islam* (that common noun) in the *muslim* subjectivity, by which alone it exists as the Islam of Muslims, be viably an object of academic discourse proceeding, even sympathetically, in a temper that is neutral?

Gibb's whole enterprise held that the answer was Yes! and, further, that the scholarship making it could bear creatively and genuinely on the interior quality of that *islam* and on the situations it faced in the flux of history. Even, further, it was his confidence that the very externality, as devotees might perceive it, was both a tribute to *their* sincerity and a potential agent in sifting its spiritual and intellectual quality. Thus the detached scholar. adequately equipped and no trespasser, could be a sort of 'believer' at some remove, precisely by an independence of mind.

Such, without doubt, was the contribution of H A R Gibb to an

---

[32] *Ibid.*, pp. 173-74.

Oxford Islamics. He assumed, as a historian as well as a linguist, that the prophethood of Muhammad and the Scripture of the Qur'an were events whose place in history was, in some measure, ascertainable and deserved to be ascertained, as far as study might discover. He also realised that the faith to which those events gave being had possessed its heritage of law, ritual, culture and politics, by factors no less capable and worthy of historical exploration. Moreover, this historical discourse in pursuit of *islam* and Islam, being no antiquarian exercise, must bear significantly on how *muslims* and Muslims responded, from within themselves, to the new times into which their continuities had brought them.[33]

He saw Islam as 'essentially a revolt against Arabian animism', elements of which, notably the sense of *taqwa* as awe, the place of *jinn* in the Qur'an and some aspects of pilgrimage, were still integral to Islam but thoroughly subdued to an uncompromising monotheism. These continuities in no way embarrassed but, on the contrary, sustained the emotions and symbols so radically transformed. There are many examples in religious history where what is vitally inaugurated wisely retains cultic survivals on its own new terms.[34]

Where Gibb parted company with orthodox Muslim understanding was in positing a personal 'originality' in Muhammad as a 'thinker facing a problem' and—by his vision and quality—lifting the whole religious orientation of his people as a deliberate project. However valid that reading, it needed to reckon with the whole significance of *wahy* possessing the Prophet with the text from beyond himself, such being the 'strategy' (if psychic events can be so styled?) by which traditional Islam comprehends the entire 'coming-to-pass' of Islam as a

---

[33] This distinction between the common noun and the proper noun is crucial. (Arabic cannot make the distinction English does by the device of initial capitals, so that, hidden, its importance has to be explicit.) It can be illustrated by the emphasis Wilfred Cantwell Smith made in *What is Scripture?: A Comparative Approach*, London, 1993, that 'Islam' is always the *'islam'* of some individual *'muslim'*. That is subjectively the case but, if pressed too far, must lead to a sort of atomism where there are as many *islams* are there are *muslims*. In that event there could be no discernible Islam by which its innumerable interpreters could be tested. Surely Smith's aphorism needs amending to read: 'The meaning lies in the text as the minds of Muslims find it.' (p. 91) This will still leave room for diversity—and indeed Muslims, disallowing other 'Muslims'—but with some sober hope of identifying 'Islam'. It seems clear that Gibb would have found that balanced formula sound. The point is very relevant for Chapter 9.

[34] The Venerable Bede in his *Ecclesiastical History of the English People* tells how Pope Gregory, when consulted by Augustine, newly arrived in Canterbury, told him to retain the pagan shrines, if well-built, after disavowing their past by sprinkling holy water and expelling the idols. By familiarity they could then still be apt for Christian worship.

divine mediation in which Muhammad played no contributory part. On this view, Islam was in no way 'the revolution wrought by Muhammad'.[35]

The intriguing issue implicit here in no way affects Gibb's register of the 'eloquence' of the Qur'an and the degree to which its music quickens and warms the intuitive religious life of Muslims and of how, from the posthumous Muhammad, the hallowing of Tradition drew both the sanction and the elements of law and ethics in Islam. These were, and are, the spiritual resources from which the ethos of Islam derived, as law and theology came to house it, reinforced from the outset by the 'steel frame' the rituals of the Five Pillars supplied.

Divine revelation had transmitted to humankind the principle of divinely regulated human existence, within which all institutions and occasions were summoned to express the divine Will. During its first three centuries, Islam was absorbed in the assimilation of conquered populations to this régime of inclusive 'Godwardness' and in the task of developing from within its revelatory story (Qur'an and Tradition) the detailed values, norms aid precepts of its ethical society. Only later did a need for speculative philosophy and theology—quite absent from that founding story—present itself as the intellectual counterpart of the faith in *Tawhid* and *Tanzil*.

Given the firm establishment of the *Shari'ah* as the divine rulebook of Islamic society, the intellectual energies were entangled in controversies aroused by the inter-action of its own founding absolutes and the speculative philosophy of the cultures into which its conquests had taken it. Despite a diversity of sects and esoteric views, the broad stream flowed within the Aristotelian tradition, so that 'Islam as a whole stands on the same side of the watershed as the West.'[36] Gibb notes, however, that—Sufism apart—Islamic monotheism is too absolute to admit of the sort of philosophic reckoning that would allow of the kind of metaphysics drawn elsewhere from a sense of things divine, as—in measure—mutual to things human.[37] It was a monotheism that needed to rely heavily on *al-mukhalafah*, a doctrine of 'difference', which pervaded, sometimes to the point of atrophy, its theological mind. Hence the emphasis on 'the unimaginable transcendence of God', of God as all-disposing will and the Qur'an as 'Allah's Word' outside normal parameters

---

[35] *Studies, op. cit.*, pp. 187-88.
[36] *Ibid.*, p. 203.
[37] *Ibid.* p. 204.

of speech and writing.

Few academic Arabists in the West have been ready to think so theologically in their ventures with Islam. Aware of the range and erudition of its scholastics in the middle centuries, Gibb was at pains to explore how their formulations related to the living traditions of piety and devotion, of how the determinants of creed were reconciled with the intuitive levels of life-experience. Was it the partnership of these that kept Islam from any strain of urgent scepticism?[38] Gibb was alert to point out how the Qur'an itself in sundry ways witnessed against the absoluteness of the dogmas scholastic theology drew from it—a point that has become ever more crucial since his day.[39]

That alertness was the clue to his fascination with Sufism and with what one of his mentors, Duncan Black MacDonald styled: 'Religious Attitude and Life in Islam',[40] namely, the quest for personal encounter with the transcendent, not against but beyond the formulations of the dogmatists. It may have been Gibb's private sense of religious meaning and the difficulty he acknowledged in intellectualising theology adequately, especially a rigid unitarianism, that explained the relevance for him of Sufism, which he defined as 'the organised cultivation of religious experience'.[41] That was, perhaps too trite and abstract a definition. For the urge to Sufi disciplines, that sought in *fana'* the 'passing away' of empirical selfhood, was always an inward impulse, whatever structural means it created in the orders and *tariqahs* it generated.

The contrast here with his great French contemporary, Louis Massignon (1883-1962), was complete. For Gibb followed his characteristic bent for broad summary assessment as a comprehensive surveyor, of a map-making mind. He saw Sufism as a 'necessary reaction against the external rationalization of Islam', where 'intuitive religious

---

[38] For sceptics have been rare in the Muslim story. An exception would have to be the blind Syrian thinker and man of letters, Abu-1-'Ala al-Ma'ari (973-1057) who breathed a Hardyean kind of poetic despair reflecting on his long years of adversity and disease.

[39] *Studies*, p. 207—for example, its steady appeal to thoughtfulness or *tadabbur*; its clear assumptions of human 'free-will'; its basic doctrine of human responsibility for the good creation; and its haunting divine question to humanity at large: 'Am I not your Lord?' See below, Chaps. 8 and 9.

[40] See the note on MacDonald (1863-1943) in Gibb's foreword to *Modern Trends in Islam*, Chicago, 1947, pp.vii f. *Religious Attitude and Life in Islam* was published in Chicago, 1909.

[41] See *Studies*, p. 204 on the problematics, p. 208 the citation.

perception became increasingly sensitive and self-conscious.'[42] That may be far from the heart-beat of Sufi devotion, but the map-making knew its territory and carefully asserted the factors inherent in Islam that gave Sufism its being.[43] Gibb appreciated both the theological significance of Sufi experience, as interpreting *Tawhid* and its complex bearing on hermetic ideas or surviving dimensions of folk-animism. He saw it also as contributing vastly to the aesthetic fulfilment of Islam, notably in painting and calligraphic arts. It also had its large place in what might be termed the 'Asianization' of Islam in India and beyond, where Semitic rigorism in theology was less congenial and mysticism already enshrined. The tensions that persisted between 'orthodoxy' and the 'initiates' of Sufi discipline remained a vital factor in the determining of Muslim identity. They also tended to the cult of 'masters' whether of legal authority or personal sainthood. Were there survivings in the latter from that sense of *barakah*, or 'blessing', which Gibb, via MacDonald, saw as abiding from the Arabian society before Muhammad? Hence, if so, the more superstitious aspects of 'folk religion' were coming close to practices those two final Surahs of the Qur'an (113 and 114) had so firmly disavowed.[44] 'Superstition', he wrote, 'is the fringe of the garment of belief' and the sciences are no less capable of it than the religions.[45]

Its presence in society requires of 'orthodoxy' a capacity wisely to let the 'tares' coexist with the 'wheat' of the religious values with which it shares the psychic territory. This is a wisdom Gibb feared 'a literalist dogmatism' too often lacks. Such

> ... in ploughing up good and bad together ... cleared the field for the seed of a secular culture which has, alas, produced a crop of newer and deadlier superstitions.

He included both seculars and rigorists as endangering

---

[42] *Ibid.*, p. 208. See also his *Mohammedanism*, London, 1949, Chap. 8 on 'Sufism'.

[43] He queried, for example, the frequent conjecture that Islamic Sufism owed itself mainly to the stimulus of Christian or Indian contacts and he stressed its credentials as both Quranic and congruent with the genius of Islam. All but anti-Sufi Muslims have cherished the conviction of the truly 'native' character of Sufism.

[44] The two Surahs 'take refuge with God' from witchcraft, the evil eye of envy and the practice of malign invocation by spells and charms—the very devices that superstition in 'folk Islam' tends to resurrect, as fears, if not features, in itself. 'Back towards animism' is always a popular temptation.

[45] *Ibid.*, pp. 215-16. The cult of 'saints', veneration of tombs and a potential charlatanery among some dervishes, are the aspects in mind.

... on the one hand the Sufi vision of the love of God and
on the other ... the springs of religion itself ...[46]

and asked: 'What will it profit the religious life of mankind?'

It was an intriguing conclusion—not one that could ever have
been, reached, or so phrased, by a mere academic. It is plain that Gibb
took a profoundly 'religious' interest in Islam both to gird and guide his
highly committed scholarship. Neither availed, as we must see, to save
him from gratuitous reproach and censure, as a dubious 'orientalist'
writing an Islam in his own distorting image. That disputatiousness only
served to delineate the issues, as a tolerant good faith has to shoulder
them, when Islam is its theme. Gibb's was a large Oxonian contribution
hardly paralleled since his day, except by one of his most perceptive
friends and pupils, Albert H Hourani.[47]

vi

The thrust of that intriguing conclusion about the counter-menace of any
'spreading to the Muslim world' of a secularity, 'gradually divorced from
the Muslim tradition' in 'a process of inner drying-up', explains Gibb's
steady concern for a contemporary Islamics. He wanted today's Islam as
firmly on the agenda of western Islamic studies as the medieval age had
so long been among connoisseurs of Al-Ghazali and his peers. This instinct
was fed by his close contact with academies in Cairo. It was evident in
the collection of essays he edited in *Whither Islam?*, published in 1933,
in response to the seismic event of the previous decade, when a new
Turkey abolished the age-long caliphate and Muslim powers were casting
around in vain for ways to re-create it.

But this interest, also reflected in his writings on recent Arabic
literature, came to its full flower in the middle of his Oxford tenure in his
Modern Trends in Islam.

Note was taken earlier of his careful *confessio* about his own
personal 'religious' vision. It was one that refused to surrender
transcendent Lordship to the 'there's-only-us' school of arrogant or
pretentious secularity, yet was alert to the implications of technology

---

[46] *Ibid.*, p. 218.
[47] See below.

and the sometime embarrassments of a crude theology affirming itself despite them. It was a 'religious attitude' to life, able to distinguish between a 'secular statehood' or 'secular law' on the one hand, and outright secularism on the other or—in the Qur'an's phrase—'the exclusion of God' from all realms of meaning and experience, as an 'unnecessary' or an 'inexpedient' or an 'empty' hypothesis.

Hence the perceived necessity for a discerning Muslim reckoning with the reality of the human role in history, as within the largesse of a still sovereign Allah to whom *muslims' islam*, in worship and obedience, would be intelligently responsive in the changes of time and place. Only so-could that *islam* fulfil the finality of its ground in prophethood and revelation.

He first outlined in *Modern Trends* 'the foundations' we have already reviewed, perhaps unduly stressing characteristics of Arab thought as struggling uncongenially with the things at stake between rationalism and intuitive attitudes that relied on a fusion of literalism and imagination. He noted that when these characteristics were brought to bear on exegesis and 'consensus' they tended to a pattern of sharp authority in law and belief. Even so, they yielded, in text and community, referents which—given the will, the will modernity required—could well serve the situation and the future. Those 'sources of law' in Islam, which had ministered so well and so long to the firmness of tradition, namely the Qur'an, the prophetic example, consensus and the 'endeavour' that engendered it, could now differently undertake the different world-scene. For the Qur'an was far from rigid in reverent hands and 'consensus', though long functioning to underwrite authority, suggested that

> religion is best left in the safe-keeping of the consciences
> of ordinary intelligent believers (with) its corollary of
> toleration of differences on secondary points.'[48]

The high hurdle there, of course, stands in who is 'intelligent', what points are 'secondary' and who is to say. But Gibb rightly identifies a principle of hope.

The next chapter in *Modern Trends* traces 'religious tension in Islam', where he cites MacDonald in underlying the familiar experience of Islamic theology in face of Greek rationality. He queries whether the

---

[48] *Modern Trends in Islam*, Chicago, 1947, pp. 14-15.

theologians truly measured what they confronted, or whether they made only a less than existential response, failing to register 'where the strength of the attack lay.'[49] The point lies at the heart of continuing vocation. Examining early Wahhabism among 'reforming' factors, Gibb observes the problem of deep entanglement in political vicissitudes and complexities.

His analysis of Muslim response to the interrogation of religious life and doctrine by the modern spirit is now half a century out of date, yet it remains relevant enough in its perception of the issues. It has not been radically overtaken by subsequent intellectual history. How far can structures of faith and law allow themselves to be virtually immunised from within, kept negligent of what should require a measure of creative self-doubt around Scripture, *Shari'ah* and social norms—a self-doubt in quest if a truer self-possession?

Gibb rightly identified two urgent aspects of this vocation. The one was the separation in education between the traditional inculcation of 'right' learning and the prevailing claims of scientific and secular skills and the many pursuits of academic freedom and human curiosity. The other was the crucial factor of 'clerical' mind-set in the turbaned world, that too rigorously willed the retention of its status as both official and personal, so that *Ijma'* and *Ijtihad* stayed safely inside its purview. The very concept of *Taqlid*, or 'hideboundness', which Muhammad 'Abduh had struggled to identify and repudiate, could easily persist in psychic form even when it was ostensibly disowned. Behind the contrasted procedures of education lay the differing concepts of 'truth', as a deposit to be securely transmitted from the past, and 'truth' as a quest reaching towards steady acquisition ahead.

If reconciling those two philosophies were not exacting enough in itself, the task at all levels was complicated by tension with the West. The secularity which made the need ineluctable came, in modern times, from the very quarter now in bitter political rejection in the lingering recession of imperialism. Moreover, this alien spur to mental change had itself been Islam's inferior pupil in an earlier era and owed something of

---

[49] *Ibid.*, p. 23. From the very origins of Islam there had been no perplexity about affirming an absolute monotheism against pagan pluralism. Perplexity was present in confronting the problems of human liability, of reason in the assessment of revelation, and of how omnipotence could be soundly understood—as these only presented themselves through contact with philosophy. Religion is often suspect to those outside it, as only answering from within a *parti pris* that has not allowed itself to think of itself outside that self-protection.

its head-start in the modern one to that Islamic tutelage. Irony, however, is rarely a solace when emotions are at the raw.

What, for present purposes around Oxford Islamics, is significant in Gibb's *Modern Trends* is not only the religious concern and academic insight of his writing but, precisely because of these, the foil he proved to be for precisely this psychic animus of resentment that took him for a 'pseudo-orientalist', a pretentious meddler in things he thereby demeaned. The unreadiness, or inability, of his critics to appreciate his motivation only served to indicate how apposite his analysis had been. For they seemed to crave for something like that immunity from self-doubt which he had tried to diagnose, as if to confirm what he had discerned in the very process of rejecting it. The situation might be merely deplored as only depressing, but that would be a faithless, unworthy reaction and one in which he would not have indulged, believing rather in the ultimate—and mutual—objectives of hope and good faith. These have to do with soul and psyche, as much as with mind and imagination.

Writing more from 'orientalist' than Islamic angle, Edward Said strangely subverts Gibb's whole perspective, seeing in his (Gibb's) review of recent Muslim intellectual history an opposition 'to any Islamic attempts to reform Islam', when his whole scholarship was a venture precisely to sustain and possibly assist such 'reform'. Said goes on:

> According to his views, reform is a betrayal of Islam: this
> is exactly Gibb's argument.[50]

That 'Islam reformed is Islam no longer' was never a dictum of Gibb's: it was a gibe uttered by Lord Cromer in his *Modern Egypt*—an ill-considered one indeed—in lofty comment on the thinking of Muhammad 'Abduh who was Grand Mufti in Cairo during Cromer's tenure as virtual ruler of Egypt.[51]

The error in the citation was lamentable yet, serves as a measure of how lost perspective can be when a psyche of enmity invades the academic scene, to pose the question:

> As for modern Islam itself, despite the complexities of his

---

[50] Edward Said, *Orientalism, op. cit.*, p. 106.
[51] Lord Cromer, *Modern Egypt*, London, 1908, Vol. 2, p. 229. It was a piece of dismissive unwisdom engaged in political depreciation of local initiatives.

otherwise magisterial understanding of it, why must it be
regarded with so implacable a hostility as Gibb's?[52]

Reactions that misrepresent are sometimes a clue to how valid
what suffers them has been.

It would not be good to leave 'the place of Arabic' and Gibb's
influence and legacy, without brief notice of his protégé, Albert Hourani.

vii

If scholars have 'mantles' as prophets do, then that of Gibb certainly
passed to Hourani who succeeded him in the Middle East Centre based
in St Antony's College, retiring in 1971. They were foundational years in
the building of that area of the college's care for the politics and societies
of Asia, Africa and the Far East. Hourani's Lebanese identity and English
nurture in Manchester and Oxford drew his prior interests into the Fertile
Crescent region, though his grasp of the whole breadth of modern Arabism
was evident enough in his two major works.[53] His mind throughout was
deeply informed by what could well be called 'the moral economy of
history', the vital dimension of spiritual impulses, however attenuated
by institutional self-interest or political guile. One of his earliest
contributions—*Minorities in the Arab World*, (Oxford, 1947) with its
care for religious tolerance and social justice—was also index to the
meticulous care he brought to the documentation of human affairs. By
essays and reviews, he exercised a wide influence on the temper of
scholarship.

In a brief early period he had found himself disenchanted with
the world of politics, where practitioners were too often the victims of
their own propaganda or at least of the need to indulge in it. Interpreters
in academic wings, however have to accept a less perceptible role in the
evolution of events. Yet, given an attentive realism, it is well to hold to
high expectations of spiritual perceptiveness as, on his own terms, Gibb

---

[52] Said, *loc. cit.*, p.106. Elsewhere he accuses Gibb of having 'entered on a career with a set
vision of the orient! (p. 277), 'writing as a coloniser,' (p. 11) and seeing Islam as 'only
Islamic orthodoxy'! (p. 278) Yet it is a relief to note that Said concedes Gibb's 'extraordinarily
sympathetic powers of identification with an alien *[sic]* religion.' (p. 263)

[53] *Arabic Thought in the Liberal Age, 1798-1939*, Oxford, 1962 and *A History of the Arab
Peoples*, London, 1991.

had done. Albert Hourani's faith-commitment, though never obtruded, was much more articulate, so that he read his academic briefs with a sober confidence in the capability of analytical honesty to disentangle the problematic and comprehend the true.

The title of his *Arabic Thought in the Liberal Age* left some readers wondering whether the 'Age' deserved the author's adjective. For Ottoman liberalism, in which Hourani was deeply interested, was never robust and often volatile in conceding the Arab autonomy that might have retained an Arab 'Ottomanism' within the empire.[54] But in the time of Taha Husain, the brothers 'Abd al-Raziq, and Ahmad Amin, the hope of an Islam alert and responsive to its contemporary tasks was brighter than it later became, when many potential 'liberals' lost their nerve and fell silent, or the counsels of *Hizb al-Tahrir* and reaction grew louder.[55] If Hourani's career demonstrated a masterly competence in the exposition of a vocation for contemporary Arabism in the 20th century, it also exemplified the scholar's frustrations in the clamour and contention of a feverish world. Yet, mentally and spiritually he inhabited no ivory tower, but clung steadfastly to the obligations that belong outwardly to the inward shrines of research. And certainly many of those whom his ideals stimulated found themselves active in political office.

Nowhere were these twin aspects of incisive thinking and inherent frustration more evident than in his writing on Palestine and the Palestinian tragedy, as both a dark measure of the politicisation of Judaism and a test case of Arabism. The political ineptness of the latter, and the painful compromise of the former, occupied much of his mind before and after 1967, when several other Arab minds fell to assessing the *Nakbah*. In the fifties he had passionately believed, like his contemporary Fa'iz Sayegh,[56] in the bright auguries for Arab nationalism. The catastrophe of 1967 had to be acknowledged as evidence of a malaise of long-standing, one that had not taken in the significance of 1948, nor understood the sad barbarisation of the high ideals of the student founders

---

[54] The issue is well explored in Hassan Saab, *The Arab Federalists of the Ottoman Empire*, Amsterdam, 1958, and in Abdulaziz A Al-Sudairi, *op. cit.*, pp. 77-105.

[55] See for example: Suha Taji-Farouki, *A Fundamental Quest: Hizb al-Tahrir and the Search for the Islamic Caliphate*, London, 1996.

[56] A Palestinian and Kuwait's Representative at UNO. See citation in my *The Arab Christian: A History in the Middle East*, London, 1991, pp. 245-46 and 256. See also: Sylvia Haim, *Arab Nationalism. An Anthology*, Berkeley, 1974, and Hazim Zaki Nuseibeh, *The Ideas of Arab Nationalism*, Ithaca, 1956.

of the Ba'th Party with their dream of a 'Fertile Crescent' in political unity. Arabism had failed to measure either the real dimensions of its encounter with Zionism, or the fractious nature of its own mentality.

Hourani realised only too keenly the irreconcilability of a Zionism determined on statehood, with the intrinsic state-seeking reality of a Palestinian nationhood.[57] Like others of his generation he could only remit the tragedy to whatever wisdom the pity—as distinct from the pride—of the religions involved might muster. As we have noted elsewhere, both Sunni Islam and political Judaism interpret adversity only as callling for (their) success. In the Palestine/Israeli conflict the tragedy is that Zionism demands to have its success unilateral.

As an academic and an analyst, Hourani saw equally clearly the necessity to distinguish between 'secular statehood' and entire 'secularity', i.e. the banishment of worship, prayer and faith from the mind and soul of society. Arabism, as predominantly nourished and educated by Islam, he saw forever alien to such outright repudiation of Allah. Yet, too often, in the name of *Allahu akbar*, Islamic assertion impeded the urgent and desirable 'secularisation' of law, or better—the inclusion within the concept of *Shari'ah* of a good, contemporary Muslim conscience, recruiting a 'lay' *ijtihad* towards a sound *ijma'*. The theme will recur here, notably in Chapters 6, 8 and 9.

In sum, Albert Hourani, in distinguished acceptance of the mantle of Gibb as of one in native right 'to the manner born', helped to set an Oxford Arabic-Islamics on its further way and to map what has become the métier of St Antony's College in respect of the Near and Middle Easts. He etched into its agenda much of what now also falls into the sphere of the Centre for Islamic Studies. His was/is the kind of mentorship that takes in—and takes up—the due relation, either to other, of religious commitment and open scholarship; the care of human rights, male and female alike, against the inroads of every kind of tyranny, intellectual and political; the testing of religious confidence in the hard school of honest agnosticism or spiritual despair; the due discipline of religious professionalism and the universal accessibility of the mysteries of faith; and the perception that, as mysteries, they have no legitimate mission except to be uncoercive and persuasive—and all these because of who and how God is in His own transcendant, ever-gentle Lordship.

From 'the place of Arabic' in these exalted measures, subsequent

---

[57] Al-Sudairi, *op. cit.*, pp. 106-128.

chapters have to take on the onus of them, in the strangely apt company of sundry figures in the past of Oxford who lie to hand for the recruitment of imagination.

Chapter 3

IDEAS OF A UNIVERSITY

i

When Matthew Arnold came in youth to Oxford its spires might be more truly described as 'brooding' rather than 'dreaming'. During the thirties and forties of the 19th century it was oppressed by an intensity of religious feeling almost beyond comprehension in the secular climate of today. Mind and soul were exercised by the Tractarians, with John Henry Newman as their most famous controversialist. The place was in ferment over due ecclesial authority and the entire doctrinal edifice of Christian belief and practice and the pursuit of piety within it.

Some twenty-five years after Newman himself had resolved his quest for certain security in the things of faith by submission to Rome and the Papacy, he wrote his most abstract work on the intellectual liabilities of truth-claims and entitled it: *An Essay in Aid of a Grammar of Assent*. By 'grammar' he seems to have been thinking of doctrine by the analogy of syntax, so that ecclesiastics—the right ones—would be the accepted arbiters of usage and meaning with, in this case, only one language with its due 'grammarians' legitimate. The grammar/doctrine analogy might work until one recalls that languages themselves are freely plural and their grammars with them.

The issue bears closely on the role and functioning of a university as, presumably, comprehensive of that plurality, yet for so long and so widely perceived as institutionally pledged to one faith-grammar, or 'orthodoxy', by which it had its mandate and pursued its role. That had been the case for centuries with 'Christian' Oxford no less than with 'Islamic' Al-Azhar in their contrasted idioms.

The problems Newman found in his 'Anglican' Oxford were no small part of his theological unease. Years after his defection to Rome, he was invited to inaugurate a 'Catholic' University in Dublin. From that context he wrote his *The Idea of a University*, in which he set out his resolution of the duty of a university to embrace all learning yet somehow also under-write the necessary truth of a religion.

Newman's relevance to Islam, in this context, is obvious.

For leaders in the 20th century of what is loosely called Islamic modernism have recognised a like dilemma in sustaining the final truth of Islam within a will to genuine openness for all knowledge, and the holding of these together in the structure of a university. Minds, both Christian and Muslim, have wrestled with the terms in which loyalty to either as a necessary 'orthodoxy' could truly coexist with the duty to fulfil the 'universal' reach of knowledge in the liberty it necessitates. The impulse to want the 'Christianization', the 'Islamization', of all truth has been present in each. There has been a parallel strategy in the reconciliation of reason and revelation, provided each is rightly read.

Thus, for example, Muhammad 'Abduh, Grand Mufti of Egypt and voice of 'modernism' in Egyptian Islam (1849-1905), sees

> ... the authority of reason liberated from all that held it bound and from every kind of *taqlid* enslaving it, thus restored to its proper dignity, to do its proper work in judgement and wisdom, always in humble submission to God alone and in conformity to His sacred law. Within its (these) bounds there are no limits to its activity and no end to the researches it may pursue.[1]

Newman's reconciling formula is uncannily like 'Abduh's.

> Right reason, that is reason rightly exercised leads the mind to the Catholic Faith and plants it there and teaches it in all its religious speculations to act under its guidance ... But Reason, considered as a real agent in the world, and as the operative principle in man's nature, with an historical course and definite results ... considers itself from first to last independent and supreme. It requires no external authority: it makes a religion for itself.[2]

Both writers, with their provisos about 'rightly', 'proper', 'conformity', seem to be hedging the academic liberty they proclaim,

[1] Muhammad 'Abduh, *Risalat al-Tawhid*, Cairo, 1897, p. 10, English trans. 'The Theology of Unity', ed. Kenneth Cragg and Isaac Musaad, London, 1966, p. 27. *Taqlid*—'blind traditionalism' 'devotion to what has always been so.'
[2] J H Newman, *The Idea of a University*, ed. C P Harrold, London, 1957, Discourse 8.

either by 'reserving' the rights of dogma or by circumscribing its realms of operation. Are they not requiring that 'universities' be 'Muslim', 'Christian', thereby exempting them from the full and free scope that, otherwise seen, is their only métier? Faiths like grammars may determine the syntax that governs them in creed and structure. Do not universities belong to a multi-lingual world?

The issue which was profoundly disturbing to Newman has been no less so inside 20th century Islam. It makes a compelling field for any Oxford Centre for Islamic Studies. Aspects of the intellectual agenda as drawn by recent Islamic thinking will be the concern of Chapter 8 in sequel to other themes that bear upon it, explored in Chapter 7, while a final Chapter 9 aims—as all faith must—to come where all discourse ends.

Here, meanwhile, the hope is to study the long traditions of Muslim education by the light of the intellectual perceptions of a John Henry Newman and their personal story. Thanks to the Oxford Movement few names come so readily to mind when Oxford religion is mentioned. There are, of course, great disparities, not to be ignored. Yet it is precisely these that can make the exercise illuminating.

ii

We begin where Newman did with a highly Anglican Oxford—an Oxford with which he found himself pleasantly congenial for years after he arrived in Trinity College and later, surprisingly, found himself a Fellow of Oriel. The misgivings he developed concerned a wholly inter-Christian issue about Church authority and history. Entire in his hostility to 'secularisation', he grew reluctant about the Anglican shape of defence against it, in view of what he came to think its dubious grounds and of its vulnerable tolerance of 'liberalism'. The Roman Catholicism in which he finally sought refuge could re-assure him about 'validity' and fortify him against 'tolerance'.

Rome would serve him to intensify what Anglican Oxford assumed, namely the religious definition proper to a university. It is important for any present discourse with Islam that the principles enshrined in Anglican Oxford be understood. They had their roots back in the Hebraic, Biblical theme of 'a holy nation and a royal priesthood',[3]

---

[3]   The First Epistle of Peter 2.5 and 9 takes up the theme of 'chosen nationhood', 'holy nation' and 'royal priesthood' from the Hebraic tradition of a 'people' with whom God dwells and through whom His Name is to be known. Cf. pp. 16-17 above.

in the vital significance of those transferred adjectives. One would expect to read 'a royal nation' (Davidic, Solomonic, monarchical) and 'a holy priesthood' (Aaronic, Sadoqite). Not so: the nation, the power-realm, should be 'consecrated' no less than the 'clerisy', while 'priesthood' as the vocation to 'consecrate and be consecrated' should. extend through all the corridors of power.

In Hebraic terms, this vision pre-supposed a single divinely 'covenanted' people. In New Testament terms of an open peoplehood under God, no longer isolated in a single ethnicity, no longer tied to birth and land and private culture but accessible to all and sundry, 'bringing their glory and honour into it', the 'holy power, hallowed nation' concept lay—a hidden clue—awaiting its future. This the Church willed to be.

Through three formative centuries, that open Church 'people of God' in wholly religious, non-political terms sustained its life as *illicita* under pagan Rome, exposed to intermittent persecution and entirely innocent of power and politics, until Constantine and his imperial adoption of the Christian Church. Those three centuries of Christian 'secular' jeopardy have always remained as a potential monitor of mind in scrutiny or disquiet around the implications of Constantinian empowerment.

When empire—for its own ends—married the Church the new, and for long ambiguous, situation could hardly be read as other than providential after the dark trauma of an oppressive Rome. And that ancient formula of 'holiness *qua* power' and 'state *qua* sanctity' lay readily to hand in the Biblical tradition. Could 'empire', then, now be 'sacred' and the Church the counterpart of politics? The long idea and ideal of 'Christendom' were born. It took shape, after the brief reversal of Julian the Apostate, in the long 'Rome of East and West', in Byzantium, and Charlemagne and 'the Holy Roman Empire'. The horizons are familiar enough. When the ferment of the Reformation disturbed the power-equation of the medieval Church in also repudiating its politicised dogmas, and when the Counter-Reformation replied by reinforcing imperial means, the Reformed expressions of faith and Church inevitably took refuge in state-patronage within the territories which had themselves generated the doctrinal reform. When Rome aimed, via agents like Emperor Charles V and Philip II of Spain, to assert a single hegemony of dogma and power, resistance to the dogma in turn recruited the national organs of power.

In such terms—and broad brevity—Elizabethan England became 'this Protestant realm'. Through its own incidence in the story Oxford followed suite, becoming both the victim and the beneficiary of these tumultuous events. By the time of Newman there was a certain sedateness about its Anglicanism, though the secularising influences of Benjamin Jowett lay close ahead. Every college had its own chapel. Dons were clerical, celibate, pledged to the Thirty Nine Articles and the Book of Common Prayer. 'Dissenters' were still excluded—and women also. Until as late as 1931, all students had to pass Responsions, a mild examination in Holy Scripture. The 'ideal' of the university was unmistakeably 'Anglican' with 'Divinity' still the Queen of Sciences' and the mentor of the arts—'Divinity' according to the doctrine of the Church of England.

Yet, 'England', as the Civil War and the Commonwealth in the 17th century had demonstrated, was far from unanimously 'Christian' in Church of England terms. There were long-suffering Roman Catholic 'recusants', Methodists—shaped by two great Oxford Anglicans, John and Charles Wesley of Lincoln College, and only severed from the State Church by its obtuseness—and, of far longer vintage, the sectarians. Even so, the 'national' ideal remained of an English Church somehow coterminous with an English people.

For all its entrenched status and the staying power of its monopoly, it had a certain instinct for tolerance which, indeed, was part of Newman's growing distrust of it. It ought to have been far more seriously exercised about 'validity', far more vigilant about what it conceded of 'the rights of God' or 'the truth of Christ'. The classic exponent of its virtues had been the 'judicious Richard Hooker' of Elizabethan times, whose *The Laws of Ecclesiastical Polity* had reasoned patiently with sectarians about the discipline of sweet reason and had invited them into a Church dedicated to 'sound learning, Scriptural loyalty and personal holiness', each corroborating the other. Figures as famous as Edmund Burke and as late as the young Gladstone still thought of a nation in which the 'subject' and the 'communicant' could be one and the same. The ideal was the very essence of Anglican Oxford.

In his sonorous prose Richard Hooker had stated its 'genius.'

> Let it stand for our final conclusion that, in a free Christian State or Kingdom, where one and the self-same people are the Church and the Commonwealth, God through Christ directing the people to see it for good and weighty considerations expedient that their Lord and Governor in cases civil have also in ecclesiastical affairs a supreme

> power ... the light of reason doth lead them to it and against
> it God's revealed Law hath nothing.[4]

Of course it could not survive. Something more pre-Constantinian would have to displace it. Growing secularity, the gathering disquiet about forms of faith we have seen in Matthew Arnold, the onset of scientific positivism which found a haven in Wadham College later in the century—these influences would steadily dissolve both the solidities and the genius of Victorian Oxford.[5] Minds like Dean Richard Church, set to perpetuate Hooker's 'holy intellectualism' in a different age, would be hard pressed to hold the university firm against the inroads of scepticism and the alarmism of both the Tractarians and the creationists.[6] Newman's influential flight into authority as a haven, rather than as a tryst with truth, only deepened the task.

The Oxford of that mid-century, one might say, was in a truly 'islamic' situation, however odd the suggestion seems. By the long Biblical tradition we have reviewed, state power was still under-writing an 'established' religious faith. The propriety of this inter-play of creed and polity, though entering into anxious doubts, was still assumed in institutional form. It was deemed right and due that the Crown should hold the faith, and believers/subjects hold to the supremacy of the Crown. The warrant of a faith was entrusted to the governance of a realm and that governance pledged to that faith. The 'islamic' quality is obvious. Was/is not 'the royal supremacy' a sort of 'caliphate', a régime to which is entrusted the care and the fortunes of a religion?

---

[4] Richard Hooker (1554-1600), *The Laws of Ecclesiastical Polity*, ed. 1841, Oxford, Vol. 2, p. 514, i.e. Book 8, Chap. ii, paragraph 6. Hooker acquired the title 'judicious' for his careful use of reason, his peace-loving, peace-making instinct and the patience of his prodigious argumentation. He thought it possible to reconcile all reasonable people once dissuaded from counsels of bigotry or sectarian pride. His work earned the praise of Pope Clement VIII. His case for 'the royal supremacy' saw the body politic as a 'commonwealth' of things spiritual and political, in one with the Throne as *'intra ecclesiam non supra ecclesiam.'*

[5] Thanks to a notable tutor named Richard Congreve (1818-99) who had adopted the philosophy of Auguste Comte, reading human religion as emerging out of pagan superstition, via traditional theology, into 'the religion of humanity' as a secular humanism that had 'grown out of' those earlier 'illusions'.

[6] Richard Church (1815-90), Dean of St Paul's, *Occasional Papers*, London, 1897, Vol ii, pp. 390-91. 'What he wanted to find, what it was the main object of his life to find, was a great and effective engine against liberalism. When he made up his mind that Anglicanism was not strong enough for the task, he left it for a system which had one strong power—which claimed to be able to shut up dangerous thoughts.'

But there is one subtle difference. Islam arose with no antecedent concept either of 'a holy nation' or a 'royal priesthood'. For, unlike Jewry and Judaism, it did not originate in covenantal ethnicity.[7] Nor did it share the sacramental principle implicit in 'priesthood' as feasibly a political dimension. Its marriage of *Din* and *Dawlah*, its evolution via the Hijrah from 'preaching' to 'rule', were entirely practical and pragmatic, making it uninhibitedly political by a logic of events. The theory of the caliphate came later through the crises of succession to Muhammad. He had become a ruler by dint of the perceived necessities of being a successful prophet. The legitimacy of the process was never called in question, though Shi'ah experience disputed the course it took.[8]

With these contrasted Biblical and Quranic antecedents, there is a radical distinction between the Christian and the Muslim perceptions of power in religion. Its nature makes it no small part of contemporary discourse between us. Broadly, we might set the contrast down as, for the Christian Church, the consecration of power, for Islam 'concurrence with power', the one seen as 'sacramental', the other as 'complementary'.

It is well known that Islam and Muslims have great difficulty in relating to Christian sacramentalism, there being 'no priestcraft in Islam'.[9] The meaning has to return to the Biblical source we have examined. The external world is a theatre for human hallowing, so that 'what we do with what there is,' acknowledges and takes it as meant for sanctity, that is, material to be received with gratitude, wonder, and a sense of entrustedness. It is like a raw material awaiting what, by our right utilising

---

[7] Arabism has always been a crucial element in Islam (Cf. Ismail al-Faruqi, *'Urubah and Religion*, Amsterdam, 1962, and his (with Lois al-Faruqi), *The Cultural Atlas of Islam*, New York, 1986. Islam, however, has no ethnic 'Sinai' in Hebraic terms but, rather, goes back to Abraham and presents Muhammad as 'a mercy to the worlds.'

[8] Shi'ah Islam derived from political disputing of the caliphal succession over the prior claim of 'Ali which was only allowed after three predecessors whom the Sunnis regard as 'the rightly guided caliphs.' That issue was further embittered by the tragic deaths of 'Ali, Hasan and, most of all, of Husain at Karbala'—whence there came a theology of holy martyrdom unique to the Shi'ah. There were also questions about the shape of Quranic exegesis and the role of the Imams in ensuring the truth of Islam. See Chap. 7, pp. 135-43.

[9] The Qur'an speaks of Christian clergy only as *ruhban* ('monks') alongside Jewish *ahbar* ('rabbis') (9.31) and takes no cognisance of the pastoral, sacramental 'office' of men so 'ordained'. Surah 57.27 disowns *rahbaniyyah* ('monasticism') as a wrong 'invention' on human part, though the same passage commends Jesus' followers, as having 'hearts of compassion and mercy'. The religious 'officers' in Sunni Islam are those of law and learning, not of rite or liturgy, though the 'sacramental' dimension is there in e.g. prostration and pilgrimage but always personally 'administered'.

and possessing, we confer upon it to fulfil that for which it was divinely meant in creation.

Thus 'all that is, is (potentially) holy' and how we act decides whether it will stay so according to the spirit and temper of our usage of it. This sacramental sense pervades sexuality and social experience and action. It is focused in intensive ways in ritual hallowing, in liturgy and festival. These belong 'extensively' in all the ways and walks of life. The conception—and the practice—are thus at once susceptible of claiming translation into the realm of politics, so that governing, ruling, legislating, controlling, are understood as necessitating a presiding sense of power as 'sacred', divinely delegated only in those terms and only in those terms duly exercised.

Islam is no stranger to something of the sacramental, for example, in ablution and prostration in *Salat*, in pilgrimage and fast, when things deliberately done in the body transact meanings meant in the heart, so that in measure, the meanings 'happen' and only so, via the doing done. To exclude this dimension would make any and all religion impossible.

While power as a trust *can* belong with Islamic theory, it seems fair to read power in the traditional caliphate as rather the practical 'complement' of the faith than its sacramental task, given and received as such. No doubt, either way, power can be travestied and lapse into tyranny and self-interest.

But it will be relevant how such violation is seen—and whether it is accused in duly corrective terms. Either way, *Al-Mulk li-Llah*, 'Sovereignty is God's.' Does it complement faith, or can faith consecrate it?

Things political, in any event, turn on themes doctrinal—due to be our concern in Chapter 8. The long venture of Anglican Oxford in 'established' Christianity returns us to the theme with which we began as to where we go, from minds like Newman and Muhammad 'Abduh, about an ideology of a university, the place it has for a faith, the duty it has to all knowledge.

iii

It is well throughout to remember that we 'cannot buy wisdom with less than wonder,'[10] and that 'wonder'—among the ultimate sanctions of religion—is sometimes forfeit in the setting of scientific and technological self-esteem. Laboratories need indeed to be known as sanctuaries, but they cannot well operate by recourse to prayer and praise. Moreover, the autonomies that all sciences properly demand, the freedom to pursue evidences wherever they lead without restraining limits external to their pursuit, have often rung alarm bells in the citadels of faith, lest their implications should threaten orthodoxies and the ways of life they inculcate.

An accentuated form of the old tension between revelation and reason, between religious authority and the free quest of knowledge, resulted from post-Renaissance sciences and was deepened further in the late 19th century by new disciplines of sociology and psychology. These attempted to transfer the techniques and ideas of the physical sciences to more intractable realms closer to religious susceptibilities. A further ingredient of freedom *cum* alarm stemmed from an increasing 'law-unto-ourselves' mood in the arts and literature, thrusting out from under the aegis of religious auspices and obligations.

Universities with the instincts of an Oxford or an Al-Azhar were the obvious spheres in which these tensions throbbed and where they demanded institutional solution, interrogating, as they did, the entire 'idea of a university'. Calendars—east and west—in no way tally but the issues do. Something of what is long past in the one is still to culminate in the other.

There is, therefore, a fascinating parallel between Newman's desire in *The Idea of a University* to keep all learning duly Catholic and the efforts in Muslim circles to have all knowledge in due 'Islamicized' care. There is a similar concession to the right of free enquiry, yet conditioned in differing ways by the over-riding prerogatives of the religious faith.

It was ironical that Newman made his case for 'the Catholic University' in reaction to what he saw as Oxford's feeble Anglicanism—a thing compromised by its 'Christian' fallibility—when his own new Roman allegiance owed its freedom to new Anglican measures of Catholic

---

[10] Memorably said by G Wilson Knight, *Neglected Papers*, London, 1971, p. 235. He is writing about Arnold's 'Thyrsis'.

emancipation which he had himself stubbornly opposed. Such ironies, however, are frequent in religious tensions. It needs to be remembered that his *The Idea of a University* was published as Nine Discourses to the Catholics of Dublin and Occasional Lectures and Essays to Catholics of the University. Thus he was addressing adherents in order to fortify them. Even so, his case-making indicates his whole philosophy of 'right' education.

Discourse V, which was omitted in the edition of 1859, seven years after the first in 1852, was the most solicitous for faith protection. Academic freedom was the right of the sciences but the scientists should 'show a Catholic spirit' and be judiciously prudent. 'The Church was necessary to their integrity,' and served to 'steady' the scientific task. Ecclesiastical authority had to be the supreme guide, to be 'an *ipso facto* confutation of any reasoning inconsistent with it.'[11]

> A university, so-called, that refuses to profess the Catholic
> Creed is, from the nature of the case, hostile both to the
> Church and to philosophy.[12]

A loyal Catholic spirit was thus obligatory. Newman was obsessively alert to 'the infidelity of the age' and the susceptibility of humankind to moral weakness and intellectual confusion which secular teaching too often abetted. Hence the urgent role of a protecting faith and Church, as 'visible antagonist'. He was even ready to anticipate that dogmatism would experience something like that 'ebb' on Dover Beach, (though the poem was not quoted) but the faithful should not weaken. 'Large tolerance of theology' could be in 'union (with) an intense hatred'.[13] He castigated the newly planned university in London as liable to be 'a sort of bazaar or hotel, not the majestic vision of the Middle Age' There was pretentiousness in 'striving for a science comprehensive of all the sciences'. For science needed the context that only right theology could supply. It was 'right in (its) proper place as portions of one system of knowledge, suspicious when detached or in bad company.'[14] So science had to make its peace with the claims of theology. For 'not to be at peace

---

[11] John Henry Newman, *The Idea of a University*, ed. C P Harrold, London, 1947, pp. xxvii and 11.

[12] *Ibid.*, p. 406.

[13] *Ibid.*, pp. 384, 306 and 288.

[14] *Ibid.*, pp. 393, 398.

was to be at war' and a half-truth, even a nine-tenths truth, was still untruth.[15] Freedom of thought had to be rescued from its own suicidal excesses and the only capacity to do so belonged to

> The representative society and civilisation of the human race, as its perfect result and limit ... that supernatural society and system which our Maker has given us directly from Himself, the Christian polity ...[16]

'The idea of a university' meant

> ... a wisdom safe from the excesses and vagaries of individuals, embodied in institutions which have stood the trial and received the sanction of ages, administered by men who have no need to be anonymous, as being supported by their consistency with their predecessors and with each other.[17]

Newman's prescripts were certainly clear and, for him, indubitable. A university should promote intellectual excellence in line with a judicious orthodoxy. That he was writing expressly of his vision for Dublin does not diminish what he saw as universal to universities.

iv

Years had passed since his departure from Oxford and there is significance in his migration both of place and mind. What is intriguing for present purposes is the echo his counsels find, all unconsciously, in the minds of Muslims during their late 14th and into their opened 15th centuries. There is the same claim to liberty of scientific thought and experiment, the same caveats about due conformity to the authority of *iman* and *Shari'ah*, the same claim to 'confutation' of what errs, the same will to confrontation with what the due canons find 'suspicious'.

The main difference has to do with how the issues have intensified and how the pace of them has accelerated for recent Muslim experience, as compared with the slower, more domestic, incidence of

---

[15] *Ibid.*, pp. 389, 401.
[16] *Ibid.*, p. 222.
[17] *Ibid.*, p. xxxviii.

technology in the Western setting.[18] More particularly the hazards—and so the protection—of youth figure more crucially than in Newman's day. Muslim educationalists have been exercised by how the social sciences tend to undermine the sense of religious absolutes. The focus of sociology on phenomena, on how rituals behave and pieties habituate, implies that they are purely relative to human emotions and have no absolute reference to objective truth.

Or the psychologists discredit dogma by comprising its warrant wholly in mental processes of fantasy or fear or sexual urge. Believers—indeed all social beings—can come to be seen as 'puppets' in a bizarre scenario by which they can know it so, and yet be totally incapable of having it otherwise. Such notions of how their fidelity should really be read can be devastating to the integrity of faith and to the disciplines of obedience.

Or, again, there is the increasing awareness of inescapable diversity in religious versions of the world. Why so many creeds, now so far and so disconcertingly aware of each other? If there is, indeed, either accident or optionality in what one holds, so that birth elsewhere, or education different, would have left me other than I am, how can finality belong to what is mine and allegiance to it continue mandatory? Youth in universities are, of course, strongly susceptible to these faith-disputing, if not disrupting, factors. It must, therefore, seem to some to be part of their function to resist and offset them by being vigorous champions of an 'orthodox' Islam, its creed and practice. But do they then fall short of the ideal of a university as mother of all the arts and mentor of all intellectual enquiry?

That issue extends into the fascinating theme of 'futurology'— the shape of the Islam that is to be, or needs to become. Given the finality of its revelation, the ultimacy of its Prophet, and the irrepeatability of its Qur'an, how are its universities to ensure that, in the pace of change, its norms do not become obsolete and its centuries overtaken? Given the strong sense of self-completeness and of self-assurance that has long been characteristic of Islam,[19] indebtedness towards, still more

---

[18] 'Domestic' here in the sense that the modern factors in ocean navigation, engineering, industrial production, and experimentation were 'on home ground', whereas—by and large—they impinged on Islamic cultures from external relations and did so at a greatly accelerated rate, e.g. in the Gulf via oil and in Egypt, earlier, via Napoleon and Muhammad 'Ali's emulation.

[19] Deriving from a 'final' revelation, the view in Surah 30.30 that Islam ideally fits human nature, the thesis of the partial corruption of other Scriptures, and the re-assuring completeness of Muslim conquests and wide global expansion.

dependence on, non-Islamic sources become the more uncongenial and problematic. For the more recent ventures of science and of ethics that pre-occupy the faculties of learning stem largely from outside *Dar al-Islam*, in pointed contrast to how it was in what Newman called 'the Middle Age.'

As a passionate Tertullian once asked: 'What has Athens to do with Jerusalem?', so the loyal Muslim might query: 'What has Oxford to offer to Mecca?' The great Tunisian Qairawan was splendidly remote in its physical locale, its vast swirl of desert territory serving its vigilance against attack. Should it then symbolise the right guardianship entrusted to such academies—if only the times could allow?

That the times do not is part of the dilemma. Can it be met by something like Newman's ideology, in some 'Islamicization of all knowledge' such as has been called for in the last quarter-century? What may be legitimate in those western social sciences that hold such menace for the weak of faith, must be taken out of the purview of western secularism and pursued within the constraints of loyally Islamic norms. There has to be an Islamic counterpart to UNESCO, fulfilling duly Islamic norms for Muslim intelligentsia and Islamic nation-states. Muslims can absorb whatever is legitimate in sociology, psychology and media sciences, by ensuring that they are kept within the constraints by which Islam is sufficient to itself. University education can and should be instrumental to this purpose. Technology may foster secular habits of mind but should not be left to do so without Islam as the entire corrective.

This requires what might be called an Islamic epistemology, that is, a due aligning of the criteria of truth with the principles of Islam. Reason must concede that there are revelatory, i.e. Quranic, sources of guidance to which reason must be humble to defer and which reason of itself could not attain. These, by the same token, leave open territories proper to reason which faith will validate and admit, provided they are properly taken. The Muslim task was somehow 'to recast the whole legacy of human knowledge from the standpoint of Islam'.[20] The principle of *Tawhid* could be invoked on that behalf, in the sense that 'the unity of Allah' meant the unity of all truth and, thus, of all sound scholarship. It would be possible, as it were, to disavow secularity by enfolding the sciences that conduced to it, and the arts that reflected it, under the mantle

---

[20] See, for example, the work of Ismail al-Faruqi (note 7) and his advocacy of the Washington Institute of Islamic Thought in his *Islamicisation of Knowledge: General Principles and Work-Plan*, Washington, 1982. More generally the publications of the Islamic IESCO.

of Islamic religion, intelligently held and practised. Divine sovereignty comprehensively acknowledged in Muslim terms, intelligently followed, could rectify the moral and spiritual aberrations that western techniques provoke and bring social norms, public and private, to proper sanity and due social health. Earlier 20th century modernism of the 'Abduh style had been too sanguine in its aims. There was a need to reach more fundamentally into the abiding adequacy of the essence of Islam.[21]

Could this posture be akin, if only remotely, to how Newman meant to resolve the role of a university? The two scenarios are years and idioms apart. Yet both are answering what is seen as threatening. Each is falling back on an all-embracing structure of fidelity that is claimed to be capable of resolving all else, given that its warrant is fully conceded. Yet are not the questions present in effect given back as answers? Both philosophers and theologians down the centuries have been known to do as much.[22] There still remain at issue the credentials of the all-inclusive structured solution, its historical claim to acceptance and its susceptibility to contradiction whether from other doctrine or from agnostic instincts.

'A Vocational Study' in Chapter 8 is intended to explore more inclusive intellectual themes for a Muslim presence in Oxford arising from this chapter's general concern. Perhaps we have to ask whether religious faith-systems do not have to 'live and let live' alongside a technologising secularity, rather than busy and weary themselves putting the world to rights by lights communal only, or mainly, to themselves.[23] Neither Islam nor Christianity could readily consent to that. But before we pass to why—and how—not, it will be well to measure—in deliberate paradox—the relevance of their irrelevance.

v

The physical sciences are great levellers or neutralisers of religious convictions, in the sense that they are pursued within their own parameters

---

[21] Cf. discussion by Fazlur Rahman 'Islam: Challenges and Opportunities', in ed. A T Welch and P Cachia, *Islam: Past Influence and Present Challenge*, Edinburgh, 1997, pp. 315-30.

[22] Notably the great Abu-1-Hasan 'Ali al-Ash'ari (873-935) who 'resolved' the issue of free-will and divine *Qadar* by holding that 'Allah willed in the will of the doer,' reinstating the two, but avoided pressing further to ask whether the doer could 'help' willing it. Examples are numerous of problems conceded and abandoned.

[23] As D H Lawrence commended in reproaching Jesus for being too busy 'doing good' at so great cost. Cf. *The Man who Died*, in *The Short Novels*, Vol. 2, London, 1956, pp. 3-45.

of research without reference to Jerusalem or Mecca, to the Bible or the Qur'an, to Chalcedon or the Creed of Al-Nasafi, in respect of their tasks, their queries or their findings. Laboratories proceed by reference to their own criteria and these do not require them—in a professional quality— to consult church or mosque. If one is dealing with botany, or epidemiology, or aeronautics, or anatomy, or pathology, one does not need attendant adjectives like Hindu, or Buddhist, as one would in addressing philosophy or culture. There is no distinctively Islamic way of flying a plane or conducting a post-mortem on the human body.[24]

It is this sheer operative neutrality *vis-à-vis* religions of the sciences and the skills of technology that must give pause to the ambition to bring *all* that universities must undertake into the purview of religious belief. Is not this situation only clear evidence of the real and actual autonomy that Christianity and Islam always affirmed humankind to possess by the gift of 'dominion' and *khilafah*? Must it not follow that, in this sense, humankind has to be allowed to be free to be 'secular'? If so, it must further mean that religion must be committed to the independence of the techniques of science—a situation which must circumscribe their desire to be categorical, though still vigilant, in this area of their relationship to knowledge.

Vigilance has to bear upon the fruits and implications of such autonomous sciences, the ethical issues they raise, the cultural and social consequences they entail. With these any secular autonomy ends. For, these technologies pass into realms where everything becomes more than secular, everything is a candidate for holiness. It is in this vocation that religious faith comes back into its own as in some sense its mentor, its guardian, its carer and disciple. Then the *Tawhid*, the 'unity' Islam affirms, the 'Lordship' of 'God in Christ', pass out of mere—if necessary—assertion and move as dynamic service, as the will to consecration. Transcendence is then understood, not simply as an affirmation dogma needs to make, but as an enabling summons in the soul.

Such a reading of *Allahu akbar* needs taking further in a final chapter. Here, concerning 'the idea of a university,' the clue seems to lie in Ludwig Wittgenstein's words to 'define' religion:

---

[24] This is not to deny the contributions religious thought and culture have made to the progress of the sciences. Cf. A N Whitehead, *Science and the Modern World*, New York, 1925, who finds 'the habit of definite exact thought ... implanted in the European mind by the long dominance of scholastic logic.' Chap. 1. Medieval and Renaissance science had large debts also to Islamic stimulus.

> A religious belief could only be something like a passionate commitment to a system of reference. Hence, although it is belief, it is ... passionately seizing hold of this interpretation. Instruction in a religious faith, therefore, would have to take the form of a portrayal, a description, of that system of reference, while at the same time being an appeal to conscience.[25]

He sees what he calls 'this combination' requiring the student personally to take passionate hold of what he has glimpsed out of 'hopelessness' so that, though led to it by a tutor, he/she 'runs to grasp it.' Only so doing does it become their own.

This makes religion not, as for Newman, 'a grammar of assent' but instead a passion—informing, to be sure, but possessing heart and mind. Faith may then be something like what T S Eliot understood to be the nature of a music.

> '... heard so deeply
> That it is not heard at all, but you are the music
> While the music lasts.'[26]

'Last' it will—given its own energy as love. It must follow, then, that the 'passion' Wittgenstein commends is only and always interior to the disciple, not external as the thrust of an imposition in the manner of bigotry and zealotry. Instead of pontifically enjoining, it is its proper genius simply to avail, to be accessible, to live for commendation beyond its own communal authority, as that which wills faith-hospitality. It is then 'public truth' by virtue of its open intelligibility and its universal relevance, not as that which must impose its warrant to acceptance by dint of institutional aggression.

vi

If the conclusion is sound, any 'Islamicization of knowledge' must be of this order, not a will to make Islamic norms or precepts the condition of

---

[25] Cited from L Wittgenstein, *Culture and Value*, ed. G H von Wright, trans. P Winch, Chicago, 1980, sect. 1947.
[26] T S Eliot; *The Four Quartets*, 'Dry Salvages', London, 1959, V, p. 44.

every intellectual quest and every scientific finding. If we are thinking in terms of grammar, perhaps we should see religious faith as rightly in the subjunctive mood *vis-à-vis* where technology goes, yet urgently affirmative about what technology owes to God and society in the disciplines of ethics, justice, compassion and truth. Only those affirmatives will rightly take it into the imperative mood with 'Thus says the Lord,' seeing that there can be no valid *islam* that is not freely brought.

This will be no compromise of what has long thought itself 'an imperative religion'.[27] For the autonomy that was commissioned in the divine enterprise of human 'dominion' has never been coercive, witness the absence—strange by other criteria—of any divine veto on genetic engineering, the internet, the intrusions of pharmacology into sexuality, or all the myriad devices of human 'colonialism',[28] or even on blasphemy itself. All these remain feasible to us despite the sundry ways in which they jeopardise or repudiate the trust we carry for all the values they may compromise or fail to obey.

Religion, then, in loyalty to its deepest warrant as faith, must be ready to de-tyrannise any role it means to play in the world, to realise what writ its symbols, rites and meanings possess, and to have them present as only echoing Allah's own question: 'Am I not your Lord?'[29]

It is uniquely difficult for contemporary Islam to have this esteem of itself, given the long centuries as an insistently 'categorical' religion, more essentially politicised than any other. Yet must not the intended intercourse of Islam and Oxford, or of Islam and any other dimension dialogical, be of this order? It will not mean any abandonment of the ancient inter-obligations of *Din* and *Dawlah*, nor any forfeiture of the role faith must play in any body politic. Explicit issues here belong with Chapter 6. It will be the interior fervour in which its 'system of reference' is held by its faithful adherents that must identify and sustain the clues it needs for a sound polity and for the integrity of politics in the care of *falah*, or well-being.[30]

---

[27] See Fazlur Rahman, *Major Themes of the Qur'an*, Minneapolis, 1980, 'The Qur'an the Command of God for man ...', p. xi, '... works by its own laws, which have been ingrained in it by God ... the aim is man and his behaviour', p. 3.

[28] In the sense of Surah 11.61. 'God has made you colonists *(ista'marakum)* in the earth.'

[29] The pointed question to all humanity in Surah 7.172 put in the negative to expect—and await—the answer Yes! which all humanity has made in a cosmic acknowledgement of their entrustment under God.

[30] *Falah*, the term used in the call to prayer—the *adhan* of the muezzin. 'Come ye unto good' or 'well-being'.

Nor will it mean that all has receded into the neutrality of academicism from which 20th century Muslims have often felt they have suffered. To say that 'the passionate commitment to the Islamic system of reference' is properly interior to the believer is in no way to have its passion retreat into a private realm. For then it would have ceased to be either passion or commitment. It will not mean that faith hibernates away from any of the pursuits of a university or that it accepts to be merely tolerated by academia that think it antiquarian or obsolete and treat it as a mere relic. Nor will it concur in the notion of some 'orientalists' that Islam can be simply a research field that lays no claim on belief, and whose history, theology, biography, are phenomena like rocks for geologists or ruins for the archaeologists.

On the contrary, 'faiths have their reasons' and rightly seek the scrutiny of a learning that is more than a neutralising academic interest. The gentleness of its academic presence, for which we are arguing, must not be mistaken for apology about itself. Just as the sciences must be allowed their due autonomy of enquiry and pursuit, so faiths have to be intellectually articulate in the very integrity of their 'passionate commitment'. Just as a laboratory is more than academic, so also is a sanctuary. In some sense they have each to dwell in the other.

vii

It would seem that two questions remain to occupy in their several ways ensuing chapters. The one is: 'What can be meant by passionate attachment?' The other: 'What is the theme of "the system of reference?"' There needs to be some interrogation of both phrases. It is remarkable about all religions how far they can admit of wide disparity about what allegiance means and demands. Ambivalence here is notable in universities. Variants of Christianity, varieties of Islam, abound in every walk of life. Islam, to be sure, had/has a stringent 'law of apostasy' by which no born-Muslim, or convert to Islam, may explicitly renounce Islam or otherwise call in avowed question any of its cardinal items of faith concerning the Prophet, the Imams, the Qur'an or the *Shari'ah*. Given that the legal penalty for apostasy is death, there is here a grievous intimidation, a grim threat to freedom of movement of belief and enquiry. No religion claiming to be one, should equip itself with sanctions that so conspire against all integrity of allegiance.

Yet, short of explicit apostasy by word or gesture, there are endless approximations to, or departures from, a full Islam. These pass muster and prevail, despite the efforts of rigorists and purists to incriminate them. The problem, present in all religions as to what identifies a 'right and true' adherent, was alive for Islam from its first century. Inasmuch as unworthy Muslims ought to be disqualified from ruling, the Khawarij disputed the Umayyad claims. Did the *Shahadah*, on lips alone, suffice or should it be accompanied by ritual and moral acts before it constituted a 'valid' Muslim? If it did not, who should adjudicate? Or were the Murjites right in leaving the issue to hope and to Allah?

Thus, through long centuries, rigorists and sectarians and militants apart, there have been constant partial 'apostasies' either tolerated or—by any agreed standards—undetectable. Accepting the situation to be such, and striving spiritually towards a due attainment of Islam in its viable and ideological criteria, are a large part of Muslim vocation in a university. More specifics belong in Chapter 8.

What, though, for Muslims, is 'the system of reference'? Summary answer has perhaps best been suggested by the Chicago scholar, Marshall Hodgson, when he wrote:

> For Muslims, being based on revelation means being in response to a total moral challenge, as it is confronted in an explicit divine message handed on through a loyal human community.[31]

That certainly incorporates the Qur'an, the *Shari'ah*, the *Ummah*, *fiqh* and *Shahadah*. It embraces the implicit reality of creation under creaturehood, human entrustment and the guiding ministry of prophethood. The Islamic State may be read in the 'loyalty' of community, as also may the Pillars of Religion. All are summed up in 'divine message'. Law will then be the fundamental 'referent', with accompanying confidence about human amenability to the divine will, and the awesome reality of transcendent presidency over the entire human scene. Precisely for its inclusive and imperative theism,[32] it must always have in the frame the patient magnanimity that, albeit so sovereign and competent, has left—

---

[31] Marshall Hodgson, *The Venture of Islam*, Chicago, Vol. 1, 1976, p. 29. See below, Chapter 8.

[32] In the sense that the more inclusive the theism, the more sublime the transcendence, the more wondrous the reality of human autonomy and the liberties it is allowed to pursue.

more and more evidently left[33]—to human trust and test the latchkey of so good, so fragile and so vulnerable an earth.

Were we to ask about 'the Christian system of reference' (so pale a word in either case), it would embrace the same creation, creaturehood and trust and test, along with law and guidance and divinely rooted ethic. But it would entail a more radical view of how amenable we humans are to moral law, a greater realism about our capacity to usurp rather than subdue to God our undoubted sub-authority. And so, in turn, it would take into the being of God's sublime sovereignty the burden of our wrongness in this vulnerable earth. That would make the earth at once more compellingly sacramental and the divine presidency more inherently redemptive.[34]

---

[33] The more evidently by the degree to which technology has developed and thereby tempted many to conclude the 'obsolescence' of God seeing that we seem to be, so manifestly, 'on our own'. Islam has always been 'absolute for God' and, therefore, confronts this situation more disconcertedly than any other theism. It is not that we are to be less 'absolute' but rather, more intelligently so, which means letting the meaning of secularity register.

[34] Is it not all caught in that New Testament phrase about 'the God of patience'? (Romans 15.5)—behind all things an infinitely gentle, infinitely generous Reality? See pp. 103-108 below.

Chapter 4

TUTELARY SPIRITS: 'GREATS' AND EMPIRE

i

Rudyard Kipling had his 'graduation' in the bazaars and press columns of India but when he became celebrated Oxford honoured him at an Encaenia in the company of none other than General William Booth of the Salvation Army. Mark Twain was with them. As they processed in scarlet robes, the General said to Kipling: 'Young feller, how's your soul?'[1]

He might well have addressed the question to the university itself. For 'souls' they certainly have, with endless speculation about how Oxford's differs from that of Cambridge.[2] What are the tutelary spirits that hover around Tübingen or Basle, Varanasi or the Azhar, Padua or the Sorbonne?

Part of the answer for Arnold's 'dreaming spires' would have to be their long devotion to the Greek and Latin classics and the role it played in the dream and the reality of Victorian and Edwardian British imperialism. Muslims across wide realms of that suzerainty had long reason to interrogate, resent, resist and realise that power-invasion of their souls. To realise meant to concede its irreversibility, as an ongoing factor in their history and their identity. Oxford, with its imperial dreamers passing from quadrangles to viceregal thrones, was always in the forefront and contributed more than any other university to that pursuit of power. It was all, in its English way, a deeply 'Islamic' thing in that it saw, and took, power as somehow in itself 'religious'. There will be strange irony if the Centre for Islamic Studies is finally achieved on the centenary of the death of Rhodes in 1902.

---

[1] Ed. Thomas Pinney, *Rudyard Kipling: Something of Myself*, Cambridge, 1990, p. 62. Kipling warmly admired the general.

[2] Much is speculation but some have spoken of 'physics' and science on the Cam, with 'metaphysics' on the Isis, or Oxford's rather mystical sentiment and the capacity to produce 'prophetic' figures—said to be rare, or rarer, further east. The air of Cambridge would never have engendered an 'Oxford Movement, and it had no equivalent of All Souls' College, founded to 'pray for the souls of the slain in the Hundred Years War', while being an apogee of academic élite.

Kipling's salute to Rhodes' burial told of 'dream devout by vision led,' how 'his immense and brooding spirit still shall quicken and control,' and his ' imperious hand ... perfect the work he planned.'[3]

Whether in the sub-continent, in Egypt and the Sudan, in Palestine and sub-Saharan Africa, Islam underwent the power equation it had itself, from Umayyads to Ottomans, so sedulously explored. Retrospect on the experience in the more sober, sombre light of present politics needs to assess the aftermath of a dis-empowered Islam and the shape of renewed autonomy in the nation-states. For the reaction the Muslim mind had to bring to its enforced forfeiture of the *Dawlah*, or 'rule', dimension it had always held to be definitive of its Islamic identity as *Din*, took its religious self-interrogation to the very heart of faith in terms which, otherwise, it might never have undergone.

For, in effect, what British imperialism—via Oxford in such major part—did for Muslim thought and society was without precedent in Islamic experience. The western Crusades in the middle centuries had only briefly disrupted Muslim power, while the faith had effectively absorbed the Tartar and Mongol conquerors and taken their prowess to itself. Tradition had it that there was no more 'emigration' after the Prophet's own Hijrah from Mecca to Medina—the Hijrah that led to power-dominion. But now Muslims were in the psychic equivalent of 'exile' because of their subjection to a non-Islamic rule, and Oxford was to the fore in fashioning the ideology that made it so.

ii

It was not an ideology bent on subjugation in terms of the Ottoman heyday in the Arab provinces and the Balkans. Rather it willed to educate and elevate. John Ruskin, inaugurating his first term as Professor of Fine Arts—a Chair he held between 1869 and 1884 (with an interlude between 1879-83)—gave it eloquent voice.

> There is a destiny now possible to us, the highest ever set
> before a nation to be accepted or refused. We are still
> undegenerate in race ... not dissolute in temper, still have
> the firmness to govern and the grace to obey. We have a
> religion of pure mercy. She must found colonies as fast and

---

[3] Rudyard Kipling, *Definitive Edition of His Verse*, London, 1943, pp. 209-10.

as far as she is able ... seizing every piece she can get her feet on ...

As for 'subject peoples', 'in every vital matter the right opinion is the majority of one, i.e. the empire's agent in place.'[4]

By a variety of factors Oxford came to be the seed-bed of an imperial romanticism and through several generations aspired to be the Athens of an empire and, by the turn of the 20th century, the nursing university of a 'Commonwealth' of peoples, as empire's worthy and emulating successor. The liberalism that the Tractarians had so firmly despised blossomed into the noble politics of empire. Islam, across all the places of its dispersion in Asia and Africa (French North Africa and the Dutch East Indies apart), was, with Hinduism in the sub-continent, the major recipient of Oxford's imperial ministries, cultural, intellectual and educational. When the commercial aggressions of the East India Company gave way to the British Raj, the Indian Civil Service took Oxford for its chief recruiting ground, so that Oxford supplied more imperial personnel than any other single university. Benjamin Jowett's Balliol College, for example, emerged as a nursery of world administration. How zealously its Master cherished, with correspondence and friendship, the men his house of study had launched upon their way! For he had deliberately fashioned his long tenure to create, not only an organ of change inside the university, but of vision concerning *humanitas* at large.[5] Even the regulations as to age of entry etc. of the ICS open examinations were adjusted to satisfy the university's calendars of degrees.

Pre-eminent in Oxford's role in staffing an imperial concept was the 'blue riband' of academia, the four years of 'Greats' or *Literae Humaniores*, which took aspirants through the Greek and Latin grammars and classics, the wars and politics, the grand philosophers of the ancient Graeco-Roman world. It must be one of the most astonishing features of educational history that the place of a tradition and theology so deeply Christian should have been so totally dedicated to the supreme value and spiritual relevance of 'pagan' histories and literatures. It would be hard to find any parallel in Islamic history of a core-faith so far tolerating, indeed recruiting, arguably alien territories for its intellectual themes, its mental preference in the nurture of the generations.

---

[4] John Ruskin, *Collected Works*, 1903f, Vol. 20, p. 61 and Vol. 31, p. 505.
[5] Peter Hinchliff, *Benjamin Jowett and the Christian Religion*, Oxford, 1987, is a perceptive study of the ideals and influence of Jowett's Balliol.

It might be said that Islam's long modern exposure to western culture and philosophy has required it to admit into its educational perimeters dimensions which its interior doctrinal system instinctively excluded. That process, however, came under a certain duress of historical necessity and only faintly resembled the entirely deliberate option for all that 'Greats' symbolised in 19th century Oxford as to the co-existence of Sophocles and Socrates with the pulpit strains of John Henry Newman in St Mary's and their high Christian moralism, the grave pathos of their devotion.

It all had to do with concepts of compatibility inside religions that are—as it were—intellectually 'established', through doctrines *de fide* and legal/social institutions held strictly normative of identity and of practice. Despite tensions, Islam has long been 'established' in just such categorical terms. It is now steadily confronted with what it may, or should, accommodate within itself and with how it may participate in attitudes or dimensions a rigorous view of what is *de fide* would have to reject.

The Oxford factor did, in some measure, foster a readiness for that question in the setting of the post-1857 trauma in Muslim India. Sayyid (Sir, as he became) Ahmad Khan laboured to relate Muslims in India to the aftermath of failure in the incipient War of Independence and reconcile them to the seeming perpetuation of British rule. Such rule, of course, violated the principle that only Muslims rule Muslims. How, then, could India be *Dar al-Islam* without that vital element of Islamic power? Yet the mosques were open, *Salat*, *Ramadan*, the Pilgrimage were all operative. The 'Pillars of Religion', power apart, were intact if only by grace of Victoria Regina. They constituted *Dar al-Islam* sufficiently for Muslims to come out from under deep depression and gross defeatism.

One ingredient of this, Sir Sayyid thought, would actually be the emulation of Britain, a greeting of the spirit for its scholarship and culture, as assets Muslims in India could make their own without compromise and so rehabilitate their spirits and their society. In these terms, after visiting England, he became strongly Anglophile and, emulating Oxford—or was it Cambridge?—founded the Anglo-Mohammedan College which later became the University of Aligarh.[6] He visualised it as a place of learning to revitalise Muslim education

---

[6]   Founded in 1877, it became the Muslim University of Aligarh in 1920 and has passed through many vicissitudes since. On Ahmad Khan see Aziz Ahmad, *Islamic Modernism in India and Pakistan, 1857-1964*, Oxford, 1967, pp. 31-56, and J M S Baljon, *The Reforms and Religious Ideas of Sayyid Ahmad Khan,* Leiden, 1949.

along English lines. In playing this role to good purpose, its vicissitudes served to indicate how crisis-prone the whole ambition was. Its first Anglophile character could not survive sterner years of *swaraj*, of Congress and the Muslim League. Yet its story remains as a gesture between Islam and Oxford whose significance abides. Meanwhile, those successions of 'Greats' men would be manning their dispersed posts among the heirs of Mughal India.

iii

'Greats', as an academic institution with these imperial outworkings, needs to be further interrogated. Why was its authority so ardently cherished, its domain so long upheld? It was clearly a major factor in the weaning away of the university, Jowett-style, from the dominance of medieval and Tractarian pre-possession. It also tallied with a certain, intellectual aristocratism which—as we see elsewhere—felt itself above mere useful disciplines, and held to that loftiness, despite warnings from Government and business that its human products were unskilled in necessary arts of diplomacy or administration.

The theory was that, somehow, the saga of the Greek cities, their wars and treaties, could educate the neophytes of empire all the better for being ancient and remote. The minutiae of languages and grammars trained the mind in accuracy and rigour, attention to detail and a mystique of sophistication. Did not Plato and Aristotle between them share the whole wisdom of the ancients? Was not philosophy circling for ever around their discoursings?

A Christian/classical compatibility—if still urgent to keep it in view—was, of course, served by the fact that New Testament studies profited from classical Greek. It could also be argued that a deliberate academic discipline, outside believing theology, could leave the latter free from undue or incisive scrutiny, so that a relaxed adherence could continue unruffled by undue earnestness. This was the more fit to allow, given the inroads of Darwinian and other influences into the composure of the routine faithful. It was feared that an over tense theology might tend to scepticism, if not tempered by voyaging elsewhere and where better than Homer and the *Odyssey*, Thucydides and Athenian heroes? Eternal themes could do well to be enshrined in another world and breathe a different air. John Ruskin ventured the view that 'the Greeks might even teach Victorians to be better Christians.'[7] In his forays into comparative cultures, Matthew Arnold assured himself that what he termed Hebraism and Hellenism could be readily combined. In the mind of Gladstone—no more ardent political Christian than he—the Bible and Homer could be co-tutors of integrity.

It was, after all, in the soil of the Greek mind that early Christianity had come to articulate its Hebraic Messianic assurance as, at length, the Christ of Chalcedon. The Reformation also, in its due time, could be read as indebted to the intellectual quest of the Greek spirit, as well as to Paul-like concerns about a pure heart, via divine righteousness through grace. It had belonged to John Colet and Erasmus as well as to Martin Luther and John Calvin.

A notable Victorian exponent of this 'Bible and the Greeks' ethos was Bishop Brook Foss Westcott of Durham, who read a vital providence in the Greek heritage as a *preparatio* for the Gospel and the Church. 'Pagan' as a term antagonistic to 'Christian', ought to be scouted. For there was a genuine something in which they could be kin. Even John Henry Newman, while warning himself against any sort of Keatsian indulgence with the Greeks, in a poem he wrote after his Sicilian journey, ventured the view that 'the Greek poets and sages were in a certain sense prophets.'[8] 'A certain sense', of course, needed careful definition but at least some affinity was authentic. That the Greek and Roman classics could be formative of Christian faith persisted into the thought of T S Eliot.[9]

In its own different idiom, Islam has undergone a comparable experience of having seemingly 'alien' dimensions enter—either as enemy or friend—into its first Arabic, its growing 'Abbasid, Mughal and Ottoman, identities. It can be argued that the bearing of Oxford 'Greats' on Oxford Christianity constitutes a fertile exemplar for Islam's own negotiation with fields for its options not congenial to its existing self-perceptions. The point will recur more suitably in Chapter 8. Oxford, it will be said, chose to 'go for Greats' in the freedom of its own calculus of education, whereas what the West has to mean for Muslims is in large

---

[7] John Ruskin, *Lectures on Architecture and Painting*, p. 120.

[8] John Henry Newman, *Apologia Pro Vita Sua*, ed. M J Svalgic, Oxford, 1967, Chap. 1.

[9] There are useful analyses of classicism and Christian faith in Richard Jenkyns, *The Victorians and Ancient Greece*, Oxford, 1980. See also Charles Lucas, *Greater Rome and Greater Britain*, London, 1912; and James Brace, *The Ancient Roman Empire and the British Empire in India*, London, 1914.

measure no option but rather destined by history. Increasingly, religions have to disabuse themselves of any entire self-sufficiency and at least explore, if not decide, the shape of their inter-compatibility, partial as it will always remain, *vis-à-vis* a world increasingly shared.

At all events, this dominant bent of Oxford education through mid-19th to mid-20th centuries, via the dispersion of its graduates into colonial-style administration, was calculated to exert a powerful intellectual influence on the mind of Islam, notably in the sub-continent but also in the Arab world. It is customary to date the impact of Europe in dramatic terms from the French invasion of Egypt in 1798. It certainly stimulated the response that Muhammad 'Ali symbolised, with his emulation of military arts and his appetite for Napoleonic ideas. The impact of what Oxford brought to bear on Islam lay in the sustained assumptions of liberal education and patterns of civil rule disseminated and mediated through hundreds of local officials habituated to those norms.

It was a strange mingling of histories, an imperialism emanating from Britain, so far redolent educationally with Athens and Rome, yet impinging steadily on the thought-world, the ingrained ethos, of Islam. Gilbert Murray, the long-Chaired Professor of Greek, held that 'At home England is Greek: in the empire she is Roman.'[10] To be sure, empire— whether Roman or British—was doing things *to* or *for* its 'subjects', not *with* them. Such is the case with empires. Yet in this triangular way, it was doing things in them through a steady penetration of attitudes and instincts, liable to come to fruition in the very factors by which empire would terminate, the associations that could argue its transformation into a Commonwealth—a concept in which Oxford also played notable part.

Civil servants apart, there was extensive inter-action about education between existing or emerging universities, via the Oxford University Press in the publishing of texts, and the fostering of translation, and via a pattern in consultation over degrees, syllabi, and the inter-change of personnel, and by visiting academics both as lecturers and examiners. The cumulative impact could hardly extend beyond the educational scene while vast masses of human illiteracy lay outside its scope. Nevertheless, a certain Oxford benison—albeit compromised on many counts by human distortion or lethargy—reached towards a sharing of its tutelary spirits where ever ran its writ.

---

[10] Quoted in Jenkyns, *loc. cit.*, p. 337.

Lord Curzon, when Viceroy of India—and in all roles he was always supremely conscious of being Lord Curzon—addressed the University of Calcutta in 1899, in his other capacity as its Chancellor. His words had a characteristic hauteur and doubtless overdid their theme, but they gave sonorous expression to a situation real enough, if more modest than his rhetoric.

> I am struck by the extent to which, within less than fifty years, the science and learning of the western world have penetrated into the oriental mind, teaching it independence of judgement and liberty of thought, familiarising it with the conceptions of politics and law and society, to which it had for centuries been a complete stranger.[11]

iv

His last sentence was grossly inaccurate, if he meant his centuries to include the splendours of the Mughals before they had declined into the harsh militant rigorism of Aurangzib. Curzon had never read, or misread, the great Akbar.[12] More soberly, our assessments of what was transacted between Oxford and Islam, between a would-be 'Athens of empire' and the heirs of caliphs and Imams through the centuries, need more penetrating sympathy.

There was, of course, the irony to which we will return, that Oxford's benison—if such it were—owed much to Islamic debts from a far past. Deferring that feature, exploration might begin with a warning from the pen of H A R Gibb, whom we have noted in Chapter 2 as Oxford's eminent Laudian Professor. Arguing that 'natural science and technology' were readily transmissible as 'the only truly international element in human culture', he wrote that

> Every society jealously guards its own and, although not

---

[11] Lord Curzon, *Speeches as Viceroy and Governor-General*, Calcutta, 1904, Vol. 1, p. 23.

[12] Emperor Akbar, who reigned from 1556-1605 and, besides vastly extending Mughal rule by conquests across North India and into Afghanistan, moderated his Sunni Islam to a more esoteric Din-i-lahi, that brought Jesuit Fathers to discussion at his court, adjusted Islamic *ijtihad*, and sought accommodation with Hindu Rajputs. He encouraged the study of Sanskrit, abolished the *jizyah*, or poll-tax on non-Muslims and—to a degree—harnessed Islam to his own office and person.

wholly impermeable from without, will absorb elements from other cultures only within a limited range and in forms adapted to its own temperament and psychological structure.[13]

But had he not begged a large question? There were analogies current among Muslims in the Gulf in the wake of oil development which ran that Muslims could readily unpack the crates that delivered the machines and the expertise, while leaving in the crates the materialist philosophies that underlay the product. Or, in more gross terms, Muslims could do as they do when eating melon seeds—spit the rind on the ground (i.e. the 'secular' West that kernelled them) and enjoy the nut inside (i.e. the technology). Could the one be so easily detached from the other? Might not the mentality that conjured the invention prove—over time— to be inseparable from the technique, namely a rationality liable to oust any awe of God, as an impression of competence leaving no room for prayer or worship? If, in Gibb's phrase, technology was uniquely 'international' could it stay so and not bring secularity, as a likely common culture, so jeopardising the separate immunities he had stressed? Technology certainly has much other baggage with it, especially when it comes hand in hand with the imperial factors with which we are here concerned. 'Jealous' Islam might be for its own, but how it would adapt its own temperament and psychological structure was—and remains— precisely the issue most at stake and in no way out of range.

If we return, briefly, to Napoleon in Egypt, the point is immediately clear. Reflecting on its significance some fourteen decades later, Sayyid Qutb, martyred mentor of the Muslim Brotherhood, read its meaning in the most drastic terms. As an alien incursion, and 'the greatest rupture' in Islam's history, it had spelled 'an appropriation by human beings of God's attributes of exclusive sovereignty and lordship.'[14]

Reaction in those terms was entirely in character. Islam, in Qutb's 'jealous guarding', read the technology and arrogance Napoleon brought and symbolised, as usurping the 'sovereignty' that could only be Allah's.

---

[13] H A R Gibb, 'The Influence of Islamic Culture on Medieval Europe', *Bulletin of John Rylands Library*, Manchester, Vol. 38, Sept., 1955, p. 98.

[14] Quoted from Christopher Coker, *The Twilight of the West*, Boulder, 1998, p. 158. The author of a large Commentary on the Qur'an (*In the Shade of the Qur'an*) Sayyid Qutb was executed in 1965 under 'Abd al-Nasir after a long imprisonment during which he proved a staunch leader in the cause of the Muslim Brotherhood. See my *The Pen and the Faith*, London, 1985, pp. 53-71.

The French emperor was an outrageous *mushrik*. It needed to be Islamically said. Yet, what would be the implications of arguing that divine prerogatives had been imperially usurped? Had God been unable to prevent it? What then of the sovereignty? Might there not be a clue in the deeply Quranic theme of 'entrustment' of *khilafah* to humans—a 'dominion' none the less real, and none the less unrevoked by God, because Napoleon was defiling it? Was it not more sane and reflective to read the event, not essentially as men 'becoming God' even if they behaved as if it were so, but as a gross violation of human trusteeship under God and reprehensible as such, leaving divine prerogative not only unassailed but more duly asserted?

The point is only intended here to insist on how invasions of cultures do not leave them impermeable to fundamental interrogation or their very psychology impervious to challenge. What was being required of Sayyid Qutb, as his Muslim loyalty in the face of desperate thoughts, was a sense of a need to align his reading of Allah's sovereignty, as one that had always left room for the role of humans, however perverse might become their exercise of it. The very core of the Qur'an was at stake and needed a more perceptive 'jealousy' for its ultimate meaning and, by the same token, a more worthy Islamic response to what had been undoubtedly a gross and grievous challenge, both to its culture and its soul.

In their quieter, more expansive way, the inroads of imperial Oxoniana, via 'Greats' and overseas duty, were much of this order. The self-image of Muslims was alerted to its contours by the growing awareness of how it was viewed by other parties, the more so when these were in positions of political control. It began to matter—as it would not have done in their absence—what perceptions were being aroused through their presence and how these might tally with inner reality, as known only on the inside of Muslim culture. What was the authentic Islam, to adjust or correct or pre-empt the alleged one, in response to visiting 'educators' acting on their own impressions, whether as rulers, academics, travellers or missionaries? Cultures were far from immune to radical self-scrutiny even in their most radical will to resistance in the face of invasion. Inside that experience was the taxing question: Who was to answer?

Thus, for example, Sayyid Ahmad Khan, in his pro-western prescripts for Muslim renewal in India, had wanted to jettison a great deal of Hadith, or Tradition, so as to simplify the criteria of Islam by assigning them far more wholly to the Qur'an. He also championed the right to *ijtihad* for the personal believer, in hope to end the inhibiting monopoly of its exercise by pundits so often resistant to change. For the liberation of ideas demanded the freeing of the organs of their definition. Islam, in short, was finding itself in the throes of valid self-definition. His heirs would be doing so amid the growing political agenda towards self-government.

In that sort of debate there were those who sought for means to security. Two Muslim Oxonians provided a telling case-in-point after the Treaty of Versailles in 1919 and the termination of the Ottoman caliphate at the beginning of the Atatürk régime. The brothers, Muhammad and Shawkat 'Ali, of India, saw the maintenance of the caliphate as vital to the Indian Muslims, as a symbol of Islam as a worldwide entity. Its demise would imperil the future of Indian Islam. The Khilafatist Movement which they headed was ill-fated. Almost concurrently with its frustration by the secularising Turks, an Egyptian scholar 'Ali 'Abd al-Raziq would be arguing in his *Islam wa Usul al-Hukm*, that the caliphate had never been integral to Islam which would be more truly its religious self without it.[15] Such radical disowning of the caliphate's rightful place in Islam, bitterly disputed as it was in Egypt, only made the Indian wistfulness for its re-assuring shield around them the more desirable. It was both dismaying and ironic that fellow Muslims—Turks in their 'de-Ottomanising' of their history and 'liberals' in Cairo—should be abandoning an institution their Indian Muslim brothers valued so highly. The Khilafatists had reason to feel betrayed and, with them, the still massive numbers of Arab, African and Asian Muslims who were in no mind to concede the demise of an institution that had endured since the Prophet's death as his due political heir.

It is not suggested that 'Greats' in Oxford, and its role in imperial romanticism, are to be held responsible for this epochal change in Muslim perspectives on their past. The armed campaign through Gaza from 'British' Egypt had more to do with it, while the philosophy of Ziya Gökalp that underlay Atatürk's secularisation had quite other origins.[16]

---

[15] Cairo, *Islam wa Usul al-Hukm*, 1925, 'Islam and the Principles of Government'. The brothers petitioned Versailles over a retention of the caliphate, despite the fact that Arab nationalism by that time was bent on independence from Istanbul. The caliphate has never been renewed.

[16] Ziya Gökalp (1875-1924) was the major exponent of the theory behind 'Turanianism', or Turk-identity as an ethnic culture in which 'Islam' was merely incidental. Hence the end of Ottoman, caliphal vocation and the secularisation of law and society. He drew on the sociology of Durkheim and saw religion as a social construct by no means absolute either as theology or law. See his selected essays, trans., in *Turkish Nationalism and Western Civilization*, ed. N Berkes, London. 1959, also entitled: *The Development of Secularism in Modern Turkey*.

Yet the sense of mental and emotional exposure to uncertainty that motivated Khilafatism came through the long abeyance of Muslim power-control that the British Raj ensured and which its ethos presided over, especially for the Muslim intelligentsia. For the very presence of (British) empire and—until the thirties and forties—the ever-deferring prospect of its termination, only served to underline the condition of political powerlessness so uncongenial to the Muslim soul. If neither Ahmad Khan's 'loyalism', nor the will to Pan-Islam in Khilafatist form, was the answer, whether in Lahore or Cairo, what else might it be?

Political self-repossession, and—as Islam believed—all else with it, should be the only solution. The logic, and the action, are best studied within the Indian scene, where the pride of antecedent glories and the time-length of their forfeiture had been greatest.

The story of the will to partition in India on the Muslim side and of the painful emergence of Pakistan is complex and ever controversial. Its supreme architect, Muhammad 'Ali Jinnah, was only converted to it as a policy in the late thirties, but thereafter his determination was relentless and his skills decisive. Highly 'secular' as he was, he had no direct debts to Oxford. His studies were legal at the Inns of Court, where—it is said—he chose Lincoln's Inn because it contained a large mural in which Muhammad, in green robe and turban, figured with Moses among great lawgivers of the world.[17] His great associate, however, in the All-India Muslim League from 1936 to 47 and first Prime Minister of Pakistan was an old Oxonian—Nawabzada Liaquat Ali Khan. His mind and his career are as good an index as any to the ideology of Pakistan, just as his tragic death in October 1951, at the hands of a Muslim assassin, foreshadowed like a heavy cloud the tragic aspects of its future.[18]

Born in traditional princely affluence and a pupil in Aligarh from 1909-19, he spent the three following years in Exeter College and his commodious apartment in The High, where he belonged congenially with a coterie of distinguished Indians of that generation and with Oxoniana in general, excelling in tennis, and presiding over the Indian Majlis. On

---

[17] See Akbar S Ahmed, *Jinnah, Pakistan and Islamic Identity*, London, 1997, pp. 4-5. Portrayal of the Prophet was, of course, highly reprehensible, yet its celebration of Muhammad as a 'lawgiver' contributed to the campaign for Pakistan by setting its presiding genius on to a legal career. Not seldom things a faith frowns on as improprieties can also serve it as useful assets.

[18] The motives of his assassin, Said Akbar, seem never to have been successfully probed. Was it a lone act of violence only reflecting the hostile passions around the Muslim character of Pakistan, vented on its most symbolic figure so soon after the death of Jinnah?

return to India he espoused Muslim nationalism in preference to a career in the ICS, being convinced that Islamic identity, at least in areas of majority dominance, demanded separate nationhood. For otherwise they, his people, would be inhibited in their culture and live in perpetual fear of the majority. Since the sad demise of the Mughals, Islam had been dislodged from power and Muslims must become a single state as the panacea for their entire cultural identity.

His thinking was in direct contradiction to the reading of Islam by Maulana Abu-l-Kalam Azad (1888-1958) who argued for a 'composite nationalism' shared by all religions. Azad had shared a Khilafatist view, while chances were remote of a British withdrawal, but when this prospect came above the horizon and any Pan-Islam was remoter still, he saw Muslims as faith-and-duty bound to co-operate as an Indian 'community'.[19]

Not so Liaquat Ali Khan. He was wholly committed to Jinnah's perception of the political incompatibility of the two faiths. As Quaim-i-Azam—Jinnah's honoured title[20]—he was well-served by Liaquat as Quaim-i-Millat, whose philosophy found voice in a speech to the All-India Muslim Educational Conference in 1945. Here one can almost hear the whispers of a departed Jowett strangely undertoning a robust Islamicity he could only have deplored.

Liaquat paid tribute to the educationalists as largely the inspiration of the Muslim League itself. He praised as right for his time the mind-set of Ahmad Khan and his Aligarh. For that liberal sense of duty to truth must undergird all society. Its protagonist had nobly withstood the bigotry that made 'Aligarh for long the *bête noire* of pious Muslims'. But his loyalism was now obsolete, indeed reactionary. Islam required the state concept. Democracy itself, western-style, needed a homogeneous country. This a united India could never be. Islam rejected *ahimsa*, or

---

[19] See M M Siddiqi, *Religious Philosophy of Maulana Azad*, Hyderabad, 1965, and Ian H Douglas, *Abul Kalam Azad: An Intellectual and Religious Biography*, ed. G Minault and C W Troll, Delhi, 1978. Born in Mecca, a deeply devout Muslim and author of a notable Urdu Qur'an Commentary, Azad was a very different Muslim from the westernised Jinnah—a politico through and through, who saw separatism as the popular option, while Azad read Islam as religiously co-operative with a Hindu majority in a united sub-continent. In the passions that shaped Pakistan he suffered much obloquy. The issues between the two figures go far into the long tensions within Islamic self-definition.

[20] Meaning 'the Great leader', with Liaquat's epithet as 'Leader of the Entity'. *Millah* normally meant 'community' which Pakistani ideology averred Muslims were not: 'sect' was still less applicable. The *Millah* had to be the 'nation'.

'non-violence', a Hindu device 'only meant to root out from Muslim youth their martial spirit and traditions.' The *Akhand Barat* idea of purely 'territorial' identification of communities offended all Islamic norms of identity by creed and culture, and might imply that 'the holy Prophet was confined to Arabia.' India was not a mere territory: it was a dominant Hinduism and Islam 'abhorred the caste system.'[21]

Yet this Islamic state had 'no room for theocracy.' It stood for 'freedom of conscience, condemned coercion and had no priesthood.' Was Oxford in his mind when he added: 'We have learned much about ourselves'? For he went on—in sentiments all the more poignant in the retrospect of Pakistan's half century since they were delivered, in May 1950, to the National Press Club in Washington:

> In a world of conflicting ideologies, nations that have recently achieved full sovereignty are likely to be the victims of mental confusion and consequent instability. Is it not, therefore, a matter of supreme satisfaction that at least one nation amongst such nations should not suffer from confusion and should, as a matter of tradition and belief, be pledged to clear international principles of democracy and social and economic justice?

Pakistani Muslims were a 'people free from disintegrating doubts and clashes' with 'the surest safeguards against disruption'.[22] Within a year and some months, he had died, like Gandhi, at the hand of one of his own religious kin. Clearly an Oxford furnished with Rhodes Scholars and pondering a 'league', if not a 'commonweal' of nations and musing on the Treaty of Versailles, had imbued Liaquat Ali Khan with something of itself and a tradition of democracy. It had not initiated him into suspicions of despair like those of Matthew Arnold in 'Dover Beach'. Had he never crossed The Broad to talk with a visiting Arnold Toynbee— thirty-years-old and then deeply occupied in post-First World War peace issues—and to savour a Christian realism as to the amenability of humans and nations to their 'principles' however formally 'pledged'?

---

[21] See Liaquat Ali Khan, *Muslim Educational Problems*, Lahore, Pakistan Literature Series, No. 7, 1952 (Speech in 1945). Also ed. Ziauddin Ahmad, *Quaid-i-Millet: Liaquat Ali Khan: Leader and Statesman*, Karachi, 1970 (a memorial tribute). Cf. also, his own, *Pakistan, the Heart of Asia*, Karachi, 1953.

[22] *Educational Problems* (note 21) p. 235.

The 'self-verdict' or the 'mind-event'—if we may so speak—that the creation of Pakistan both tells and upholds, as to the nature of Islam being inseparably *Din wa Dawlah*, is as eloquent for ideology as its grievous half-century of travail has been for the elusiveness of human good faith. The idea of 'an Islamic state' kindled the decisive will to reach it on the ground. What the ideal of it should be has thus far eluded the definition of its constitutional lawyers and the attainment of its sundry rulers, civilian and military. Even before the heavy blow of the death of Quaim-i-Azam Jinnah and the grievous loss of Liaquat, the Basic Principles Committee failed to reach consensus about how Islam was to be expressed in a Constitution, or 'non-repugnancy to the Qur'an' written into it in terms that satisfied both 'democracy' and the authority of the *'ulama'*. Hence the unhappy succession of régimes and coups, the ravages of corruption and the ever-present weight of all that partition symbolised of suspicion, enmity, rivalry and zealotry.

To recognise the illogicality of Pakistan[23] is in no way to diminish either a patience with its overwhelming odds or a compassion for its burdens. It had been, in Muslim terms, a very 'Zionist' solution, a 'salvation' bare politics could achieve. It has tragically incurred comparable contradictions and self-violations.

v

It has been convenient to trace the tutelary spirits both Oxonian and Islamic, in the context of the sub-continent. British imperialism, by which Curzon, Rhodes, Cromer, Milner and all their kin aimed and claimed to manage the world, and the English 'Athens' that, for some of its ideologues, aimed and claimed to educate them for the role, was most long-lived in India and the Raj. It was more ambiguous, and briefer, in Egypt and the Sudan, differently problemised in Islamic Africa, while never explicitly present in Persia.

---

[23] 'Illogical' in that it exposed Indian Muslims to jeopardy in a potential 'Hindustan' (should secular Nehru-style ideas falter in India) which its own rationale said would doom Islam. Did not Pakistan imply that India should emulate it and be a 'Hindustan', i.e. Hindu-dominant? At its creation, Pakistan enclosed a larger proportionate minority of non-Muslims than Muslims constituted in a single India, thus offending against its own principle. Even so, was it not better to be master where one could, than be permanently 'minor' parties in a larger whole—and have it so whatever the human cost in tragedy and hate? The question lives in the two nations as a stark legacy.

The theme to which we have now to turn is that legacy of democratic principles which Liaquat Ali Khan had proclaimed, and which was meant to undergird any eventual mutation of 'empire' into 'Commonwealth'.

Oxford had lively tutelary spirits here too. Rhodes had not consulted the university about the terms of his will, but Rhodes House and Queen Elizabeth House for Commonwealth Studies came to employ his munificence to implement a gentler vision.[24] Reginald Coupland (1884-1952), the second Beit Professor of Colonial History, and Margery Perham (1895-1982) were zealous proponents of democratic ideals throughout the successor nation-states to which the imperial past should be destined to give way, as the benison in the relinquishment of empire. If Benjamin Jowett had aspired to educate the educators of the world, this would be the graduating lesson for all who had experienced that tutelage across the world. If history knew of few empires willingly 'demise-ing' themselves, this British one would do so in terms that, hopefully, might perpetuate its polity as the monitor of independence.

It was a laudable vision in which Oxford wanted pride of place. With the largely Anglophile, English-speaking dominions, via a Statute of Westminster, it was eminently feasible, in mandated Palestine—despite a lingering Zionist notion of Commonwealth membership—a vain illusion. What of elsewhere, what, for present purposes, of *Dar al-Islam* and democracy? What of it, too, as a legacy from an ousted imperialism that had supplanted Mughal glory, ignored Muslim history and inflicted that ultimate humiliation—Muslim powerlessness? Could active tutelary spirits that had clashed in terms so deep, now engage the one with the other in fruitful concert? What of democracy if Zia al-Haq or Idi Amin were the custodians of Islam? How sanguine could even the long tradition of 'Greats' men be, as a precursor of 'Commonwealth', given all they knew about city-strife and Thucydidian war?

The social and economic pre-requisites of a viable democracy are familiar enough—a solid 'middle class' with tolerably adequate incomes so that their votes are not a selling commodity, and a relatively sound level of literacy and education and press liberty, so that they are not easily manipulable by perverse propaganda and surrender independence of mind. More vitally yet must be the quality of personal character and civic virtue, tending to integrity and honour at the core of

---

[24] Though Queen Elizabeth House did not profit from Rhodes' will and was dogged by financial exigency.

politics. All these criteria prove extremely formidable among ever burgeoning populations, deeply burdened economies and widespread poverties that inhibit strong social cohesion and deter personal ideals. A global *Dar al-Islam* varies between abject deprivation here and opulent education there, turning on state resources and the strange incidence of geology with oil.

Given all these variants and their often deteriorating fortunes, what of the equation, 'Islam and democracy' in intellectual and religious reckoning? Scrutinising the answer needs first to appreciate how the setting of post-imperialism affects it. Democracy, commended by departing and alien masters, faces a double hurdle in sharing 'Commonwealth' in the aftermath of 'empire'. There is the sharp sense of long injured pride, refuting invocation of an honoured past, and there is the urge to make independence psychologically as well as politically complete—even with the knowledge that, globally, it can never be so.

We have noted the sense of grievance about 'being supplanted', of 'foreign rule as a cramping force', in the words of Liaquat Ali Khan, while those of Jinnah were still more forthright and stentorian. They were only asserting their memory of the great Mughals. When Muslims in India after partition were denied that *sine qua non* of an authentic Islam by the case-making of Pakistan itself, the urge for a psychic self-esteem was the more keen for the experience of departed prestige.[25] Elsewhere, in the Middle East or Africa, resentments had their own differing impulses, but everywhere Muslims knew that the overwhelming advantages Europe enjoyed in techniques and politics were partly owed to Islamic skills and sciences in the Middle Age. The genius of these in sundry fields had been reaped by the West from their masters in Baghdad's *Bait al-Hikmah* and other notable academies through translation into Greek and Latin. Tutelary spirits whispered that earlier masters had been bettered by their own pupils. There was, therefore, a hint—if not a pain— of psychic injustice in being invited to take further lessons in the art of statehood, the governance of their liberated world.

Yet, as we have seen, the protestations of democratic intent were loud and sincere. Oxford academics took a lively part in hailing them.

---

[25] The aura of the Mughals—disastrous as the last of them, Aurangzib had been—seemed to justify a Muslim superiority complex *vis-à-vis* Hindus, from among whom anyway Islam had recruited itself, following Babur's conquest and for whose caste system, Muslims could only feel disdain. This complex was also kindled by a pervasive sense that the British Raj 'favoured' Hindus.

The creation of Pakistan was marked by a spate of pamphlets of the 'Islam and ...' order, expounding its potential role in peace and justice, education and welfare, society and the arts, civic ends and moral means. Being a whole way of life and not a bare dogmatic system, Islam could readily embrace all human needs as their sufficient mentor and provider, even their panacea.

But, in that role, how democratic could it be? The issues proved vexing enough for Pakistan but emerged everywhere else in local form. They had to do with how democratic processes, moving through popular suffrage and elected assemblies, could be reconciled with the claim of non-elected *'ulama'* to subject all measures for scrutiny of their Islamic validity—a scrutiny only such pundits could bring. This bedevilled Pakistan's 'Basic Principles Committee' and Constitution-drafting from the beginning. Having been explicitly created to shape Islamic statehood for an Islamic nationhood, Pakistan had coalesced a miscellany of ideas concerning its definition, in the drive to achieve partition and gain its separate existence. That political pragmatism had known that defining would be divisive and so had argued: 'Let us first obtain and then define.' It was a logic with a nemesis. For it meant that views ready to defer solution pending attaining, conflicted in the sequel. The consequences have plagued the story of Pakistan for half a century.

If its law and order, its society and courts, had to pass muster with Quranic and *Shari'ah* orthodoxy warranted to veto its Parliament, how would that leave the sovereign organ of democracy? Or could due Islamicity be left to the verdict of a Muslim electorate and its elected representatives, suffrage itself taking care of Islamicity?

The answer to the first question must obviously be: 'compromised'; to the second 'certainly' or 'hopefully' or 'by no means', depending on how one read *Shura* and *Ijtihad*, two arguable principles of development in Islam. Surah 42.38 said of Muslims: 'They conduct their affairs by mutual consultation.'[26] The term *shura* which gives its title to the Surah suggests a debate to ascertain what each thinks and has been cited to sustain the modern notion of democracy. *Ijtihad* has been intensely discussed. For, on its interpretation, both the liberty and the limits of Muslim thinking about Islam critically turn. It has to do with the initiatives by which Islamic society may reach 'consensus' or *Ijma'*, by

---

[26] As 'a drawing forth of ideas' the term certainly fits the *majlis* idea where rulers are available for what a tribal member wishes to air with them. In the immediate context in Surah 42 it may have to do with the devout believers being conciliatory with each other.

which, as a further source of law, 'common Muslim mind' might supplement, but never override, the primary sources in Qur'an and Tradition.[27]

Who is warranted to exercise this *Ijtihad* and pioneer constructive change in society? Might a Muslim parliament aspire to it, if it inheres as a right in any and every devout Muslim? Not so, said those Muslim 'clerisy' who required for this role skills of exegesis and minutiae of *fiqh* which only they, as experts, possessed. If only these—as the phrase went—could turn 'the door of *Ijtihad*', Islam would stay rigorously conservative. The role of such *mujtahids* would be vital to the self-preservation of Islam and should figure in any state constitution, leaving democracy impaired if not thwarted.

But if *Ijtihad* was towards *Ijma'*, and if *Ijma'* really meant to recruit from an entire society (based on the Prophet's tradition that 'My community will never converge—agree—on an error'), how could the means to it in 'initiatives' be monopolised by *'ulama'*? The question presses the more, seeing that the themes and areas demanding urgent guidance concern more and more the 'laity' in Islam, the scientists, engineers, geneticists and medicos, whose devices set the moral problems and the social changes.

Moreover, that ruling aegis of the Qur'an itself is potentially far more pliable than classic commentary allows. What readership must bring to the authority of Scriptures is no less keenly present for Muslims than elsewhere among 'revealed religions'.[28] Tradition, too, is urgently capable of radical flexibility in what it yields, given due attention to its origins, credentials and sources. Has it not long been a way of Islamicising much custom into law? Need that process not persist via absorptive capacities in current society? Doubtless due safeguards must exist but who is to identify and apply them? Might not the *Shari'ah* itself come to be seen as, enfolding in theological sanctity, the mind of Islam at large, working out its confident 'finality' in a contemporary continuity, for lack of which its very finality would be forfeit? In receding from centuries, or decades, of political control, European imperialism had not left *Dar al-Islam* unchanged. Perhaps there were aspects of its legacy to be absorbed for

---

[27] Hence the theme of 'non-repugnancy' in Pakistani debates, a term easier to satisfy than positive 'conformity to'.

[28] It is one that has come increasingly to the fore in recent philosophy. However sacrosanct in status, a text is beholden to what the readers make of it and cannot 'answer back'. Such is the hazard in all authorship, even heavenly.

sound reasons consequent on its departure. So thought the Commonwealth enthusiasts in Oxford. Democracy—Muslim-style—would vindicate a long power-tenure and the final exit. 'Greats', too, would reap a due harvest, thanks to Demosthenes and Pericles.

vi

It was a worthy, but also a sanguine, vision. In much of *Dar al-Islam* legacies from before the days of empire and the crises in their ending precluded the conditions democracy needs to enjoy. More deeply still, there have been instincts relating to power, explicit in Islam ever since the Prophet himself and bearing his enormous sanction. They have to do with perceptions of leadership and authority which, in face of all the foregoing about *Shura* and *Ijma'*, tend to dominate rather than authenticate the private individual in his or her Islam. The demand for the State of Pakistan demonstrated this instinct forthrightly. Being Muslim—at least in majority areas—was not a private option to be sustained by personal religion (as it had to be in India): it was a power-system both to shield and fulfil religious faith.

This power principle fulfils itself across the world of Islam, whether in caliphs, sultans, amirs, kings, nawabs, tribal chieftains or military generals. These it proves problematic to democratise against the grain of age-long habits of mind and historical norm. What is distinctive about the Shi'ah experience of being powerless under Sunni rule is that it must be undergone as *taqiyyah* only *until* what is alien to their Islam can feasibly be overthrown. Insurrection must not be abandoned as a duty: it must in its own interests be delayed until it can succeed.[29] Meanwhile the heart does not succumb to any inward recognition of a wrong order. The power-anticipation remains paramount. Not even the Shi'ah can well exist 'just as a religion' in a passive innocence of power.

Islam in Asia and Africa shows the historian and the political scientist a diversity of régimes in a medley of vicissitudes. Through them all a built-in dubiety about democracy abides. The high-principled Ba'th movement in Syria and Iraq, intending the democratic renewal of the

---

[29] The root verb *waqa* means to 'guard, preserve, safeguard or shelter', and these carry forward into the abstract noun *taqiyyah* with the Shi'ah pattern of response to adverse régimes, namely to 'conform by dissimulation' until the time when it would be possible to gain (or regain) Shi'ah power. By this means 'heart consent' is withheld, the 'evil' is only tactically 'tolerated' and 'hope' stays loyal to its goal. See further p. 140.

Fertile Crescent by the student vision of Michel Aflaq and Samir al-Bitar, in a Christian-Muslim concert of vision, quickly succumbed to men of power.[30] When Dr Akbar S Ahmed makes his robust—almost panegyric—tribute to the founder of Pakistan, *Jinnah. Pakistan and Islamic Identity*, he sub-titles it: 'The Search for Saladin' who, for all his magnanimity, was no democrat.[31] How could he be?, we may well ask, in the 12th century.

Perhaps it is futile to stay wistful about the fortunes of democracy, seeing that even in the most conducive situations it is in itself no panacea. Maybe there is about Islam more than a ken of Thomas Hobbes of Malmesbury, and graduate of Magdalen Hall, 1608, in terms of an absolute power present from consent. In his case, it was the once-for-all, irrevocable consent of the individual to hand over his otherwise anarchic powers to an all-powerful ruler, subduing everyone's privately potential anarchisms to ensure an unchallenged security for all. It was a desperate logic, a cruel philosophy, the murder of democracy.

The consent to power of, and in, Islam is of a different order. It belongs with the submission to a divine revelation that incorporates in power the means to its authority in the human world. For those who belong, there is a double subjection. What ordains the faith for the mind established the régime for the will. Sovereignty is Allah's. Its meaning is told for faith through prophethood. Its exercise is committed to faithful hands, as political power bequeathed to what was once caliphal and is now statehood territorially possessed. The two are inherently one Islam. The perennial question is how numerous, how feasibly consensual, how loyally accountable, how accountable to loyalty, those faithful hands can be.

Only in these terms can the theme of democracy in Islam be duly summarised. Muslims are not starting from John Locke or John Stuart Mill. A rich sprinkling of their intelligentsia has frequented The High and The Broad. Oxford has been conspicuous in the governance and administration of their national haunts. The strong inter-association abides and makes a Centre for Islamic Studies party to a mutual significance that, with these long antecedents, leaves a map for its wisdom to read.

---

[30] See further my *The Arab Christian: A History in the Middle East*, London, 1991, pp. 161-66.

[31] Note 17. Dr Ahmed relates all the hazards and frustrations of Pakistan's first half century to the failure of Jinnah's heirs to match his prowess, his vision and his example. The case is made with a disciple's fervour. Has this obscured how far the contrary argument could be mounted, namely that Jinnah's 'Pakistanism' was unequal to the demands its implementation set for it—and still beset it?

Chapter 5

THE VIEW FROM ST EBBE'S

i

Early in the 20th century, citing the Biblical cry: 'See what manner of stones and buildings are here!' an enterprising writer proposed to tell *The Story of Architecture in Oxford Stone*.[1] He believed he could find in the spires, their churches and colleges, an entire handbook of architecture. In *Islam among the Spires* we are attempting something comparable in— theology. Norman stone took the other author to the Church of St Ebbe, now hard by the Westgate Shopping Centre, but long the mother parish of the old poor quarter west and south of Carfax, adjoining the Castle and the Mill. It boasts no spire but it has long been the abode of evangelical, missionary dreams translating into action across the eastern world.

For a brief two-year period in the 1870s, between several sojourns in India, there was a Rector of St Ebbe's, whose biography, before and after that interlude, deserves to stand among the most significant responses to Islam by any Oxonian. Thomas Valpy French, born in Burton-on-Trent in 1825, was of Norman blood and Huguenot extraction. *Valet pietas* explains his middle name. A schoolboy at Rugby, he became a Scholar of University College in 1843, won the Chancellor's Prize and later was a Fellow of the College. His Oxford credentials were thus as sound as those of Matthew Arnold. He was to demonstrate a lifelong capacity for intellectual acumen and spiritual leadership and emerges as an outstanding figure in the story of 19th century Christian mission.

Taken then, symbolically, he prefigures an intriguing question concerning a minaret among the spires. What would have been his reception of a Centre for Islamic Studies in the heart of his university? How, more pointedly, does the thinking of his generation look in perspectives that are ours? It is only given to the generations to serve as how and where they are. Yet Thomas Valpy French and—later—W H

---

[1]   E A Greening Lamborn, Oxford, 1924.

Temple Gairdner, a Classical Exhibitioner of Trinity College and an apostle to Cairo, belong with Oxford no less than the Arnolds and the lexicographers and the literati.

Personal equations apart, to muse in these terms on 'the view from St Ebbe's' takes us into difficult issues about the bearing of a faith that obeys mission on the discourse that debates relationship. How does the warm mutuality that is academic consort with the convictions that are forfeited if they are not confessional? Or do we think they are forfeited? We are not enquiring, blandly, whether French would approve of an official house of Islamic studies.[2] We cannot well align disparate periods of history. Yet only historically are they disparate. The question remains how necessary witness lives with genuine coexistence.

It seems clear that French, Gairdner and others would want to ask whether abeyance of witness does not somehow mean a treacherous privatisation of conviction when, at the core of conviction, there is the trust of a universal relevance. The posture of dialogue seems to be that what I represent was/is meant only for me and mine. It is a communal identity which I still confess but only as characterising me and mine, i.e. ours with the 'us' that we are. I am not anticipating more than a discursive interest in my identity, while I take an equally detached interest in the faith-identity encountered elsewhere.

In this guise, of course, I part company totally with my own New Testament as, indeed, this way Muslims likewise are not tuned to their own Qur'an as an imperative summons to Islam. Both of us are in danger of having finally academicized religion and faith, or disloyally turned them into a phenomenology. Do we arrive at the paradox that the more faiths come together the more they neutralise what they bring and somehow distort themselves from within? Yet how preferable to bigoted advocacy is a discursive coexistence! How can the loyalties to meaning, on the one hand, and to meeting on the other, be reconciled?

ii

We have studied in Chapter 3 the complex shape of faith-founding in the soul, the subtle ways in which convictions can be found intrinsic in their truth and how all bears on the institutions and structures of religious

---

[2] There was lively sensitivity around his encounter with India and it is idle to conjecture how the lights he lived by there and then would guide him here and now.

authority. All this we need to carry forward now. It will not be in expectation of an answer to *our* problem that we look to Thomas Valpy French, but rather for a perspective from which to start, the criteria his story suggests.[3] Well placed by his College Fellowship for an academic career, he was drawn instead by his student association with St Ebbe's, and other factors, to volunteer for service in India, being recruited by the Church Missionary Society. During periods there through more than three decades, two spheres of ministry came to carry the imprint of his mind and spirit. They were the College of St John at Agra and the Diocese of Lahore, with its impressive cathedral on the Mall of that city. After a brief initial period in Calcutta, he settled at Agra, as teacher in its Christian College.

There was both a thrust and a sensitivity in the cast of his mind. He wrote of the College as being, in his view, 'one of the most advanced posts into the enemy's country', yet he was alert to the majesty of the Taj Mahal, that most exquisite tribute of the love of man for woman, of which the poet sang:

There is but one God for the soul
And but one moon for the sun.

St John's, he thought, 'raised the signal of the Cross as the pledge and earnest of the character of its teaching.'[4] He was eager, as he busied himself with Hindustani, to discover how to 'enlist for Christianity', as he put it, 'all the associations connected in the mind of the Hindus with their venerable and beautiful language.'[5] Augustine of Canterbury among Kentish pagans in the 6th century had comparably puzzled how to purge and adapt all that culture held in ambivalent tension between asset and debit, things potential and inimical.

When overtaken by the physical hazards of what his nation dubbed 'the Indian Mutiny'—though local-wise a 'war of independence'—French grew more puzzlingly aware also of both asset and debit, in the Raj that gave him occasion and liberty. The dangers were escaped but, despite the tenacity of his will to evangelise, there were points at which the problematics sharply emerged. It was easy to employ the 'Woes ...' of Matthew 23 against the Brahmins or to think of

---

[3] French's career is fully accessible in Herbert Birks, *The Life of Thomas Valpy French*, 2 vols., London, 1895.

[4] Birks. *op. cit.*, Vol. 1, pp. 29 and 43.

[5] *Ibid.*, p. 44.

'pagans' as 'made to dance at the will of deity as are dolls in a puppet show.' But how should one react when a classroom incident disclosed a subtle paradox of communication? He invited his mid-teenagers—a Hindu class—to comment on Mosaic laws as they chose. One essay, opting for the one about 'taking Yahweh's Name in vain', enquired: 'Why take the name of any god in vain?' French could have done better than count it 'a little pre-concerted outburst of Hindu feeling.'[6]

More was at sake than boyish teasing. Moses had been read with Hindu eyes. Reverence for reverence was the instinct of perceptive India. Moreover, without this Hindu reaction, would the Bible-inured have read the command as licensing the reviling of gods, rather than enjoining the mutual exclusiveness of Yahweh to His people and His people to Yahweh? Meaning, like beauty in the eye of the beholder, is ever in the ken—at first—of the hearer. French had yet to learn that we only know what we have communicated when we hear how people comment. Of the Gospel for which he cared so deeply, the odds of misconstruing were heavier still than with the Decalogue. The New Testament had so much more in trust.

Such experiences, until truly digested, are liable to quicken assurance, if they do not arouse self-question. To seek in others the replication of one's own faith—if we see this as the aim of mission— does not easily consort with sensing scruples of our own. Witness is fortified in its warrant by its very obstacles. When a kindly *moulvi* hinted to French that all faiths might, in some way, be 'true', French responded with Hinduism and Christianity being as far apart as earth and heaven with no compatible 'truth' between them. It was painful to have another *moulvi* take delight in how Jesus was forsaken at the last by his disciples.

These and like exchanges, in the context both of class teaching and itinerant preaching (for French encompassed both with urgent energy) give evidence of much discourse, of Hindu entry on to the New Testament and of French's language fluency. He encountered the familiar query as to why only he and his like had ever come with such tidings, whereas the British Raj had brought a whole retinue of Sahibs and Correls, making it 'hard' for him 'to be part and parcel of (his) Government's proceeding'.[7]

In due course, he became aware of experience posing issues about fidelity to the Word and, with this, the matter of 'image' in official eyes. Among Hindus he found himself 'not insisting on divine unity'—

[6] *Ibid.*, pp. 44 and 58.
[7] *Ibid.*, 'Correls' = Colonels; pp. 75 and 78.

no doubt in growing awareness of how barren controversy could be—
and so pleaded with a Christian friend not to let the fact be noised abroad.
'It is difficult to explain clearly in writing and I might be supposed to be
infringing the glory of the Saviour's divinity.'[8] The orthodoxy, which
may be easy in its heartland, often becomes troubled when it aims to be
among strangers to its mystery. And then there are always the vigilant
eyes of its armchair guardians. There comes into perspective 'the
loneliness of the long-distance messenger'. Muhammad too knew what
it was to seem, to his hearers, to be addressing them from a long way off.
(Surah 41.44)

Beyond brief sojourns in England, including his tenure at St
Ebbe's when he taught Hindustani in the university, French's career moved
forward to its climax as bishop of the vast diocese of Lahore. Interim
travels in Persia, via Muscat, during which he was enchanted by the island
of Hormuz, kindled again the inspiration he had first taken as a student
from Henry Martyn (1781-1812). Martyn, too, had keenly known the
trauma of having the New Testament faith in trust for the sub-continent.
In moments of near exasperation, translating it, he had cried: 'Where in
all this [the New Testament text] do I find India?' and 'What would Paul
do in my condition?'[9]

It was falling to French sixty years later to take this 'translation'
into the arena of diocesan leadership when Martyn's East India Company
had given way to the British Raj. French was determined that the cathedral
at Lahore should represent, in stone of worthy beauty and design, the
single meaning of the body of Christ across the tensions of nation and
empire. Numerous other edifices in cantonments around his jurisdiction
and the steady increase of an Anglo-Indian population, told the same
ambivalence. For mission could never exempt itself from the exigencies
of time and place.

More vital than an architectural expression of the Church he
served was the matter of its human ministries. For these he cared in the
modest 'Divinity School' he established in the precincts and in which he
taught. His intention was that its nurturing of clergy should be thorough
and far-reaching, with church history from apostolic times a vital
dimension from which to address the issues of an Indian future. His

---

[8] *Ibid.*, p. 85.

[9] *Journals and Letters of Henry Martyn*, ed. SWilberforce, London, more fully explored in
my *Troubled by Truth*, Durham, 1992, pp. 15-31. French wrote in 1882, 'I wish I may pick
up a little bit of Henry Martyn's mantle.' Birks, *op. cit.,* Vol. 2, p. 48.

contacts with Bishop B K Westcott and Frederick Robertson, notable 19th centuries leaders of mind, had made French acutely aware of the importance of 'eastern sympathies' for Christian theology. He found himself thrown back on to the metaphor of 'wrestling Jacob'—the theme Charles Wesley had captured in a memorable hymn: 'Tell me Thy Name and tell me now!' What was it to be crippled before one could understand? French wrote: 'I must try to show how barren, empty and naked the idea of absolute deism is.'[10] He agreed that the Islamic principle of *Tawhid*, or 'unity' 'was the heart of all truth' but that it could not be rightly asserted in a form, or from a mentality, so radical that it violated the dimensions— within it—of human creaturehood and the mission of prophets. These surely demanded that the divine *action* they signified had to be derived from within the divine *being* and were, therefore, essential. A too radical, precipitate dogma of *Tawhid* only falsified what it wanted to affirm (as bare deism did). Any intelligent theism must incorporate what was implicit for the being of God in what perhaps we may describe as His human enterprise, i.e. the created order and the abiding 'dominion'.

It would seem that T V French—like many medievalists before him and moderns after him—feared that somehow Islam was incorrigibly 'deist'. Emphatically this is not so, given the centrality of that 'human enterprise of Allah' so central to the Qur'an. The theme is one to which we will return in Chapters 6, 8 and 9. It is supremely crucial business for a lively Islam amid the spires of Oxford divinity.

Late in his life French wrote to a newly appointed English cleric: 'Day-dawn may break on what is perplexed and overclouded.'[11] One final symbolic episode remained. Retiring from his Lahore and his cathedral—perhaps in an instinct to counter all seeming care for prestige— he returned to the Muscat he had visited in 1882, to be a mere evangelist and now a veteran of sixty-five. He did not long survive. His physique could not sustain the rigours of heat and travel and the weight of the inward urge with which he lived. He died on 14 May 1891 and was buried in a tiny cove of sand between the dark cliffs of the Omani shore. He lay among the graves of forgotten sailors, his resting place accessible only from the sea.

---

[10] *Op. cit.*, Vol. 2, p. 57.
[11] *Ibid.*, p. 389.

iii

That final gesture—it was no more—deserves to come into the perspectives of these chapters from the non-academic bit of Oxford where French once belonged. Before moving into the significance of 'what is perplexed' precisely in being so assured, it can be briefly underlined by the life of Temple Gairdner (1873-1928), a lively undergraduate, student leader, and talented servant of the Church in Egypt until his untimely death.[12] His father was a distinguished physician in the University of Glasgow, his nurture warm, artistic, genial and intelligently Christian. It was in the Oxford of the nineties and the high peak of Victorian assurance that he came to a deeply passionate, yet always questing, Christian commitment, one which increasingly embraced and employed his high gifts in music and the arts. His life-long zeal for letter-writing is telling witness to the range of his interests, the liveliness of his pen and his vigorous literary criticism.[13]

But the ardour and the solid power of his personality were firmly enlisted by his Oxford years for the obedience of mission. Cairo was to be its exclusive venue, certain Sudanese and other journeys apart. His concept of ministry married the two aspects of his spirit—a genuine hospitality in the human world with all its wealth of scene and culture, and a decisive conviction of the Christian Gospel, as making him a debtor inside all that his imaginative love seized on in appreciation. That Egypt via Cairo should be the place of this eager expenditure of personal dedication to its folk, its music, its drama, its Copts and Muslims, became both his pride and his pain.

As the years passed, there came a note of weariness into his diary which he shared with his nearest associates and family.[14] For Islam presented itself to him, not out of any crude crusading cast in his mind, as grimly unrelenting in its usual posture towards Christianity. Given how genuinely the likes of Temple Gairdner merited some Muslim

---

[12] See Constance Padwick, *Temple Gairdner of Cairo*, London, 1929, where there is a lively evocation of Gairdner's Oxford, pp. 3-62.

[13] See *W H G T to His Friends*, ed. by his wife, M D Gairdner, London, 1930, notably his lively critique of Thomas Hardy, H G Wells, Elgar's music and his family intimacies.

[14] Even prior to his marriage he had reason to write from Cairo to his betrothed in Scotland: 'I seem to have left ... the boyhood of my life behind forever ... and I see the same in front—this apparently hopeless effort to cope with Islam ... For this is a call to enter into the very inner chamber of the sufferings of Christ.' (Strange sentiments inside a troth!) Padwick, *op.cit.*, p. 95.

replication of their quality towards Islam, perhaps the Oxford Centre may ponder what it could now be. His early maturing publication entitled *The Reproach (or Rebuke) of Islam*,[15] registered, in gentler tones than many predecessors, the familiar negations Islam 'seems' or 'means' to urge against the Christian significance of Jesus, the writ of the New Testament Scriptures and, most of all, the Passion and 'the bread and wine'. That there could be heartache around what is more than barren controversy, and beyond all polemic, has always been remote from Muslim souls but vividly real to such as Gairdner and his colleague, Douglas Thornton (1873-1907).

Like French under the British Raj, they had the debit/asset of the British presence, making street preaching and open dialogue possible. They launched a monthly *Orient and Occident* to widen the reach of these debates. Gairdner wrote a sequence of plays for church performances around Biblical/Quranic figures like Abraham and Joseph/ Yusuf. He searched out and brought into use numerous local tunes and harmonies. Scholarship being always crucial to his vision, he composed a series of New Testament Commentaries in the style of the great exegete of the Qur'an Al-Baidawi (1226-1260) and a collation of the Passion story in Arabic script with margins and ornate markings akin to those used in Islam.

But was he right in holding, at least initially, that the Unitarianism of Islam was 'Deistic'?[16] That might well be true of much popular, folk Islam, yet the clear and central 'humanism' of the Qur'an, creaturehood and 'dominion/status' surely excluded it. In his working context, with growing—and sadly unrelieved—burdens of administration and pastoral cares, Gairdner, with all the will, had all too little occasion for relaxed study by which to monitor the growing interrogation in his soul.

In 1910-11 opportunity came. He learned German in Potsdam and spent precious academic time with Duncan Black MacDonald at Hartford, Connecticut, and with the Jewish Islamicist, Ignaz Goldziher, in Budapest. The temptation was keen to bring his vast field-experience and his Arabic expertise into the sweet permanent haven of a scholar's study. Cairo summoned and vocation forebade. But the year of leave had tempered his vision. He published his study of the *Mishkat al-Anwar*

---

[15] London, 1909, 'Rebuke' on reprint 1912. The nouns signify primarily Christian 'failure' but also, as a minor key, things reproachworthy round the mosque. See 18.

[16] Padwick, p. 160 where he wrote of 'Contact with unitarian Deistic Islam ...' leaving open whether he saw the second descriptive inseparable from the first.

('The Niche of Lights') of Abu Hamid al-Ghazali (1058-1111) which was its only literary fruit.[17] His widening awareness of the mystical tradition gave new perspectives to his evangelism yet, *vis-à-vis* what he met on the ground, only sharpened the pain,[18] compounded as this was by the lack of newcomers to share his task and the trauma of the 1914-18 War with its tensions in Egypt.

Readers are referred to Constance Padwick's biographical celebration of a signal ministry, its wealth of sacrifice, its love of Copts and music, its devotion to the arts and its central responsiveness to Islam. The very zeal and promptitude of her writing might—to the uninitiated —seem misplaced. On the contrary, the one ardour was the authentic tuition from the other. If, from both, there is any ongoing appeal to an Islamic response, it might be captured in an incident among the many she records.

It tells of a Palm Sunday procession in Old Cairo, bearing palms and singing an Arabic poem, written by Gairdner to music of his own, adapted from the Hebrew melody of Bruch's 'Kol Nidrei'. 'A grizzled, bearded (Muslim) fellah', a patient of the hospital was sitting at the back.

> I noticed he had disappeared. Soon after, the procession of palm-bearers passed ... and there at the tail of it I saw the old man carrying his branch. I think it was the most moving experience I ever had.[19]

This was exactly what Paul had meant in writing to his Corinthians about following in the train of Christ, replicating in discipleship the Galileans flocking into Jerusalem to inaugurate, so paradoxically, the thorn-told kingship of Jesus.[20] The old fellah had understood that the procession needed him, and that he should join it in the spontaneous impulse of his Muslim being.

---

[17] Published in *Der Islam*, Strasbourg, 1914, and reprinted as a pamphlet, London.

[18] Such as a sharp attack on the person of Jesus to which he replied in his most 'assertive' writing, *Ecce Homo Arabicus*, Cairo, 1918.

[19] Padwick, p. 262.

[20] Corinthians 2.14 where Paul is echoing the Palm Sunday entry. Our 'being led in triumph' is no way about 'never being confounded,' but that we are captive to Christ, not as the sullen victims of Roman pride on cruel display but ready subjects of redeeming love.

iv

Temple Gairdner's life-work was minted in Oxford. He was no less a
fruit of it than others of his generation—Mark Pattison, Walter Pater,
Charles Gore, Henry Scott Holland, J R Illingworth and the Lux Mundi
worthies.[21] The church built in salute to Gairdner's life in old Cairo was
named 'the Church of Jesus, Light of the World'.

Romance may be, in truth, a heady wine. Yet without it there is
no honesty and, with honesty, it knows how to keep close to a sober
realism. How should a different Christian generation, sensing its
inferiority, take for heritage the Oxford legacy we have invoked T V
French and W H G Temple Gairdner to symbolise? How might it signify
for minds in trust today with their own Islam?

Answer to either question must require that we explore what
seemed to French and Gairdner and their times the incorrigible enmity of
Islam to all they held dear from their New Testament. Need we still now
think of 'the enemy'? What mitigations might we find to frontal
contradiction and mutual alienation, assuming that mitigation is the apt
word for what we seek?

The instinct of professional academics to dismiss outright any
need to reciprocate the sort of devoted quest for the other religion as our
symbols painfully pursued could easily be assumed. Sympathies, even
allowing them, do not belong in other than strictly intellectual terms. For
there is a certain irony, as we have seen in Chapter 3, around any institute
both functioning in a university and also, in some measure, sponsoring a
religious faith. Yet the history of mission, either way, remains a significant
part of the equation, leaving a neutral indifference itself a failure in
academic integrity.

A cluster of issues propose themselves. Was 'the enemy' a right
assumption about Islam? Was its emergence as a post-Christian religion
necessarily antithetical, if we probed aright all the circumstances of
Muhammad's prophetic development?[22] Did the long controversy around
the Trinity, Jesus' 'Sonship' and the status of Scriptures (of both faiths)

---

[21] The last three names belong to a notable group of Oxford theologians, joint authors of *Lux
Mundi, Essays on the Incarnation*, London, 1889.
[22] See, for example, the doctoral dissertation, in Dutch, of Willem Bijlefeld; 'Islam as a Post-
Christian Religion'—English summary in *De Islam als Na-Christelike Religie: een
Onderzoek naar de Theologische Beoordeling van de Islam in het bizonder in de Twintigste
Eeuw*, The Hague, 1959.

lose its way in a sorry tangle of minutiae and an over reliance on the supposedly primary role of dogma? Did the dogmatic instinct create and perpetuate a culture of loyalty to loyalty that excluded any possibility of genuine reckoning with the other? We have noted T V French's scruples in this regard. A certain psychic freedom is indispensable to faith-reckoning and doctrines which may otherwise seem safer are the more incommunicable when it is absent.

Factors of the psyche that are deeply present in the matter of a given allegiance are urgently more so when conversion is at stake. Was the Christian quest for personal baptism, in all its ideal validity, too partial a reading of what Christian faith and community had availing for the house of Islam? Did it unwittingly prejudice its meanings by an individualism that sought the private soul, rather than toiled towards a hope of freedom of faith and conscience within the solidarity of Islam? Given the increasing modern ferment, and Islamic initiatives on every hand to meet it, should Christian minorities have seen more common ventures?

The perplexities ramify and some will have to spill over into two final chapters. Here two broad themes have to be made central in any inclusive reckoning with how the Christian 'evangel'—with the 'isms' stemming from it in their sundry tensions—fulfils itself in the Islamic context. They are: Allah in the due worship of a true theism and the Christ-story of the Christian confession. The two might be understood in their inter-relation, by the double sense of the Persian word *diwan* meaning 'register'. *Diwan*, as 'reckoning', is what accountants and officials keep: it is also where poets place their music.[23]

Borrowing that double sense here for our theology as both careful statement and heart-feltness, we can utilise Matthew Arnold's prose writings. In these he stressed how urgent it was to pause to ask what we meant when we used the word 'God'. He also had his own sense of what we now call the meta-narrative of Christianity.[24]

To come to the heart of the Gospel and, in the same context, to the Islamic theme of *Tawhid* or 'unity', is to measure the clue of either to

---

[23] See E W Lane's monumental *Arab-English Lexicon*, Part 3, Book 1, p. 939.

[24] The 'meta' prefix is familiar enough in 'metaphor', 'metaphysics' and denotes an inter-association between two realms, beyond and yet akin. A 'meta-narrative' in context here is had in Robert Browning's line about the Incarnation:

'What lacks then of perfection fit for God
Than just the instance which this tale supplies

the other and find that only so do we surmount and resolve what was so long, and often so tediously, at stake between our kindred, but sadly contending, theisms. We will find that—as with *diwan*—a soul-poetry combines with a caring intelligence, discerning both drama and dramatist in the acknowledgement of a true worship.

Anticipating what became even more the concern of 20th century philosophy, Matthew Arnold insisted that intelligent theology was impossible without a clear understanding of what the word 'God' was used to denote. All too often the usage reigned in total lack of real enquiry, as if the sense of the word was well known and unequivocal, whereas it conceals a wealth of implied meanings, true and false.

Attempting his own, he proposed: 'The Eternal not ourselves that makes for righteousness,' or: 'The stream of tendency by which all things seek to fulfil the law of their being.' He thought the former 'contained nothing that could not be verified.'[25] But 'verification' here cannot begin to be shown, since the criteria it needs are bound up with what the definition claims. And why 'not ourselves'? (necessary to safeguard transcendence?) seeing that we—we humans—have some reciprocal relation to the definition, given any meaning in creaturehood and 'dominion'?[26]

Perhaps we should leave endless discussion of 'the existence of God' and ponder 'the God of existence', starting from 'we-ness' in this 'here-and-now-ness', their whence and whither, and read all as received from the Will, the divine Intent, that brought—and ever brings—it to pass. Such would be both the Biblical and Quranic faith concerning the God who 'let be,' who 'let humans be' and with them the whole panorama, the durable structure, that admits their being who and as they are.

Such would be an adequate confession of *Tawhid*—the unity of a sovereignty, generous in the extreme, possessing an unequivocal intent translated into history—both nature's and time's.

We are not then discoursing abstractedly about 'the existence of

---

Of love without a limit ...?
Then is the tale true and God shows complete.'
Browning, *The Ring and the Book*, London, 1972, pp. 513-14. Cf. further, Hayden White, *MetaHistory, The Historical Imagination in 19th Century Europe*, Baltimore, 1973.
[25] Matthew Arnold, *God and the Bible*, ed. R H Super, Michigan, pp. 157, 202, and frequently, like a refrain. On being precise in using the word 'God', p. 155.
[26] It seems clear that a reverent 'humanism ' is crucial to theology, in the sense that reckoning duly with 'the human phenomenon' and the way in which our 'knowing of God' reciprocates His 'knowing of us'. This in no way jeopardises the transcendent.

Allah' and incurring endless quarrels but, instead, marvelling awesomely at 'the God of existence', the will behind all things, commissioning all that we must occupy in the inter-human scene. Then 'the unity' of God belongs, not with idols, as numerical thwarting of it, but with human pretensions, pseudo-ambitions and travesties that pretend to empires of their own. These flout divine unity, not in pluralizing a bare 'solitary' but in disputing a sovereign Lordship. *Tawhid,* in the first sense, is incapable of proven assertion. For, as Hinduism, for example, well knows, there *are* plural, diverse factors in the flux of history. These are only subdued in and through the unifying authority of dynamic will, within the mysterious 'letting be' of all that is and we amidst it.[27]

Tawhid, then, is not first a matter of something being said, i.e. 'That God is One', even as idols are not overcome in being discounted, as a mathematician might, i.e. 'counted out.' It is overcome, in all its subtle forms, only when God is believed to have His creation in sure competence against all odds, one in being undefeated in His 'let-being' enterprise. So reading the meaning of *Tawhid*, we have not compromised transcendence: we have willed to understand its meaning dynamically and in no neglect of all our ancient doubts, all our daunting fears. Believing in the unity of God has to be an act of courage, no less than of submission—and either with the other.

If so, then there has to be place for some disclosure of that undefeatedness, of that sovereignty at issue with its defiants, which have also been 'let-be' in the midst of history. The factors of human sin and wrong which make this 'necessity' central to any faith-with-courage we can take up more fully in another place. Here, in brief, let it be said:

The Christian faith holds the Christ-story to be, on every count, where and how that disclosure is, the meta-narrative that does by event what metaphor does in language, namely give otherwise opaque or obscure meaning a house and home, and so tell itself—like any literature—for the readership of trust and recognition. Apostolic writing told it as 'God in Christ reconciling …'

In his proximate way, Matthew Arnold caught something of how 'faith-*qua*-story' works when he wrote:

---

[27] Mere number, as such, can never enter into what is meant in *Tawhid*. We are not 'counting' and being required to stop at 'one ...' We are confessing a sovereignty that has all (admitted) multiplicity and manifoldness' in hand beyond, yet consonant with, the privilege entrusted to humankind. The point is developed, under nine themes or aspects in my *With God in Human Trust: Christian Faith and Contemporary Humanism*, Brighton, 1999.

Literature and Dogma had altogether for its object ... to show the truth and necessity of Christianity and also its charm for the heart, mind and imagination of man ... For the power of Christianity has been ... in its engaging for the government of man's conduct, the mighty forces of love, reverence, gratitude, hope, pity, awe and all that host of allies which Wordsworth includes under the one name of *imagination*.[28]

In some strange way, however, he wanted to see it only as 'the language of poetry and emotion'. Popular faith was astray in what he called 'the preternatural', i.e. rooting it in actual event. That, for Arnold made it 'superstitious' as being, thereby, 'unverifiable'. Authentic (courageous) Christianity has no such misgivings, seeing that the actuality in Jesus, around which Arnold generated his poetic emotion, gathered to itself most comprehensively what most needs to be central, if we are to have any viable assurance of God in His unity, namely the sin and wrongness of the human world. For it is these that most tellingly confront the sovereignty of God and any conviction concerning it.

As for the 'verification' that Arnold thought unattainable *qua* history but unnecessary *qua* poetic emotion, that surely turns—as noted earlier—on what 'verifying' means. Historians have long looked on history as a mode of metaphor, so that explanation by narration has been their métier. The New Testament, in its own idiom, summons us to interpret the narrative of Jesus being the Christ, as divine narration of 'the God of existence' in utmost relation to what most urgently waits for that very story as the clue and believes to find it where faith says it lives. Received as such, it becomes the supreme re-assurance to us of the Oneness of God.

If we reflect on the genesis of the Gospel in the context of the Passion of Jesus, we can see this very process happening, whereby a particular eventuation, abiding as a narrative, generated a community of faith. The story-ing that all history is, breeds different reactions and differing assessments. To some it tells entire comedy, to others unrelieved tragedy, to others a dialectic of reason, to more again a cyclic futility. For verdicts to be reached at all, they must be selective, imagination 'homing' where it will. Significance turns, in part, on the will to its recognition,

---

[28] Matthew Arnold, *God and the Bible*, ed. R H Super, Michigan, 1970, p. 377.

lest we arrive where 'the only history that counted was that which heightened ... the necessity of ignoring history altogether.'[29]

It we read New Testament faith as 'meaning by narration' and the thing narrated deriving from within the unity of God, we have identified the source and the impulse of the two representative Oxonians we have studied. So doing we have not only located them and theirs firmly in the ongoing discourse of the university, we have also freed ourselves from much obfuscation in Muslim/Christian encounter. To understand the unity of God, fully under-written in the meta-narrative of 'God in Christ' and to commend (the New Testament favoured verb) what that 'Lord's-story' warrants, is to be out from under the abstract discoursings about 'nature', 'essence', 'substance' and *Tawhid*, that so long and laboriously pre-occupied the participants. To see it so, does not repudiate their cares but only aims to measure them more wisely. It honours them the more by striving to lift their burdens into a surer reckoning.

v

It would, however, be too simple to say that we read metahistory, rather than busy ourselves with metaphysics. For the Greek-style mind has its claims and long inter Muslim/Chrlstian relation has taken that course, so that we cannot expect to escape its legacies. Yet if we see that what Christians call Christology has its definition at Gethsemane, before we ever come to Chalcedon, we must take the latter's ontology—its care about status and logic—as only and always a philosophical acknowledgement of the former. Given the clear Hebraic aura of Messiahship and given the Semitic cast of Islamic religion in a certain common quality,[30] it seems vital to understand Christology as the divine Self-evidences in the action of love.

For that metahistory is what was always meant when faith said: 'The Father sent the Son to be the Saviour of the World,' or that: 'in Him was light and the light was the light of men.' It is pointless to let the

---

[29] Hayden White (note 24) referring to Schopenhauer, p. 242.

[30] This theme of Hebraism (or the Semitic mind at large) as in contrast with Hellenism was a favourite topic with Arnold. In 'A Persian Passion Play', a heavily attended lecture in Liverpool, he spoke of the Qur'an as 'an independent testimony to the essential doctrines of the Old Testament, rather than a plagiarism from them.' *God and the Bible*, *op. cit.*, p. 36.

Incarnation ever descend into querying about how what was 'God' could fall asleep, or use the toilet, or acknowledge a mother, or 'breathe his last.' To say: 'the divine was in the human: the human was for the divine'—readily intelligible in active terms[31]—was never sanely meant to elicit such irrelevant queries. Yet they and their kind have distorted, or poisoned, reflection too long. All faiths need to ponder the nature of the questions they can sanely accept lest, allowing the impossible ones, they find feasible answers sadly forestalled.

This has to mean an alertness to the sort of questions another faith is predisposed to put since response, if only wisely to obviate a mood of partisanship in the exchanges, needs to recognise the pitfalls it faces. The Christian understanding of the Unity of God, as only duly confessed in 'the Holy Trinity', cannot be explained by staying with numbers, since these anyway have no place in theism. It can only consist in the perception—and so confession—of unity in action, like that of a music composed, instrumented and appreciated. It was, indeed, from experience of God beyond, with and in (over, for, through) the human scene in the love-source, the storied-act and the soul-sense of 'God in Christ', that the formulation of 'Father, Son and Holy Spirit' came to be reached.

Similarly, the confession of Christ as 'the Son from the Father' was historical and experiential. It became a creed only in having been seen as an event. The 'Son' word was almost synonymous with the 'servant' word, both language-wise and creed-wise. Via that twin meaning, the faith's perception was that there had been a depth of 'service' such as only a 'Son' could bring—or God by His own devices.[32] Given the Greek mode, the long ventures into metaphysical definition were simply concerned for a right confidence that what was confessed was verily and truly from, in and through God, and not some human construct of imagination. Imagination, in any sense employed by Wordsworth, or his disciple Arnold, could well kindle in turn to apprehend it, but only as hailing, not creating, its reality.

---

[31] At the heart of theology is the relation of 'being' to 'doing, within what is affirmed of God, the interrelation of 'nature' and action. The formula here (using the adjectives as if nouns) is plainly a reality in all prophethood. It deepens in Messiahship where the 'in' of the 'agency' at time and place belongs integrally with the 'in' of unity. So the Creeds hold in their conviction that 'the action is God's' and that 'God's is the action.' (Cf. Paul in 1 Corinthians 3.23b) See Chapter 9 on *Allahu Akbar*.

[32] In a purely legal sense, this is the point of the Parable of the Vineyard and the Husbandmen. 'I will send to them my son ...', seeing that only 'the son' could assert his Lord's ownership which the tenants' violence had put into calculated threat.

It is well to realise how this same desire to be able to say '… of God' about the religious 'event' is no less crucial, and no less metahistorical, with respect to the 'uncreatedness' of the Qur'an for Muslims.[33] As doctrine, it is no less elusive, no less mysterious, than Christ's Incarnation. To be sure that the indubitable Book is God's, it must share His eternity, never having been 'acquired' but inherently with Allah *min al-azal ila-l-abad*.[34] The philosophical form this necessity took involved deep philosophising around how what was clearly earth-time-located could also have been eternally complete. In the end, the long debate could only conclude by appeal to divine action that had willed it and brought it to pass. Its *Tanzil* and its *Wahy*, its 'descent' by 'revelation', was metahistory, an earthly event as the shape of divine action. However the pundits resolved their philosophic speculations, that was what they meant by them.

Their efforts, like those of their Christian counterparts before and long after Chalcedon, were praiseworthy. There is no denigration of them here. They were legitimate *if* theirs were the questions it is fitting to pursue, if—that is—the concern in them is not more fitly taken on, or back, into the event quality on which faith turns and on which faith relies. For, however meticulously we enquire—by such lights—into how the Qur'an could be both earth-had and heaven-sent, or how Jesus as the Christ was 'man for God' or 'God in man', the more the quest takes us back beyond 'how?' into 'whether'. A faith's affirmative answer may seem to the sceptic 'a dream among the minarets', 'a dream among the spires'. Either way, a verdict is involved. The 'verification' is an act of will, a decision to rely upon credentials that strenuously exclude all wishful thinking and yet finally take, as intrinsic to its founding history, the conviction they deserve. How can faith be otherwise, reading itself 'imaged' by—and so warranted through—the history it identifies?

vi

This does not make it a bare 'faith in faith' as some might say. What carries the weight is outside the human will yet, by the very nature of religion, can only be saluted there, with mind and heart in tune. We need

---

[33] A radical issue which divided Sunni Islam into rival camps whose sharp acrimony spilled over into the caliphate when it patronised the Mu'tazilite School of its 'createdness'.

[34] Arabic has the two expressions denoting 'eternity from' and 'eternity to …'

not debate here the vexing Muslim question as to how far the human will is 'free'. Perhaps those over-tedious questions, too, were abstruse and self-frustrated. Bible and Qur'an alike agree that humans are addressees of God—a sense of things which leaves no place for cowardice or evasion. *Islam* would be meaningless without a will to it.[35] What we have is a 'faith via faith', i.e. a *fiducia* through a *fides*.[36] Part of the former may well need a readiness to 'come clean' about the metaphysics we involve. Yet the crux will always be in the metahistory we recognise and round which our 'imaging' of God has focused. In such wise, a Christian would say of the Christ-drama with words that once greeted the face of nature:

> 'There I beheld the emblem of a mind
> That feeds upon infinity, that broods
> Over the dark abyss.'

Wordsworth went on to write of its being 'mid circumstance awful and sublime that ... men see, hear, perceive.'[37] Such, in the Cross, was the 'mighty vastness', the quality of 'God in Christ'. An analogy here for the Church is 'a rising meditation' kindling to 'the perfect image'.

Muslims would need assuring that we are using 'imaging' and responsive 'imagination' here in terms akin to those of Matthew Arnold, though confessional—as his were not. The valid point in the total Islamic veto on *shirk* refers to the plural worships, the idolatries, that violate divine unity. The term, in that context, is in no way contravened in the lively sense of the last paragraph. Moreover, there is 'a hidden *shirk*' in all worship of Allah that is not an end in itself. Hypocrisy at prayer violates God's unity no less than crude idolatry. To think or theologise unworthily of the theme is to bring falsehood into worship. Meditating on God's 'eventfulness', in the shape we have explored, makes the accompanying 'imagery' authentic, being understood as 'God-granted'.

What is meant in all the foregoing about 'God in a divine history' may be studied in a personal *diwan* of Dr Daud Rahbar—a 'register' that

---

[35] Cf. Chap. 2, note 33, re the common noun to be distinguished from Islam (capital 'I') with the Qur'an and the Five Pillars which e.g. Abraham and Moses—though in *islam* as *muslims*—did not have. 'There being no compulsion in religion' the *islam* of every *muslim* has to be willed.

[36] A distinction often made between a 'deposit' of belief and the fidelity which holds it—the two senses of the ambiguous English word.

[37] William Wordsworth, *Poetical Works*, London, 1905, 'The Prelude', Book xiv, lines 71-73 and 85-86.

is, of a new sense of sight about God, had through the perceived meaning of 'God in Christ'. It was, in part, a sequel to an experience of Muslim prevarication or hostility concerning due academic integrity in Quranic studies.[38] More deeply, it sprang from a son's register of a father's devotion which deserved to suggest a costly Fatherhood in God. A deeply religious scholar and *'alim*, Daud Rahbar's father had set aside his beloved studies to care in widowerhood for his several sons. The significance of the sacrifice was not lost upon the youth, nor the debt owed to it by his own subsequent academic prowess.

By these antecedents and an interest in Christianity, he homed upon the concept of the ultimately 'worshipable', namely, that which supremely deserved to be accounted 'worthy'. In the light of the full sense of *shirk* (just noted) it was a right Islamic logic. With thoughts like Browning's 'Shall the creature surpass the Creator',[39] he concluded that the love of God, believed to be 'imaged' in Jesus as God's Christ, was the most truly and duly 'worshipable' reality and, therefore, the place of confidence about those supremely Quranic things, namely the justice, power, mercy and compassion of Allah.[40]

We have come a long way with 'the view from St Ebbe's'. Any Centre for Islamic Studies in Oxford becomes part of the city-scape that view includes. Reciprocally the ongoing Christian 'Islamics' to which French and Gairdner gave representative expression a century and more ago have to be taken on in the Oxford of today. For they were devotedly her sons.

---

[38] During a Conference in Pakistan in 1958 at which he was asked officially to withdraw the text of his paper on 'The Ethical Doctrine of God in the Qur'an', when it was feared it might disturb certain influential delegates. To Rahbar it seemed a strange compromise of Muslim academic integrity. It shook his confidence radically. See the published work, *God of Justice: Ethical Doctrine* etc., Leiden, 1960.

[39] Robert Browning, *Poetical Works*, Oxford, 1940, 'Saul', Stanza xvii, p. 231.

[40] In a private paper, Hartford, Connecticut, 1960.

Chapter 6

QUEENS IN THE HIGH

i

How beautiful is all this visible world!
How glorious in its action and itself!
But we, who name ourselves its sovereigns, we
Half dust, half deity, alike unfit
To sink or soar, with our mixed essence make
A conflict of its elements.[1]

The sentiments are Byron's but in the mouth of his Manfred standing in awe on the Jungfrau among the Alps. He was not. as he might have been, standing somewhere between Queen's and Oriel looking either way up or down The High whose curve makes one of the finest urban vistas in Europe. Matthew Arnold could have approved of his words.

Forget the consecrating name of the University Church and of the college guarding the eastern bridge. The 'we who name, ourselves its sovereigns'—was for centuries exclusively male, though the rest of the stanza was humanly inclusive.[2] 'Our mixed essence' referred to the 'dust, deity' divide belonging to mortality. Characteristically the poet has only unconsciously incorporated 'our mixed essence' in 'a conflict of its elements' as that of male and female. 'Our' speaks humanly, but the voice is male. There is an assumed identity of 'human' and 'masculine'—the one so long ensured by the hidden double sense of 'man'.[3]

---

[1] Lord Byron, *Poetical Works*, ed. E H Coleridge, Oxford, 1905, 'Manfred', Act 1, Scene 1, lines 37-42, p. 400.

[2] We had not 'Named ourselves its sovereigns'—though many recent reproaches of the Biblical/ Quranic 'dominion' humans exercise read it that way. On the contrary, it was never claimed or clutched at: it was bestowed as a 'trust' meant for reciprocal humility in being accountable. Humankind is 'entrepreneurial' in relation to nature and technology can hardly be disinvented. Thus the answer is not some 'buddhist' disavowal of tasks and talents but a hallowed custodianship which consecrates, celebrates and controls.

[3] It would be good if language and theology could retain the inclusive sense of 'man' as in no way 'masculine' or arrogant, as in the Hebrew *adham* and the Greek *anthropos*. For both

Oxford, as a venerable Christian institution is as fair an example as any of a tradition of male dominance—a dominance so complete as often to be oblivious of its own existence. It will be both urgent and right to argue later that the Christian principle of the sacramental nature of our sexuality always held the secret of the entire inter-equality of the human sexes. Yet truths can be so deeply implicit that their force is disesteemed. The duty, however, in this chapter is to study 'our mixed sexual, essence' with 'the conflict in its elements', as a major theme in the contemporary meeting of religions and, therefore, as a vital dimension of Oxford's Centre for Islamic Studies.

The immediate need, whether in the inner counsels of any one faith or in their interrelating around this elemental sexuality in our human condition, is for a steady mind with a social realism, one that honestly holds together the ideology it can teach and the actuality in its long story. 'The world is too much with us' in a grimly disqualifying sense when we expound a faith's management of human sexuality in negligence of what our history tells against it.

It is no less important, however, not to let such honest realism lapse into an ironic sort of cynicism that for ever finds the ideal statement either futile or hypocritical. For then no issue is sincerely joined. Nor is society ever remotely addressed in its deepest yearnings.

One effective example of the first technique of sanguine exposition is to hand in Muhammad Abdel-Haleem's *Understanding the Qur'an: Themes and Styles*, where Chapter 4 on 'Marriage and Divorce' opens with the words:

> Islam is the religion of marriage and only allows divorce in
> order to create better marriages ...[4]

and goes on to make a careful, exegetical and moral case which, on ground of definition and aspiration, could hardly be faulted. For it aligns the

---

language and theology get into sorry straits when they omit, or attempt circumlocutions for, the usage. But perhaps the necessary thrust of feminist case-making renders this impossible.

[4] London, 1999, p. 42. The chapter continues to p. 58. A reader in ill-will—such as might greet any claim—could say that the sentence is vacuous. Do non-Muslims not marry? What is meant by 'better marriage'? Is that 'only' honest? More importantly, the chapter quite ignores male social control over female living space. It forgets the continuing tragic family murdering of allegedly 'shamed' women, the failure of state-order to press murder charges and stamp out this violation by males of the very personhood of women—and that in the most criminally conclusive manner. For all its importance, Quranic exegesis would do well not to be so sanguine or so abstract, so purblind.

Qur'an and Tradition eloquently and reassuringly with all that a societal ideal would wish to see. Indeed, openness on all sides has to be ready for such idealisation as the form in which a faith states itself expectantly and is not to be disparaged for being such. Yet, by the same token, it is crucial that social actuality and current practice be kept firmly in the frame.

Example of an ironic cynicism might be cited from a broadcast in the celebrated *Letter from America* series by Alistair Cooke. He is commenting on the US electoral convention by which political platforms are in no way binding for actually 'running on'. He continues with an analogy.

> It is rather like the marriage service. It does not remotely describe the way the marriage came about. It defines a contract the couple must swear to ... rarely brought up again except as grounds for divorce. Between the altar and the decree nisi the parties live their own stimulating and untidy lives by quite other impulses.[5]

Not so. Any honest party to the Christian sacrament will insist. Wedded day with its pledges, wedded life with its attaining, are quite other than this politics of flux and 'tongue-in-cheek'. The reasons will come later. The present point is that cynicism must be resolutely banished from the themes of sexuality, but let religious readings keep their verdicts firmly on the ground. It is when they do neither that an urgent feminism is drawn to store its ammunition and fire its salvos with a vehemence prone to obscurantism and the excesses of frustration and anger. Any advocacy aware of strong odds against it needs to curb the temptations in its psyche from compromising the argument in its logic. Feminism is perhaps the clearest case in point, seeing that its logic, duly marshalled, has a force that needs no compromising excess of indignation.

ii

There is strange paradox about the role of women in Oxford's story. Two Marys hallow its most famous thoroughfare, name its most focal Church and dominate its skyline. For all the elegance of Christ Church, the gentler modesty of Jesus and Corpus Christi Colleges, it is women—not the

---

[5] Alistair Cooke: *Letter from America*, n.d., quoted by A C's permission.

'Master'—who share the architectural precedence. Yet the two Galileans, Mother and prostitute—as we hold the 'other Mary' to have been—for all their pride of place, availed nothing in the long assumptions of Oxford scholarship and privilege. English women had neither access nor welcome to the confines, the quadrangles and studies, that women saints adorned. The long, slow, late-Victorian battle for their admission was finally won after the First World War, with a tradition of single-sex colleges continuing into the 1970s.

The Centre for Islamic Studies has arrived, then, in an Oxford that has relinquished the old tenacious patriarchal text of things, though with some feminist pleas still to be heard by Convocation, concerning posts and tenures. It is heir to the sustained Muslim patterns of patriarchalism in their own traditional idiom, but coming increasingly into vigorous interrogation through most of the Islamic world. There is something in Islam, broadly analogous to the celebration of women saints in Christianity, namely the wives and daughters of the Prophet. Sunni and Shi'ah have differed over their significance and their relevance, no less than Christendom in its long tensions around the role of Mary, but their centrality alike in piety and moral teaching is undoubted.[6]

It was fitting in England that ancient universities as fastnesses of male privilege should be a conspicuous arena of the quest for women's rights. For education is the essential key to these, in all the other realms of action, social, political and professional. Education in the Muslim context has been arguably less crucial, given the traditional patterns of marital and family usage and the long neglect of primary female education. Much in the story of Muslim feminism springs from the role of girls and women in political resistance where, as for example in Egypt and in the Algerian Revolution or in the Palestinian struggle, several factors contributed to their recruitment. There was always the spirited example of 'A'ishah to hand to sustain womanly ardour *fi-sabil al-Islam*.[7] This has meant a different

---

[6] The Sunni/Shi'ah divergence turns, in part, on the place of the hereditary principle in Shi'ah ideology and the Shi'ah experience of suffering at Sunni hands. It also stems somewhat from tensions resulting from the timing of accession to Islam, prior to Muhammad's death, of leading persons and families. On 'Women's role'—in popular terms, see Anne-Marie Schimmel's *My Soul is a Woman*, trans. S H Ray ('The Feminine in Islam'), New York, 1999. See also trans. and ed. Nicholas Awde, *Women in Islam: An Anthology from the Qur'an and Hadith*, London, 2000. See further, Chapter 7.

[7] For how the old historians perceived this child-bride of the Prophet, see William Muir, *The Early Caliphate*, London, 1883, notably Chapter xxxvi, pp. 351-75. Still only 45, she finally 'retired' to Medina to live for another twenty-one years as a lively source of Tradition.

kind of graduation from the 'mortar-board' under which, as in contemporary Saudi Arabia, ample pursuit of academic learning still encounters sturdy barriers to its implementation in the work-a-day world, thanks to abiding forms of social practice and routine house-boundness that are slow to yield to the implications of the education in hand.

There are two immediate points to be made about the task and the temper of Islamic feminism. The one is that it must inevitably tangle with 'western' relationships. The other is that this tangle will occasion two contrasted dimensions, reaching far into the psyche as well as into the mind-search of religion. It follows, in turn, that—on all counts— there will be a deep inter-faith, inter-Muslim/Christian aspect to both study and resolution of the issues.

The tangle stems from the fact—or the charge—that western perceptions of Islam have too long and too gloatingly fastened on images of Muslim sexuality, as a means to denigrate and distort an entire culture. The ethos of *A Thousand and One Nights*, the depiction of the Ottoman harem, readings of Quranic Paradise, derogatory versions of the Prophet's plural marriages—all these have contributed to a western indulgence of superiority, seen in eastern eyes as deliberate hypocrisy. The charge looms large in such writings as the now notorious indictment of *Orientalism* by Edward Said who reads all kinds of psychic indulgence in, for example, Gustave Flaubert's eastern eroticism.

> Woven through all of Flaubert's oriental experiences, exciting or disappointing, is an almost uniform association between the Orient and sex. In making this association Flaubert was neither the first nor the most exaggerated instance of a remarkably persistent motif in western attitudes to the Orient ... (it) still seems to suggest not only fecundity but sexual promise (and threat), untiring sensuality, unlimited desire, deep generative energies ...[8]

Even the ever indefatigable Edward Lane, an Arabist who did more for Arabic philology and lexicography than any Arab of his generation, falls within this category of unqualified reproach in Said's writing. He, and his kind, literati, scholars. pundits, novelists and savants

---

[8] Edward Said, *Orientalism*, New York, 1978, p. 188.

in the utterly prejudiced West, only 'saw the Orient as a locale requiring Western attention, reconstruction, even redemption.'[9]

With the theme of sexuality so prominent in this appraisal of a 'western-Orient' a strong element of umbrage and slighted worth goes far to characterise eastern management of the issues around sexuality in inter-cultural discourse. The situation is too loaded with suspicion to admit of any ready access to mutual truth. The West has a chronic superiority-complex to overcome before it can ever discourse with Muslims, about a theme its literature and its pride have so grossly distorted.

Edward Said and the likes of Flaubert apart, Victorian moralism contributed no less to the verdict the English, at least, were liable to reach about Arab and Ottoman Islam. The Gladstone of political passion around massacres had a profound corrective fascination about prostitutes.[10] Thus a strange irony comes into view, making for the second psychic dimension in sexual perceptions. It has to do with how far pre-occupation with sex has gone in the West in the mid- and late 20th century. It might be dated arbitrarily by *Lady Chatterley's Lover* or *O Calcutta* but it had much to do with the vastly read *The Naked Ape* of Desmond Morris in 1967.[11] From his obsessively biological angle of vision, he pointed out how far humans differ from other primates in sexual appetite and competence, far in excess of the mechanics of reproduction. Extended sex is possible every way, seeing that women, hiding all signs

---

[9]   *Ibid.*, p. 206. Lane (1801-76) was a monumentally industrious, meticulous scholar whose *Arabic Dictionary* represented a major contribution to Arabic studies, while his *Account of the Manners and Customs of the Modern Egyptians* (1836) eye-witnesses life around the Nile in those years with a wealth of detail. Neither his scholarship, nor his assiduity, save him from the strangely vicious criticisms Said makes of his 'cold distance from Egyptian life' only 'delivering the Egyptians without depth in swollen detail' (p. 162). Said has the outrageous comment that Lane 'literally abolishes himself as a human subject by refusing to marry into human society' (p. 163), when he declines the offer of an arranged marriage in Egypt. It is odd that such strictures as those in *Orientalism* should come to fruition in the very bosom of occidental haunts of education. For a different assessment of the labours of Lane, see A J Arberry, *Oriental Essays, Portraits of Seven Scholars,* London, 1960.

[10]   Or rather the 'rescue' of 'fallen Women.' See Roy Jenkins, *Gladstone*, London, 1995, pp. 104 f.

[11]   Desmond Morris, *The Naked Ape*, London, 1967, a book that rapidly enjoyed a phenomenal circulation as might be expected from a pen saluting us as 'the sexiest primate alive' and exciting a fascination with our prowess in the anatomist terms that went far to plant 'having sex' and 'being sexist' in day-to-day parlance, in ways from which the earlier modesty he despised would have refrained instinctively. Now 'instinct' had a freer run.

of ovulation, are sexually attractive all the time, unlike species that are so only when liable to conceive.

That human facility has, of course, been heavily corroborated by newly available techniques, offsetting older liabilities around child-bearing and allowing of ever wider indulgence of sexual capacity beyond what were formerly physical or social constraints. Media patterns, aggressive advertisement, shifts in ethical perceptions and the ever growing enthronment of the 'gene-factor', have made for a burying of awareness of mortality in a riotousness of 'sex-alive'. The sheer ineluctableness of the West's ubiquity means that—via travel, tourism. the inter-net, television and all 'the devices and desires' of an irresistible technology—this ethos invades, if it does not pervade, the world of Islam.

It means that the Muslim will to feminism needs to differentiate its urge for liberation from what, by sure Islamic lights, could never be for imitation. The very nature of 'liberation' comes itself to be at stake—as between equality of marital rights and the legitimacy of a female professional fulfilment, on the one hand, and any coveting or admiring of Spice Girls and the fashion industry on the other. So it is that Muslim feminists need to discriminate, for example, about how they assess the veil, and other dress usages, lest what is desirable about 'unveiling' be mistaken—and reprehended—for libertinism and arrogant sensuality. Some deliberate retention of the veil comes to seem wise and right, if only as evidence of a modesty that aspires after equal personhood, but is urgent to abjure what, thanks to the West, such aspiration might be mistaken as intending. So there has been, and remains, a western 'connection', complicating and disconcerting Muslim feminism in a shape quite contrasted with 19th century disparagement.

Thus an intellectual Islam, engaging with a sociology of sexuality in contemporary terms, has this double aspect of every western nexus to overcome, namely a deeply felt resentment at an actual, or alleged, exploitation of a Muslim 'shame' all too readily castigated as such by a western 'orientalism', perceived as empty pedantry or vicious misrepresentation, now aggravated by bewildering lengths of sexual license endlessly exportable to more conservative societies. It is as if Islamic resources may not meet their own challenge without pressures, either of subversion or seduction, from non-Islamic attitudes from which there is no refuge or exemption. The long Islamic sense of an all-sufficing religious completeness is sharply tested by things unprecedented in modernity around our human sexuality. The Iranian Revolution proved as emphatic as any gesture could be against any capitulation to the moral menace it registered in the vagaries of the Shah's world. That the right response is hard to seek—and harder still to achieve—is evident enough, both from the depth of the issues and the conflict of the remedies.

iii

However self-reliant a religion wills to be—and none more instinctively than Islam—it must follow that the external origin of its dilemmas ensures that these can no longer remain purely domestic in their incidence or their interrogation. Where all now are, as in the human theme of sexuality, precludes any unilateral handling of the stakes. We rightly assume that Muslim and Christian theisms are brought together in discerning how either reads its responsibility and brings its lights to bear.

At once there is one common conviction to hold firmly in place, namely that of the 'trust' quality in all the powers we exercise, by dint of the physicality our creaturehood enjoys. The *khilafah* of the *khaliqah*, human 'dominion' in a gifted creation, is the vital Biblical/Quranic reading of the human condition. Whatever attainments our technology reaches, they never carry us beyond the obligation to recognise them as God's entrustment into our hands for due consecration. They can never become a mandate to conclude that 'we are on our own,' warranted to think our powers and competence exempting us from all transcendent reference or relegating Allah's sovereignty to limbo.

Yet all such due liability to a wondering gratitude, an entire submission, remains within our will—a decision that has to be made—and kept made in steady volition, 'letting God be God'. The familiar doctrine among Muslims that all nature is in a state of *islam* requires the distinction that, whereas chemical substances 'obey' their 'laws', automatically, and animal nature theirs biologically, each and every human *islam* is volitional. We humans have to agree to 'will God's will'—this principle being inherent in the delegacy given to us over the external world. It is also plainly inherent in the whole necessity of prophethood, whereby we are 'guided, reminded, warned, and exhorted' to such willed conformity. These central ministries of messengers would be pointless were we puppet-like things jerked from outside.

It follows from this basic truth of human *khilafah* that, however far genetic knowledge may take us in appreciating the biological drive that makes our sexuality in its human shape so engrossing and so crucial, it never means that we are exonerated from the trust it represents. Nor are we free to argue that genetic factors dissipate all moral factors in our gender relations. What is substantially biological in intercourse and, through it, in procreation, is essentially spiritual in the personhoods transacting it. Muslims and Christians alike know this well from their respective Scriptures, in the differing idiom we must explore. Only when personhood, in the due dignity of a commissioned creaturehood, is in conscious and reverent control of sexual exchange is its active possession secure from the sin that violates the truth of it. For sexuality and personhood, being mutually at risk, are only mutually fulfilled. To debase the one is to deny the other.

In the liberties that modern techniques afford, and in the libertinism to which they tempt us, both—indeed all—faiths face a common fact of contemporary life, distinct as historic cultures may be. What techniques offload on to society may have sought no consent to do so. Such are the ways of science. But, having come to be, they are not for disinvention. There are no sidings of culture into which they can be shunted and ignored. To believe in divine Lordship in history, as Muslims and Christians do, is to concede that technology's products lie within divine intention via human invention, and all inside *khilafah*. The duty of consecration remains, therefore, unremitting, as a 'war in which there is no discharge.'

'Consecration' *(takris)* may seem too expressly Christian a term but it is close to *al-ma 'ruf*, the 'fittingness' so basic in Islam, except that the sanctions are sacramental rather than social, drawn from divine action rather than divine law. To explore the meaning, we might say that Islam, concerning sexuality, has traditionally been a 'shame' society, where the female—seen as a perpetual source of male temptation—has required to be protected, managed and shielded, within parameters that needed the proxy enforcement of male liability for them. Hence the familiar social patterns whose roots can be traced back to the Qur'an itself.

The corollary has been a strong distrust in male capacity for genuine honour and sexual restraint. Hence the sundry Quranic advisings and injunctions to the muting of sexual charm and—though doubtless from other factors too—the prevalence of the veil and the chadour.[12] The

---

[12] It seems clear that cultural and pagan factors lie behind the veiling of the face. Surah 24.31 enjoins veiling the bosom and care lest adornments provoke, through ostentation or collusion with potential male fascination. Numerous passages forbid the exhibition of private parts, and limit male-female cohabitation to the inner family.

latter could well be read as a radical vote of 'no confidence' in the ability of the masculine world modestly to venerate, rather than callously or lustfully to violate, the female world. Hence also the special liability for female custody on the part of the intimate family masculine circle only, fathers, husbands, brothers. Hence again the tragic incidence of 'shame' murders of 'errant' women by these 'next of kin' as required by law and custom, violating the very citadel of personality—life itself. The deplorable incapacity of legislation, across the Islamic world, to outlaw this pattern and to requite the perpetrators justly, is tragically eloquent of how far this norm of day-to-day Islam offends the compassion of Allah in 'male and female making He them'.

Unbridled forms of secular sexuality, the sorry exploitation of the female body, and wild indulgence, might vindicate the Muslim mind in the logic of its traditional severity, but it would be a wayward conclusion, born either of panic or despair. The only ultimate solution lies in the affirmation of equal personhood and the entrustment of the mutual complementarity of human gender either to other, inside the inclusive 'trust' that is *khilafah*. To be sure, sexual intercourse was always more than procreation—increasingly so now that devices so readily make possible their separation. Yet the Qur'an has always been insistent on comprehending parenthood within the *amanah* by which all creaturehood is dignified.[13] It must follow that the powers known in all sexual exchange deserve the same sense of awed wonder and spiritual esteem that belong with the mysteries that attend on embryo and womb. Only an un-Quranic vulgarity would think to divorce them.[14]

If, then, personhoods, female and male, are truly read, received and fulfilled by light of this comprehension, the female need be neither the subversive 'temptress' under imprisoning social 'guard', nor the male the incorrigible 'tempted', required to constitute a closed circle of relationship within which only she and he are 'safe'. For perpetuating that melancholy counsel of prudence or despair will deny the liberties of a just society, deprive the social order of the wide ministries of women, and inhibit both their personal achievement and the due moral stature of the male.

---

[13] The nouns *khaliqah* (creature) and *khalifah* (trustee) are both feminine but denote both sexes. That apart, it is clear that the status is indiscriminately shared. Thus the case for personhood in autonomy is one for man and woman. This fact must control all else.

[14] From a first Surah (96) the Qur'an constantly wonders at the womb's gestation and stresses the mystery of procreation Cf. also Surah 7.189 where a couple came through a pregnancy when they had prayed for 'a goodly child,' only to revert to pagan gracelessness afterwards.

To be sure, the resulting society will be vulnerable, the more so with a secular sexuality going its own brazen way, but not more vulnerable—to different enmities—than it always was in the old, traditional way. But the risk will be consonant with the primary truth we must Biblically and Islamically hold to be paramount, namely that of a human *imperium* in which the sexual entrustment of gender, both ways, is seen to be firmly within the divine grant of autonomous being to us all. It could be no part of that perception of our human meaning under God if the sexual dimension of it, as the female knows it, is made hostage to male dominance and so forfeiting broad social, personal opportunity and fulfilment in all the varied realms of aptitude, skill, talent and interest, for the enhancement of society. It falls within the joint capacity of such *khilafah* that all the evident areas of female primacy, in childbirth, weaning and nurture, can be consistently satisfied, with no fatal compromise to traditional home-making roles and with the added benison of a more compassionate male self-image, freed of heart-hardening, even brutal, prescripts of power.

iv

If that desideratum is duly argued from the basic Quranic premiss of personality in *khilafah*[15] it would seem to follow that its Muslim realization in *tahrir al-mar'a*[16] indicates one of two half-contrasted policies. The one would be to stay firmly within the Qur'an's rubrics, maximise their 'liberal' potential and present the clearest textual case for what is sought any way. Is it not inevitable in all religions that we go to Scriptures for what we will to find and, indeed, are invited to do so?[17] For no sacred text can be sublimely immune from the private or communal mind of its loyal readership.

The other strategy would be to consider the sacred Scripture too far pre-possessed by a traditional—even reactionary—officialdom and

---

[15] See note 13. It is noteworthy that the noun *khalifah* yielding the English term 'caliph' is never used in the Qur'an in its assumed political sense. Apart from a single reference to David, the term, both singular and plural, applies only to all humans in their personal dignity as 'presiding over things as themselves under God'—'regents by volition'.

[16] 'Woman's Liberation'—the title of Qasim Amin's pioneer work back in 1900, incorporated in Vol. 2 of *Al-A'mal al-Kamilah li-Qasim Amin*, Beirut, 1976.

[17] Cf. 'Do they not reflect on the Qur'an or are there locks on (their) hearts?' Surah 47.24. Cf. also 4.82.

opt away from it, for what might claim to be a 'lay Islam', holding a faith in better loyalty than self-interested custodians. This may well seem a more radical tactic to those who have long felt disappointed or frustrated by an unyielding conservatism, those who see their enterprise as needing totally to confront what it must decisively disown, albeit claiming to do so 'in the name of Islam'.

It is fascinating to muse about 'queens in The High' in such terms and within the remit of the Islamic Centre. Maybe a measure of partnership between the two strategies could be feasible, inasmuch as both appeal to a Scriptured template of their society. In that event again, certainly the possibility of inter-faith converse emerges, seeing that Christians, as many Muslims see them, are deeply, their Christianity perhaps mortally, flawed by the sexual febrility of the western world.

There are two exemplars of these approaches, the one earlier cited in Muhammad Abdel-Haleem's *Understanding the Qur'an*, the other in *Women and Gender in Islam* by Leila Ahmed.[18] The former devotes a whole chapter to 'Marriage and Divorce', in which the maximal case is made for a lively exegetical feminism, necessarily abstracted from the current practice it must deplore. Exposition could not do better than follow it closely and with admiration for its impulse.

The decisive passage on love in the marital relationship is Surah 30.21 which sets marriage among 'the signs of God' and continues:

> He created for you *azwajan* from among yourselves, that
> you might live in joy with them and He ordained between
> you love and tenderness.

Azwaj denotes both parties to the marriage contract, variously translated as 'mates', 'helpmates', 'spouses' or 'wives', with feminine or masculine entailed in the pronouns. 'His mate that he might rest in her' is like an echo of the meaning in 7.189. The 'mutual society, help and comfort that the one ought to have of the other' of The Book of Common Prayer might be read here by the sense of *taskunu ilaiha* of 'souls inter-dwelling'.[19] Clearly there is to be total mutuality within marriage, with a

---

[18] Note 4 above. Leila Ahmed, *Women and Gender: Historical Roots of a Modern Debate*, Yale, 1992.

[19] The verb *sakana* can be read as much more than physical 'co-habitation', carrying the sense of mutual 'ensuring' of personhood, either the one 'sanctuary' of the other in inner security and trust. On the sacramental (Christian) dimension as understood in *The Book of Common Prayer*, see below.

contractual bond as the only legitimate context of sexual exchange.

Taking this affirmation in its fullest emphasis means reading the Qur'an elsewhere in its light, despite accents which seem to imply male superiority. The validity of polygamy occurs only once (4.3) and is capable of exegesis as a 'virtual prohibition'.[20] Surah 4.34-35 has to be read in the marital context in describing men as *qawwamun* over women since they are 'privileged relationally' *(faddala Allahu ba'dan 'ala ba'din)* 'because they expend of what is theirs for them.' The case made is that husbands undertake economic liability for their wives so that the translations about 'in charge of' and 'superior to' or 'excelling' have missed the exact sense which is not essentially 'inferiorising' women. It is merely stating a marital situation. A feminist might insist that this is still ignoring her whole case against assumed economic dependence and the felt subordination it induces. Accordingly she would need to abandon the whole passage to its actual Quranic world.

As for husbands. 'fearing *nushuzahunna*' (wifely contumacy), being obliged to 'admonish, banish and beat' them, *Understanding the Qur'an* appeals to linguistic analysis and to Tradition to have the passage mean that husbands should refrain from converse in cases of flagrant wifely failure to be *hafizat* (i.e. chastely behaved) and suspend marital relation meanwhile. It notes that 4.34 is the only reference to 'beating' and reads it as a last resort when silence and apartness have been tried. In any event, the verse is dealing with things inter-personal only when these have become strained as, in all marriages, they are liable to do. It should not be read as any kind of charter for male malignity or marital tyranny.

Many would suspect a degree of special pleading here, the more so when the author seeks subtle difference between 'beat' and 'strike' or 'batter' and 'slap', or when he adds:

> There are still more circumscriptions round the permission
> to 'hit'. Many Muslim scholars are also of the opinion that
> hitting is only permissible if the husband is sure that it will
> bring the right results, otherwise it should be avoided.[21]

---

[20] Depending on the reading of *in ta'dilu*, i.e. whether the equal 'justice' which is the proviso to the permission is materially feasible or emotionally unattainable. In the latter case, the permission lapses. Elsewhere more than a 'virtual' prohibition would be appropriate.

[21] *Loc. cit.*, p. 54.

Muslim feminists. as opposed to 'Muslim scholars' might well say that the very form of the apologia only deepens its reproach. There is clearly an issue of strategy in pursuit of desirable change between retrieving all one can from the Qur'an or jettisoning it altogether. There is something to be said for the former, if one concentrates on the positives (as in 30.21) and ascribes the problematics to a place-time these deserve to over-ride.

Muhammad Abdel-Haleem's case around divorce in the Qur'an is that every mention of it commends 'revocation' and 'upholding the limits set by God'.[22] Islam is realistic about human failure. Divorce sets tangled parties free and opens the way 'to start solid marriages' again and so strengthen the institution. All is within the prescript: 'Be conscious of God and know He has knowledge of all.' (2.230-42, 4.32-6) Divorcing carries no stigma, means no bar to re-marriage and serves rather to achieve a moral society. Its hasty instigation at the husband's whim can be circumvented by a wife's insistence on a marital contract which precludes this. It can happen then only by mutual consent, and is anyway conditioned by obligations of maintenance during and for a period after its completion. The whole rationale of Quranic marriage concepts is elaborated and enjoined by wide citations from the Prophet's example and a wealth of traditional lore. Tradition is always more a measure of coveted values than a proof of historical fact.

As for physical intimacies, there remains the oft-cited passage in 2.223: 'Women are your fields *(harthun lakum):* go then into your fields as you please, having in mind what you are garnering of deeds eternally and be aware of Allah.' Comment goes to a tradition concerning intercourse in Medina to explain what 'go to' means, while the over-riding sense of the ethical assize beyond time lifts all things 'in the body' to that judgement beyond, in order to

> ... make the marriage as God has intended, full of affection
> and mercy, and any misbehaviour in this intimate situation
> will be recorded.[23]

All can be comprehended within the inclusive rubric of 2.187: 'Hold intercourse with them and seek what God has ordained for you'—a ruling

---

[22] *Ibid.*, p. 56.
[23] *Ibid.*, p. 44.

which stays, as all such rulings must, within the purview of individual moral conscience, such conscience being, in turn, how, via the *khilafah* of His gift, the Creator has willed it for the risk it must be. All belongs finally with an effective sense of what is *ma'ruf*, such sense being the essence of the *taqwa*, or 'Godfearingness' which is the heart of Muslim piety.

Perhaps it must be said that all human relationships—those of sexuality most of all—hinge on how devout, devoted, God-aware, compassionate, loving, conscience and practice are ready to be. So much is true whatever the content, however weighty the wisdom of precepts and values, like those we have studied. Love is for ever making itself hostage to integrity in the other, doing so in the hope that the situation is genuinely reciprocal. A Muslim feminism, registering so much inequality to overtake, social assumptions so far entrenched, will probably feel that the Qur'an exegesis we have reviewed is still weighted adversely, still potential in other hands of sustaining the attitudes it wants to exclude, still implicitly dubious in the very shape of its advocacy. So it follows that Leila Ahmed, in *Women and Gender in Islam*, opts instead to appeal to 'a lay Islam', an authentic vision, 'an essential ethical message'—one which stresses

> ... the equality of all human beings and the importance of justice (which) went largely unheeded and (has) remained with respect to women, essentially articulated in the laws and institutions ...

The 'essential' message annuls the sexual hierarchy established by the initially historical, male-prejudicing it received—a prejudice which the true essence is, now, well-calculated both to dispute and effectively to subvert.[24]

The case-making is a bold one. For it can rightly move from the finality of Islam—a doctrine which can only stay credible if the faith refuses to 'museumize' itself in the time of its origins and makes good its contemporaneity with the world-scene in its own 15th century. Such 'making good', as we have seen, requires a sane answer to secular profligacy in unbridled sexuality, but also an authentic liberation from the social incubus and tyranny of a patriarchal order. That order will not

---

[24] *Loc. cit.*, pp. 242-3.

satisfactorily yield its built-in prejudices to the sort of textual apologia offered in *Understanding the Qur'an*. For it will always be open for diehards to rescind its readings and entrench dogmatically behind their own right to *tafsir*, even giving a warrant to the sacred text to ask the sacrifice to its authority of the very intelligence that queries it.[25]

The case, as *Women and Gender* makes it, is a radical one but can fall back on the rubric that 'Islam means what Muslims say it means' and 'the Qur'an what its Muslim readers find it to mean.'[26] If this challenges where the seat of authority is, it could shelter inside the concept of *Ijtihad* insofar as that organ of development and interpretation can free itself from 'learned' control and admit of some laicisation of its workings. The female half of humankind has certainly an equal claim to participation in *Ijma'* (consensus) where the pundit and the male have been allied for so long.

Boldly it proposes a discounting, a re-counting, of history.

> Establishment Islam's version of the Islamic message survived as the sole legitimate interpretation, not because it was the only possible interpretation, but because it was the interpretation of the politically dominant ... This .... legalistic, establishment, version of Islam ... largely bypasses the ethical elements in the Islamic message.[27]

The sober feminist and the right-minded Islamist can claim to be one and the same. A claim concerning 'an essential Islam' is the likelier stance for those who would be the Virginia Woolfs of Islam, striving to legitimate female participation in realms traditionally seen as male preserves, rather than invoke the kind of Qur'an exegesis which still leaves intact what they see at its irreversible bias—a bias seen to be persisting in the very shape of its case-making. The claims of 'official' *tafsir* will resist them, leaving ever open the question as in what *tafsir* consists and who—or what—authenticates it.

---

[25] The sacred text, in all religions, has often been held to warrant that kind of claim on the part of its 'official' exegetes, namely that if the 'lay' believer finds its content vexing their intelligence they should be ready to defer to it none the less, 'sacrificing' their critical faculty as the price of submission.

[26] In this field of 'women s rights' the urge to 'inread' the Qur'an according to one's intention is strong indeed, but equally so for rigorists as for reformists.

[27] *Op. cit.*, p. 239.

Such feminists. however, may well find unexpected help from unexpected sources. For, while the late Ayatollah Khomeini insisted that Qur'an interpretation depends upon the *ahl-i-'ismat*, and that 'the field is not open for anyone to try to impose on the Qur'an any idea that enters his head,' he also conceded that even he did not 'in any way claim to be expounding their ('these verses') ultimate meaning.' What he had to say was 'based on possibility not certainty'.[28] If the *ahl-i-'ismat* are not more categorical and even Ayatollahs are not so, then 'possibility' remains present. Those who invoke it will still have on their side the founding fact of their personal, human *khilafah*, or 'entrustment' which may arguably include responsibility with their given Scripture.

They can also invoke the fact that Islam officially requires a legal contract as the necessary condition of sexual partnership and denounces as *zina* all deviation from it. That vital legal status of 'the husband/wife condition', though explicitly not a sacramental one, clearly disavows a haphazardness that, otherwise, would certainly jeopardise the woman more than the man. In that fact Muslim feminists have much going for them, despite the long prevailing climate of unequal personhoods.

One of the narratives of Egyptian Muslim feminism moving broadly along these lines is Nawal al-Sa'dawi's *Mudhakkirat Tabibah*, 'Memoirs of a Woman Physician', an autobiography in the form of a novel.[29] Born in 1931 and graduating from the Medical Faculty of Cairo University, she acquired a leading role in publicising and promoting the role of women in Arab society, by means of widely celebrated literary productivity and her capacity to portray the inner experience of women under the constraints of the male world. Her professionalism, and the sphere in which she has pursued it, gave her graphic insight into women's experience of 'male gaze', as somehow both threatening and corrupting and of the male assumption about women as 'tricksters', or potential 'seducers', whom it is urgent to confine and circumscribe.[30]

She contrasts the liberty enjoyed by the male body and the inhibitions that dominant a girl's education into a social role in which

---

[28] Imam Khomeini, *Islam and Revolution: Writings and Declarations*, trans. Hamid Algar, Berkeley, 1981, p. 366.

[29] Published Beirut, 1980.

[30] See, for example, 'Sacred History as Mysogyny' in Fedwa Multi-Douglas, *Woman's Body, Woman's Word, Gender and Discourse in Arabo-Islam Writing*, Princeton, 1991, Cairo, 1992, pp. 54-66, being an exposition of Ibn al-Batanuni's *Kitab al-'Unwan fi Makayid al-Niswan*, 'The Book entitled "The Tricks of Women"', a 15th century classic of the genre.

marriage-by-order is the due destiny toward which all else is drawn. The very writing of 'Memoirs' was a sort of social 'graduation' for the author and it did much to familiarise a still sceptical world with the validity of the professional woman, the female laying siege to territories of fulfilment, whether in healing, politics, or letters, hitherto barred by usage or prejudice or religion. Her writing has steadily called Muslim misogyny into question, employing the medical sphere as uniquely given to positive exploitation, thanks to the entrance it enjoys into the intimacies of social etiquette and the trust it presupposes.[31]

Medicine apart, numerous other writers have used the autobiographical mode to make the kind of female self-gesture that Virginia Woolf ventured in *A Room of My Own*. Notable among them are Huda Sha'rawi: *Harem Years: Memoirs of an Egyptian Feminist*,[32] Zaynab al-Ghazali's *Ayyam min Hayati*,[33] and Fadwa Tuqan's several kindred works,[34] reflecting the Palestinian dimension.

While Huda Sha'rawi was the greater publicist, it is arguable that a more incisive pen in the cause was that of Malak Hifni Nasser, who was alert to the need to hold an authentic Islamic feminism clear of the western factor, in which she sensed a menace to its own Muslim integrity. Hence the case she made for some—if critical—retention of the veil. She saw the importance of an inclusive regeneration of society, seeing that, at its core, the women's hope lay with the quality and temper of male society. Much of Malak Hifni Nasser's work was published in *Al-Jaridah*, by its editor Mai Ziyada. She challenged men to redeem their moral character and to lift the issues out of mere intellectual debate, by a realism that truly measured the degree of female humiliation as creatures allowed no free opinion even about themselves.

She was particularly cogent in her attack on the very concept of a 'co-wife', brushing aside those complacent apologists who mouthed

---

[31] See Multi-Douglas, *op. cit.*, pp. 130-44, 'empowerment through Medicine'.

[32] Trans. by M Badran, London, 1986. Huda Sha'rawi, of an earlier generation than Sa'dawi, was a notable pioneer.

[33] Beirut, 1987, an autobiography treating of religious faith in tension with doubt and misgiving over authority and ethics. It would seem to have been modelled on the three volumes of the blind scholar, Taha Husain, of the same generation: *Al-Ayyam*, 2 vols. Cairo, 1929, Vol. 3, Cairo, 1973. Eng. translations: E H Paxton, *An Egyptian Childhood,* London, 1932; H Wayment, *A Student at the Azhar*, New York, 1948, and Kenneth Cragg, *A Passage to France*, Leiden, 1976.

[34] Fadwa Tuqan's writings belong squarely with the Palestinian struggle, published between 1968 and 1987. She too echoes the title of *Al-Ayyam* in *Wahdi ma'a al-Ayyam* ('Alone with Passing Days') Beirut, 1974.

platitudes about 'giving more women chance of motherhood' or handling an alleged 'surplus' of women over men in the population. 'Co-wife' she wrote

> ... was a terrible word, laden with savagery and selfishness ... As you amuse yourself with your new bride you cause another's despair to flow in tears ... You hear the drums and pipes (of the new wedding) and they hear only the beat of misery.[35]

She was clearly reaching for something like the inter-personal principle of sacramental marriage, where the very notion of some duplication of what is given and received in genuinely mutual sexuality is abhorrent and treacherous in itself, apart from any translation into fact.

These were early writers of the 20th century within Egyptian Islam, but they probed the ultimate issues with a rare tenacity and these have remained essentially the same battle in the decades since. It might be defined as a struggle to pass from a shame society to an honour society. For the traditional Muslim ordering of things sexual administers a shame culture unilaterally as one to which women, not men, are subjected.[36] Indeed, it is left to males to impose the shame régime, not on themselves but on their allegedly offending women folk, while—in this process— the very element of male honour, which might so blessedly be otherwise directed, is exclusively bent on requiting the 'shame' of women. Only a mutual 'honour' culture could ensure that 'shames' are read aright, as never unilateral and known as never truly redeemed, except by reciprocal honour. That conclusion requires that the authentic inter-personal truth of human sexuality be enshrined in something more than contract-in-law and stand in a pledged sacrament, entailing law and public notice, to be sure, but hallowing these in dimensions of the heart and the whole meaning of the body.

---

[35] Leila Ahmed. *op. cit.*, p. 182.

[36] Though the penalties for adultery, in violation of the legal bond of marriage, are prescribed for both parties (24.2) and accusation against a woman requires four 'witnesses' (4.15) and both punishable (4.16), the retribution for the 'shame' has long been, by social custom, unilateral against the women and inflicted by menfolk. The whole *Shari'ah* system has been slow to register the sexual inequalities it sanctions and state legislatures unready to re-interpret or override it.

v

Thinking that way, it might be said, brings us to the full meaning of 'queens in The High'.[37] Or at least it returns us to the question, raised earlier, whether debate inside Islam about feminism, its claims and pitfalls, should or should not, admit of inter-faith participation. The hazards clearly are many, if we think it may. Feminism has had a long and wearisome history in the Christian past and bringing the issues into comparative treatment could invite much unseemly or fractious partisanship, at all costs to be avoided. Yet 'male and female created He them' knows no frontiers. A will to honest openness has no more urgent field. If we can renounce facile verdicts and special pleadings, bringing the sexual equation into the discourse of faith-cultures can only be a salutary exercise on all counts of love and truth.

Before pondering what Christian sacramentalism might signify for Muslim ordering of sex and marriage, it will be well to anticipate its relevance by Quranic indications in the same direction—if not decisively, then potentially. The clearest comes in the final clause of Surah 30.21 earlier quoted. After 'love and tenderness enjoined' between husband and wife, it adds: 'Truly therein are signs for a people who have their minds alert.' The verb *yatafakkarun* is not infrequent with the *ayat* of God and has here the *la* of emphasis. The thought, clearly, is of sexuality within marriage, as a theme of 'mystery', an experience calculated to evoke long, ever reverent, reflection, all crudity, all wantonness, all vulgarity apart. There seems to be an invitation, an expectation, a perception, lifting the relationship out of all triviality, fickle passion, lust or profanation, into a realm of awe and gratitude. The whole—arguably— is not far from what Christian marriage comprehends as sacramental, that is, 'minded as holy'.

There is another passage which may be read as pointing in the same direction. In the context of directive about intercourse during Ramadan, Surah 2.187 uses the analogy of 'attire' or 'garment' to describe its meaning. 'Your sexuality is like a seemly garment, yours to them and

---

[37] In terms, that is, of due regard for the 'queenly' potential of the female sex. The assumption, however, of some feminism is that this means female participation in *all* that has been characteristically male 'preserve', *qua* the professions. It may well be that the truest goal is not for women to be 'as men', but rather for men to live more in the gentleness, compassion and honour they have expected of women. It needs always to be remembered that, whereas men have no wombs, women do, and much else follows inescapably and inalienably from that 'natural' fact.

theirs to you', or—in more literal translation: 'Your wives are a garment to you and you to them.' The key word is *libas*, a noun from *labasa*, meaning 'to be in intimate connection with'. 'Clothing' as a figure of 'seemliness' and 'self-awareness' is frequent in different cultures.[38] The meaning seems to be that as husbands and wives transact their embrace, either of the other's body, they clothe themselves with each other and. thereby, make all 'seemly' and authentic—'naked' to be sure but, thanks to their meaning in the act, in no way 'naked' as the term would be used figuratively, as in 'naked aggression' or 'bare lying'. For these lack all inhibition and. in sexuality, a reverent inhibition is precisely what registers its positive character.

In their sexuality each 'goes to the other' in fulfilment and so 'covers' what extra-marital crudity would brashly defile. Is *libas*, then, close to the meaning when Genesis 4.1 says that 'Adam knew his wife'? The marriage bond then 'justifies' what otherwise would be 'gross, i.e., 'uncovered, and so reprehensible.[39]

If rightly read this way, 2.187 comes close to 30.21 in hallowing the sexual relation within marriage, as the theme of an inherent significance, warranting the equal personhood that the sacramental view fulfils. To be sure, the passages speak of 'wives' plurally. They do not use the dual verb or pronoun as would the sacramental concept, so that what the parties mean is in their singularity as being 'pledged either to other' in terms each makes inalienable from the other, so ensuring that their mutuality is total, with forbearance and fulfilment equal in both directions. Then neither inferiorises the other's true personhood.

It would be foolish to claim that the verses examined make any such conclusion categorical. Yet the following phrase in 2.187 about 'what God has ordained for you,' could confirm it as a possible one, despite all that has long negated it in the cultures of Islam through history. Having the reading itself feasible, as distinct from its practice, would have to turn on the issue being open to inter-faith converse, through which the definitive Christian sacramental reading of marriage might be allowed to be on offer.

What that reading is has already told itself in reviewing the Quranic passages, namely that what is contractual in marriage adds to its

---

[38] The New Testament Letters often use it—'be clothed with humility,' 'put on Christ,' 'put off (lust etc.) ... put on (charity etc.).'

[39] There is, of course, a certain terminological paradox here, in that 'concealing' is often a term for subterfuge or deceit. (Cf. the journalistic usage of 'covering' a crisis or a situation.)

veto on adultery, and to its positive legitimisation of sex as marital, the spiritual sacredness of the ensuing 'estate', that has made 'one flesh' of wife and husband. In a 'sign' or 'sacrament' what we do carries what we mean and what we mean fulfils itself in what we do. Hence the simple, frequent 'sacraments' of daily life—shaking a hand, hugging a friend, laying a wreath, sending flowers, saluting a flag. These may be little more than gestures but they enshrine the idea of 'relatedness' via action, so that meanings are genuinely transacted and so made vivid and actual, rather than merely implied or lamely latent.

Religious faith lifts these 'gestures' into sanctions that both mean and 'perform' at the same time, like ablutions before *Salat* or prostration in it. The physical is recruited to 'do' the spiritual: the spiritual employs the physical to affirm its reality via the fulfilling deed. The sacrament of sex is of this order. 'Love's mysteries in souls do grow, but yet the body is their book.'[40] Sex becomes a sacrament when it is held to its meaning as human love, perceived and received as a divine gift of an inter-personhood, male and female, in which either is hallowed in the honouring they equally exchange and know, in doing so, both the loyalty they owe and the completion they experience.

Marriage in these terms is an act of co-inherence, a way of the soul in the sanctuary of the body. As such, it is in vital association with monotheism by virtue of its fidelity to unity. By physical nature, the body makes the place but through grace the place makes the body. Two mysteriously love each other and do so faithfully by a vow that excludes all disordered, wandering passions. That vow is their loving tribute to each other.[41] The integrity it covets to pursue becomes the benediction of society at large, by dint of how it looks on all other relationships.

It would be unrealist to suppose that this sacramental perception of the meaning of the deepest asset of human personality could be suddenly or painlessly grafted into the Islamic mind. It is at least commendable to the struggle of a feminism, so hard beset, whether by massive prejudices in its own society or by the blasphemies of a westernism that has so far disowned or discarded it. Muslims are certainly

---

[40] John Donne, *The Poems*, ed. H J C Grierson, Oxford. 1937, 'The Extasie', p. 48 (modern spelling).

[41] This must be the response to the case made, e.g. by Thomas Hardy in *Jude the Obscure*, that marriage 'licensed a women to be loved on the premises' by the husband and leave her or him—somehow—no longer free of her/his own body, either to withhold or to employ elsewhere. Such gibes miss the entire point of a mutual forbearance via a love-relation that 'desires' only by the writ of reciprocal 'desiring'.

free to say that their own historic culture ignores it, or that there is more honest realism in the Islamic tradition of feasible, even, frequent, divorce and in the patterns of male supremacy.

But, in any event, all must come within the discourse of communities and crises open to each other—a situation surely pre-assumed by any 'Islam among the Oxford spires'. For it is the ultimate concepts by which human sexuality is understood that will finally determine the course of law-reform in Islamic society in regulating all aspects in practice.

The foregoing leaves issues in that sphere where formally they belong. The concern has only been to read how religious faith and sexual understanding combine, and to bring that inter-action into ecumenical discourse in an academic scene. There is also the burdened question of homosexuality, which the Qur'an condemns in Biblically Semitic terms.[42] The debate, which its practice raises as to what is 'natural', can only be resolved by how the male and the female condition are perceived. The whole problematic might well be gathered into the oft-repeated Quranic clause concerning *qawm yatafakkarun*, 'a humanity mindful of its (right) mind'—if we may so translate the intensive sense of the verb. Where, in Islamic jurisprudence, the Qur'an is silent, much falls on the Tradition of the Prophet, but this, in turn, may be subject to communal 'consensus' insofar as this may duly emerge from a society that adequately ruminates on what its loyalties require in its ever changing outward scene.

There is a passage in a mid-18th century English novel, Samuel Richardson's *Pamela* (1740), on which many a feminist would fasten as being exactly the stereotyped role-making by which women, brides most of all, have too long been oppressed and betrayed. It reads:

> He told me afterwards that when he had done saying: 'With this ring I thee wed.' I curtsied and said: 'Thankyou, Sir,' maybe I did: for it was a most grateful part of the service and my heart was overwhelmed with his goodness and the tender grace wherewith he performed it.[43]

Precisely! says the critic. She was duped into a snare, a trap set by a delusion and did he not prove a profligate husband afterward? The story

---

[42] Only obliquely in Surah 4.15 (about women) depending on the sense of *fahishah* and the meaning of 'two of you' (in 4.16), also 7.80-81 concerning Lot where the meaning is clear.

[43] Samuel Richardson, *Pamela*, Everyman edition, 1914, Vol. 1, p. 316.

is a blatant case of masculine treachery and merits only scornful exposure of its villainy!

But suppose the curtseying—or its male equivalent—had been reciprocal? For such was the meaning of the Liturgy with its equal exchange of an equal integrity, this being the *niyyah*, or intention, of the vows.[44] An exchange of reverent gratitude is the very core of marriage. It was for this Pamela had waited, resisting all attempts to seduce her, but accepting to be loved when marriage was accorded. That, in Pamela's experience, the according of it was subsequently betrayed means no case against its rightness. On the contrary, while it could not be proof against infidelity, it stayed crucially to condemn it. For no institution is proof against human nature—which leads us back to the 'if' the sacrament was meant to resolve and hold in honest troth, as a bond which cannot abrogate itself.

It was just such masculine quality that a woman novelist, a century later captured when she wrote, of the courtship in *Adam Bede*:

> He called his love frankly a mystery ... He only knew that the sight and memory of her moved him deeply, touching the spring of all love and tenderness, all faith and courage within him ... He created the mind he believed in out of his own, which was large, unselfish, tender.[45]

Or, as a 20th century writer has it:

> Moments of their secret life together burst like stars upon his memory ... For the years, he felt, had not quenched his soul or hers ... all their souls' tender fire. In one letter he had written to her then, he had said: 'Why is it that words like these seem to me so dull and cold? Is it because there is no word tender enough to be your name?'[46]

Was it not an 'Oxford Reverie' that was initially proposed—that of 'people minding their right mind'? The crux of Islamic—indeed of all feminism—

---

44 Using the familiar Muslim term, requiring a focused purpose in all ritual acts.
45 George Eliot, *Adam Bede*, numerous editions, since 1859, that of 1980, ed. Stephen Gill., Chap. 33, p. 400.
46 James Joyce, *Dubliners*, 'The Dead', ed. 1956, pp. 210-11.

lies in masculinity. Can the male in Islam take to its soul 'A Woman's Prayer', composed by the man, Robert Browning?

> Be a god and hold me with a charm
> Be a man and fold me with thine arm!
> Teach me, only teach me, Love, as I ought,
> I will speak thy speech, Love, think thy thought.
> Meet, if thou require it, both demands
> Laying flesh and spirit in thy hands.[47]

Only if we realise the irony. It is 'Love' the prayer addresses—'Love' that comes through with the answer only when truly fulfilled by 'flesh and spirit' in the equal unison the parties bring.

---

[47] Robert Browning, *Poetical Works*, Oxford, 1941, p. 216, 'A Woman's Last Word'.

Chapter 7

THE SIEGE IN THE SOUL

i

The spires of Oxford were once girdled and guarded by walls. New College garden has their most impressive remnants. Their tight enclosure of the medieval city tended to bitter, and at times bloody, disputes between 'town and gown', with citizens and scholars baiting and buffeting each other in The High between St Martin's and St Mary's. Oxford's walls saw many investings by hostile forces in times of war and tumult. There were the disorders of Stephen's reign in the 12th century, the turmoil of the English Civil War in the 17th.

Walls under siege have long been analogy for stresses in the human soul. The theme is as old as the Bible.

> 'Innumerable evils have compassed me about' (Psalm 40.12), 'The Lord showed me His loving kindness in a state of siege. (Psalm 31.21). 'He has built up walls around me as gall and travail' (Lamentations 3.5).

Beleaguered towns are liable to haunt beleaguered souls. John Bunyan drew on the theme in his *The Holy War* for the tribulations of his 'mansoul'. In the chorus in *The Rock* T S Eliot sang of the time-kept city that forfeited its security by the neglect of its churches. Outer walls only represent a physical defence against 'the ghostly foe'. So perhaps Oxford's fortifying remnants may be allowed to symbolise sundry Islamic experiences of a 'stage of siege' through its long centuries. If so, the first and most long-sustained of them began almost immediately after the death of the Prophet and as a direct consequence of his demise. It has continued through many vicissitudes in the ebb and flow of historical fortune ever since, namely the Shi'ah exemption from the broad characteristics of what became Sunni Islam.

Given the irreplaceable and irrepeatable status of Muhammad, and the traumatic experience of his passing, it was perhaps inevitable that his political legacy should generate tension. Its emergence in Sunni-Shi'ah form runs deeper still. For Shi'ah Islam became a deep minority verdict against the characteristic Sunni assurance of success. Despite occasions of power and dominance, the Shi'ah form of Islam found itself vulnerable in terms that generated a long-standing and deeply rooted dichotomy which has long meant sincere engagement with the place of suffering and adversity in the interior experience of faith. This had to wrestle with the reality of religious prejudice and enmity, aggravated into a form of civil war and long proving to be somehow intrinsic to the faith system itself, unless relieved by a different self-perception that wills in liberality to co-exist.

Christian Oxford—witness the Martyrs' Memorial facing up St Giles—has its own bitter story of a faith at war with itself, when the pretensions of authority made havoc of 'the mind of Christ'. Yet—for all these blasphemies of the will to power—it would be fair to say that Christianity has at its core and heart what Islam contains in the very different terms of an internal schism, namely how and where the vulnerable, the victim, the vicarious, belong in the economy of God.

It is not suggested that the Passion of Jesus as the Christ, so central to the Christian theology of divine sovereignty and unity (as traced in Chapter 5), is of the same order as the tragic events where Shi'ah Islam took its dramatic rise. It is to say that—however far we must dissociate the one from the other—both belong, in their own measure, with how faith has to do with the tragic and what the tragic has to do with faith and both with the economy of God, the 'God of power and mercy'.

ii

The emergence of the tensions generating the Shi'ah separatism, hard on the demise of Muhammad, is a familiar enough story and needs no long rehearsing here, where our concern is with the aspects of martyrology in any faith as a key to its soul. There were, to be sure, powerful political factors around the true caliphal succession. Abu Bakr, father-in-law to Muhammad, took up the role, to be followed by 'Umar and 'Uthman, only then, in 656 after the murder of 'Uthman, did 'Ali make good what the Shi'ah held to be his prior claim in 632. 'Ali was the cousin and son-in-law of the Prophet and the father, through Fatimah, of his only surviving male heirs, Hasan and Husain. Given the Shi'ah reading of Surah 33.33

concerning 'the people of the house' as 'immaculate', the hereditary principle was crucial for the Shi'ah mind.

When, after the violent death of 'Ali in 661, the hegemony passed to Mu'awiya and to his capital in Damascus in the inauguration of the Umayyad caliphate, the Shi'ah 'partisans of 'Ali' had accumulated a sad tally of frustration and disaster—a deferred right, a short-lived reign, a bitter defeat and a destiny of denial, only made the more bitter by the firm régime achieved in Damascus and by the fact that these victorious Umayyads represented latecomers to Islam in the days of the Prophet's *Sirah* in Mecca.

Worse, infinitely worse, was to follow. The two grandsons had their base in Medina, still loyal to the city of the Prophet's tomb, and the symbol of his rulership. There the elder, Hasan, died, probably at an assassin's hand, while Husain waited on the future and how it might correct his fortunes. In 680 came the death of Mu'awiya—perhaps presenting occasion to restore the 'Alid claim. Believing—on dubious grounds as it proved—that his cause was popular in Lower Iraq and that he might hopefully instigate the insurrection that might overthrow the Umayyads, the bitter outcome instead was the tragedy of Karbala' on the 10th of Muharram, when Husain and most of his retinue of 'Alids were massacred by the swiftly organised forces of Yazid, Mu'awiya's son and heir, from Damascus.

The event was execrated across the entire world of Islam as the immolation of Muhammad's own precious progeny. In the realism of martial politics, it consolidated Mu'awiya's legacy and confirmed a caliphate which stretched from the Oxus to Atlantic Spain. Shi'ah Islam entered on a long encounter with the deepest of religious mysteries, the despair of those who find themselves lost in the very cause they serve as God's. They were bound to see the victors as renegade Muslims unworthy to rule in *Dar al-Islam*. Yet rule they did, only to the perplexed pain of a Muslim community somehow betrayed of its divine right—a right so totally sanctioned by divine will in being 'housed' in Allah's own Prophet's godly seed.

To be sure, the Shi'ah would come into power centuries later, notably in the Fatimid caliphate in Cairo and the rule of the Safavids in Iran. But nothing could repair the calamity of Karbala'. How ought a faith in Allah's indubitable Lordship to negotiate the meaning of a history so darkly gone awry? Why should a dire vulnerability, taking brutal shape in bloody massacre, befall the utterly virtuous such as these from the hallowed womb of Muhammad's daughter? That the experience was a minority verdict inside the distinctively successful tradition of Sunni Islam in post-Hijrah triumph, and in rapid expansion west and east, only made the riddle the more vexing.

It is precisely in this desperate paradox that the deep significance of Shi'ah Islam becomes evident. For it underlines what—for a final chapter here—has to be seen as a central theme of positive mediation between Islam and Christianity. It is that, necessarily, where faith confronts tragedy it must reach for more than palliative, more than consolation, more than exhortation. It must reach for redemption. To be vulnerable in the dire terms of Karbala' is to be constrained towards a sense of something vicarious by which adversity is mastered. This is more than a Stoic acquiescence which sullenly steels itself against events. It is more than an unyielding defiance of dire fate. It discovers to itself a 'virtue' in the very pattern of unmerited tragedy by which a saving 'merit' is released.

This is what mysteriously happened in the heart of Shi'ah Islam in the centuries after Karbala'. How it eventuated has long puzzled historians and theologians. In any time-sequence, a state of being vicarious follows every experience of being vulnerable. Things evil are undergone by victims *because of* the evil-doers that made them such. Only in some cases do they have the option of retaliation. For the doers may be anonymous and out of reach.[1] If, though feasible, retaliation is abjured, forgiveness may opt to bear the evil in its 'done-ness', as a way of taking away what otherwise would be malign, in an injustice unrequited or an enmity sustained. When this can happen there is a genuine sense in which wrong is overcome and tragedy thereby transmuted into something excelling any *status quo ante*.

It would be too venturesome to explain Shi'ah reading of Karbala' as 'The Passion of Husain' in these explicit terms. But on one supreme factor it did rely, namely the inherent 'worth' of 'Ali, Hasan and Husain. As the 'immaculate' family of the Prophet, they were believed to possess an inner sanctity so that their dire immolation at the hands of incarnate evil was entirely undeserved. They were in no sense paying for misdeeds of their own. Thus there could not fail to accrue from their blameless deaths a *barakah*, a virtue and a benison, which could avail for sinful souls if sought and pleaded with a genuine faith.

---

[1] As in John Steinbeck's *The Grapes of Wrath*, New York. 1939, where dispossessed small-holders, migrating forlornly westward, vow to trace to its last hiding place the exploitation that is guilty of their destitution. They find themselves clenching their fists in a futile gesture towards a brass plate in the financial area of New York—a faceless symbol of the evil done.

Thus there came into Shi'ah Islam the redeeming martyrology that found its expression in 'The Passion Play of Husain' at Karbala'.[2] The drama takes its profound place in the soul of Shi'ah Islam, drawing on the deepest emotions and the full thrust of religious ritual, as it re-enacts the events of that fatal day. It associates with the victims of Karbala' other hallowed sufferers, like Jacob yearning over a lost Joseph, or Jesus as one whom men sought to kill. These antecedents prepare the way for the most ultimate of all immolations. 'The Passion Play' may incorporate scenes in which travellers, pitching tents unwittingly in the holy soil, draw blood from the earth with their tent-pegs.

Deplored or decried as this tradition of Husain's Passion is among Sunni Muslims, there is no doubt that it constitutes a powerful meta-history, in that round the event itself those long centuries ago a mythology gathered which captured—as only such imagery could—the religious meaning of evil undergone and evil defied. All is an inclusive religious reckoning with the vulnerable/vicarious actuality, which, for Christian faith, has its drama in the world as a crucifying place, known so round the Cross of Jesus.

iii

If, in this way, the condition of being vulnerable leads into the experience of being vicarious, there is a vital issue latent in the sequence. The victimisation is there, in any event, but how is it taken? It will only be there as a fate, if it is not recognised as an inward travail towards forgiveness. When the great Hebrew prophets spoke of 'righteousness' they did not mean merely a static quality fatally possessed: they meant a 'rightingness' that had a task in hand in the situation it addressed. It may be thought akin to the strong emphasis in the Qur'an on the duty of *istighfar*, 'the seeking of forgiveness'.[3] This is primarily the wrongdoer's

---

[2] The Shi'ah Passion Play memorialises the tragedy of Karbala' when the Prophet's only surviving grandson. Husain was slaughtered by the forces of the Damascus caliph after an unsuccessful bid to unseat him. In his lecture on the Play (to a large audience) Arnold dwelt on the theme of 'openness to the East', noted the intense devotion aroused in Shi'ah hearts, detecting something he called 'intrinsic' and 'corresponding with the urgent wants of human nature.' He found it 'truer than the theatricality of Oberammergau'. See M Arnold, *Essays in Criticism*, 3rd ed. 1867, pp. 13-39.

[3] *Istighfar* is the abstract noun from the 10th form of *ghafara* ('to forgive') and seeks that that action be done. It is a frequent injunction in the Qur'an.

duty in self-reproach and a will to penitence. But if this is to have any meaning, there must be a will towards forgiveness on the part of those who have been wronged. Where honestly sought, it is proper that forgiveness should be had. In having it ready and offered, those who have suffered the evil pass from being only vicarious in the victim role and become vicarious in the active one that answers *istighfar*.

When Matthew Arnold wrote his piece on the Persian Passion Play that so intrigued him, he relied heavily on the French orientalist, Gobineau.[4] He and the historian, Edward Gibbon, report two traditions from Karbala'. In one, Hasan who was murdered in Medina, tells a man planning to kill the poisoner: 'Let him alone, till he and I meet together before Allah.' In the other, the Umayyad Caliph Yazid I, responsible for Husain's death, says of him: 'Allah loved Husain but He would not allow him to attain to anything.'

The former might be on the way to a sort of *istighfar* precisely in being unvindictive. The latter cruelly dismisses the pathos, sees only the power-equation, with Husain the hapless loser. No merit in sorrow, no mystery in tragedy, is glimpsed. In The Passion Play there is an episode—'The Marriage of Qasim'—which commemorates the stricken bridegroom. He says: 'Could I but wet my mouth with water, or my very blood, I would soon make an end of these men of Kufa'—the Sunni perpetrators.

In the context of a military expedition intending a bid for power, such a will to overcome was wholly in prospect. Yet Shi'ah piety, in its cherishing of Husain's tragic sorrow, lifted it into the realm of imagery around the deepest burden of the religious spirit. So doing, it left open the question whether the ultimate 'virtue' of suffering lies in the status the victims possess in their prior quality—in respect of the 'Alid three in 'immaculate innocence', or whether it finally consists in the character in action which the suffering tells.

That issue passes in a manifest way into the whole quality of martyrdom. Humans have only one life to lay down. There is surely a kind of sacrilege—as some religious zealots in all faiths have done—in courting death for its own sake as a prize to be clutched, irrespective of the stakes in the event. There are martyrdoms of courage in life, of enduring patience for the sake of God, more precious than the lurid exits of bravado.

---

4 Cf. note 2 above. Arnold tended to evaluate religions by how well they satisfied the deep, primary human affections. Cf. Iris Murdoch. See below, pp. 150-53.

Yet, given—as the Preacher said—'a time to die', there are martyrdoms incurred in the waging of war and others undergone in entire non-belligerence. The one runs its risks in taking lives, the other in a defencelessness for truth's sake. There is surely a compromise of the merit in the deed of life-forfeiture, if there is paradisial reward in prospect. For then the integrity of present issues is forfeit.

One haunting paradox of the themes that Karbala' inspires is the fact that occasions are so often plotted by religious pride and prejudice. Muslims did Muslims to death at Karbala': likewise the inter-Christian sources of the martyrology of Oxford's The Broad.[5] That it has tragically been so, both between religions at large and inside their own divergences, surely serves notice on all 'absolutes' that they must somehow learn to 'de-absolutize' themselves. For it is precisely by confidence in a custody of what claims to be paramount and final, that the temptation becomes almost irresistible to disavow and suppress all rivals. Is it in making its own martyrs, by an interior mutual rejection, that a faith least deserves the credence of the world? What to do about intolerance has first to find an inward answer and so be the better alert to external relations, lest the secular mind conclude: 'A plague on all your houses!'

Given the prolonged and deeply fraught cleavage in Islam between Sunni and Shi'ah, there emerged among the Shi'ah a philosophy of minority experience that has great significance for all siege of the soul. *Taqiyyah*—the term that defines it—was at once a policy of endurance and an ambivalent preservation of hope.[6] It has to do with a kind of 'tolerance' that, nevertheless, does not 'tolerate'. In this way, it captures a profound religious problem as a way of living with a sharp moral dilemma.

Taqiyyah has been defined as 'dissimulation' or 'pretence', but these do not do its subtlety justice. It could also be translated: 'holding out against', or, perhaps, 'how to be the durable underdog'. For all too often the Shi'ah found themselves in a position of duress and distraint, made the more onerous through the traditional triumphalism of the Sunni soul. Accordingly, they developed a posture of outward quietism or civil

---

[5] The burnings at the stake in 1555 during the Marian tyranny of Thomas Cranmer, Archbishop of Canterbury, Nicholas Ridley. Bishop of London, and Hugh Latimer, Bishop of Worcester.

[6] From the root *waqa*, 'to guard' or 'to shelter', *taqiyyah* comes to mean 'prudence' and 'caution' but in the subtle Shi'ah sense of secretly sustaining one's antipathy to a perceived 'false' régime as long as its ascendancy precludes its removal. *Taqwa* or 'piety' is a root term in the Qur'an, an inclusive denominator of Muslim being. Cf. p. 88, note 29.

submission, but without foregoing the rejection they had in their hearts for the régime they all the time disavowed.

They were in this way dissembling subjects and subjects dissembling, until opportunity came to repudiate allegiance and reconstitute their own society and faith and governance. There have doubtless been in all cultures similar policies of prudent loyalty-disloyalty, as the only prescript for both survival and hope. But Shi'ah *taqiyyah* has a quality all its own and—it might he said—a uniquely Islamic savour. For the right to power and control has ever been instinctive to Islam and, therefore, an 'Islam' that felt itself betrayed or ill-served by its 'Muslim' rulers could never—Quaker-like—content itself with perpetual pietism that, in *ahimsa* terms, had no sense of power-ambition. On the contrary, Shi'ah quietism, lasting only as long as situations demanded, nurtured the hope of overthrow. It did not capitulate in heart to what it disavowed in doctrine and polity. For had there not always been a political, as well as a hereditary and martyr, warrant for the Shi'ah as Islamic?

The stance, if it does not derive from these, can base itself on a Tradition of Muhammad according to which 'evil things' should be put right, where possible, 'by the hand', without fuss or show. Where this is not possible, they should be corrected 'by the mouth', by protest and accusation that do not allow them to persist unrebuked. Where, again, this is not possible, the believer should 'change them in his heart.'[7] Where there is never an inward capitulation, there can be the pre-requisites of a new thing. We are never defeated until we think we are.

Surely here is more than a verdict about 'siege in the soul'. 'Changing things in the heart' could even be the clue to the meaning of redemption and a ground for the *istighfar*, the forgiveness-seeking, and granting, the Qur'an commends. The pretence that is only cowardly or supine, has to be deplored: the pretence that is unbowed for truth's sake can dream of a new day and finally realise it. *Taqiyyah* in Shi'ah Islam, we may say, is more than 'siege behaviour': it is at the heart of the religious ethic.

Inside the necessary ambivalence of *taqiyyah* as possibly marrying cunning with courage, or seeming with sincerity, lay that other

---

[7] The tradition is cited in the Prolegomena of Ibn Khaldun, *Al-Muqaddimah*, trans. Franz Rosenthal, New York, 1958, Vol. 1, Chap. 3, Section 6, from the traditionalist named Muslim. 'The heart' is held to be 'the weakest of the three'.

deeply religious theme, namely what to do with enmity? As the other side of the coinage of forgiveness, enmity is the sharpest encircling confining in the siege of the soul. The hand that, in the tradition, could change evil things, can also accentuate their evil. And what of the mouth? What, in frankness, will allow itself no guilty silence, is also capable of sustained vituperation. So it was that 'the cursing of Yazid' became a long indulgence of the Shi'ah spirit. The steady malediction of the caliph held responsible for Karbala' only served to sustain the Sunni Muslims in their antipathy and so perpetuate a mutual rejection.

Giving verbal thrust to inward enmity was only the more telling because it reversed the familiar Islamic salutation of: 'Peace be upon you and the mercy of Allah'—a formula enjoined at the conclusion of *Salat* and said so as, in a gesture, to embrace the entire *Dar al-Islam*.[8] Whether in blessing or cursing, the actual mouthing of words in all Semitic tradition is held to transact and convey the sentiments for real.

Thus 'the cursing of Yazid' on the part of Shi'ah Muslims served to fortify Sunni obduracy concerning the legitimacy of Abu Bakr, 'Umar and 'Uthman, as 'rightly guided caliphs', and of the Umayyad caliphate that followed them in Damascus—the crucial (to Sunnis) legitimacy that Husain had challenged by his campaign. One Turkish Sunni Muslim in the 12th (Christian) century tells it this way:

> The Hashimites were sorely grieved, but vengeance by the sword was out of the question, so they took to using their tongues to abuse and execrate Yazid and his followers, thus slaking their burning anger. Ever since then, this grieving and this cursing have been customary among the Shi'ites and have gradually spread to the Sunnis too.[9]

The shape of the writing betrays the set of the mind. 'In the Karbala' incident' Husain and his retinue had merely 'lost their lives.'[10] Such competing perspectives and the Shi'ah maledictions led to a Sunni proscribing of all cursing of the valid caliphs. In return, the Shi'ah made their verbal enmity to Yazid, (their age-long grudge) mandatory. Happily

---

[8] In that the pray-er turns the head to left and right as the words are said, thus saluting the praying 'kindred' round all the perimeters of which Mecca is the centre.

[9] See Katib Chelebi: *The Balance of Truth*, trans. G L Lewis, London, 1957, p. 85.

[10] *Ibid.*, and detailing how the mutual recriminations and calumnies persisted in sectarian encounter through later centuries.

there were Sunni legists who conceded the crime of Yazid and did not outlaw his being accursed.[11]

It was left to the great Abu Hamid al-Ghazali in the 11th century to forbid it, adding that 'it were better to refrain from cursing anyone whether infidel or devil.' His *fatwa* was benediction in its wisdom but *fatwas* may only proscribe enmity. They cannot oust it from the soul. Yazid could continue to be the execrated as the 'Pharaoh of Islam'.[12] It is well to be content with what meaning we can give to 'the wrath of God', so that—as a principle has it—'after death Yazid was no more cursed.' How our faiths enwall and buttress, or liberate, our spirits in the state of siege can well take Oxford's Islamics to the paradigm of a great Sufi, the cordwainer 'Abd al-Mughith al-Husain ibn Mansur, known as Al-Hallaj, martyred in Baghdad in 922. His story was truly that of a soul under siege and yields crucial meanings that are the more noteworthy for their fruitfulness in both Christian and Muslim spirituality in the 20th century.

V

'The siege in the soul' of Al-Hallaj, in his Baghdad gaol and at his gruesome immolation defies all simple analysis. For it was subtly compounded by both politics and mystic-ardour. His thirst for mystical union with Allah could be likened to the yearning of the fly for the flame round which it hovers—to be consumed by what draws it fascinatingly. The attraction Al-Hallaj felt in the will to 'enter into God' undividedly in the ultimate meaning of *Tawhid*—not as the for ever 'dual' affirmation that 'God is One'—but the unitive absorption into Allah in undifferentiated oneness annihilating private identity.

It was allegedly for that articulated aspiration—*Ana al-Haqq,* 'I am the Real'—that Al-Hallaj was done to death. But political chicanery, contributed to his judicial murder, his vagaries being seen as a threat to public order as well as sound faith and even at odds, as he was, with more prudent Sufism from which he explicitly withdrew in a concern for social activism. If we have to conclude that Al-Hallaj died for love of an impossible desire, it would be doubtful to read his immolation as redemptive in any Biblical form. For there was a sense in which it was a

---

[11] *Ibid.,* p. 85. Even about Yazid 'there was no unanimity.'

[12] The analogy of Pharaoh, from the Moses saga in the Qur'an as the arch-foe, recurred again in 1980 at the assassination of President Sadat by Islamic extremists, making him the byword for vituperation, despite his being maligned as Egyptian from a 'Jewish' perspective.

provoked martyrdom arising from misconstruings he had needed to will in order to attain it, rather than from immediate issues of love confronting a malign situation, as in the crucifying of Jesus. Yet one could speak with reservation of 'the cross of Al-Hallaj'—given the pathos of his tragedy, the patience of his sufferings and the vicariousness of his story, which the subtlety of his mystical idiosyncrasy leaves undiminished. All was in sharp contrast with the military setting of Karbala'. Yet many of the elements of the Passion Plays can find echo in that other 'tragedy of Baghdad'. The meaning of an ever-wounding world as a crucifying place is present in both dramas. What they have in common witnesses to the theme of the tragic in the soul of Islam. It was a right instinct which led a contemporary Arab poet to model a play on Al-Hallaj around the Canterbury production of T S Eliot's *Murder in the Cathedral*.[13]

There is no evidence that Al-Hallaj felt Archbishop Thomas Becket's 'Fourth Temptation', that of 'doing the right thing for the wrong reason', envisaging the posthumous triumph his relics would win over his king, Henry. For their situations were in such high contrast. Yet, even so, there is abiding in the costliest martyrdom a dimension of self-interest subtly persisting in the very completeness of a self-surrender. The assimilation of the creature to the divine, which—outside the mystical—would be blasphemy spells a self-vindication in the aspirant who yearns for it. For does not the attaining of it, ending in a sought-for martyrdom, end also in satisfaction? Is the satisfaction wholly unselfed?

> I want You, I want You, not for the reward
> But I want You for the punishment,
> Because I obtained all that I desired
> Except the delight of my passion in suffering.[14]

While there was, in Al-Hallaj's immolation, a crime to 'lay to the charge' of the perpetrators—for they were motivated by a blind intolerance and cruel enmity—their heinousness was effectuating what Al-Hallaj himself had sought. His mystical yearning for death meant that his suffering could be vicarious only in the limited sense of its undergoing the hate of the world, not in the inclusive sense of redeeming that world. For a redemption

---

[13] Namely Khalil I Semaan, *Ma'sat al-Hallaj*, Cairo, 1965, Eng. trans. *Murder in Baghdad*, Leiden, 1972. On Al-Hallaj see Louis Massignon, *The Passion of al-Hallaj*, abridged. trans. and ed. Herbert Mason, Princeton, 1994.

[14] *Poèmes Mystiques*, trans. Sami Ali, Paris, 1995, No. 6, p. 31.

of that order was not within his motive. Even so, the abiding theme of 'the martyr of Baghdad' endures inside Sunni Islam as remarkably enshrining what a confident religion all too readily omits or ignores. The celebrated *Ruba'iyyat* of 'Umar Khayyam purport to banish all human grievousness in a playfulness where 'taverns' with their malt, 'do more than Milton can, to justify the ways of God to man.' Wine—or ale—to be sure may be an allegory for a spiritual 'intoxication', so that 'taverns' in such poesy need not always be associated with physical inebriation. Like the 'symposia' of the Greeks they may be serving souls not throats.[15] That mood of 'epicurean' focus on the passing moment and its occasions of mirth, or distraction from the burdens of pain or perplexity, is a far cry from the intense interrogation of suffering in the long Shi'ah tradition, even though there were times in their poweredness when the logic of Karbala' or the pathos of Husain could be left in the margins of ritual ceremony.

Even so, it is well for Islam today that the characteristic triumphalism, born of Sunni 'manifest victory' at the outset and in the sequences, should be forever partnered by the disparate traditions, both of Shi'ah pathos and a mysticism like that of the martyr of Baghdad.

vi

That 'man is born for trouble as the sparks fly upward' was the verdict of Job's friend (Job 5.7). Surah 70.19 agrees when it sees 'man created with a restless anxiety.' 'Fretful' or 'self-commiserating' are other translations of the word *halu'an*. That too, away from the implications of martyrdom and death in historic tragedy, has to be the perennial theme of religion, whether as its exegesis or its consolation.

If, via Matthew Arnold's 'breath of the night wind', we can bestride the centuries and let our human 'anxiety' have 20th century shape, there are two sharply contrasted recent Oxonians who can serve our ends. Each addressed the human condition, the one in a narrative art that unknowingly celebrated much of what Islam comprehends in the term *sabr*, or 'staying power',[16] the other in a poetic personality strangely

---

[15] In the poetry, for example, of Hafiz, the 'taverner' is the Sufi's master of devotion. The term 'symposium' meant initially a 'drinking party'.

[16] Its derivatives are frequent. Often rendered 'patience', it is the human quality within the virtue of *taqwa* as durable, steady and sober 'submission' to Allah as both the ally and the disposer of the faithful soul.

symptomatic of our human malaise. They differed also in their allegiance to Oxford and for that reason belong with 'the siege in the soul'. The one is J R R Tolkien (1892-1973) long a Fellow of Merton College, the other Philip Larkin of St John's College (1922-85). If the choice seems arbitrary, its justification will be evident enough in the sequel.

Tolkien's mythopoeic story-making revolves around the central theme of goodness striving against evil from the land of darkness and hate. It gained enormous popularity and must surely rank as the most distributed and translated product of Oxonian scholarship of its century. Tolkien was a highly committed Roman Catholic[17] but while Christianity may have girded his moral sense, his inspiration came, via philology, from the fascination of Anglo-Saxon folklore, the field in which he held a Professorship through three and a half decades. His interest in mythology had been kindled in part by James Frazer's twelve-volumed *The Golden Bough* (1907-15). Joined with Anglo-Saxon saga, as yielded to his mind by the language-web of philology, his academic pursuits—arcane as they could well have been—were steered into active myth-making as, perhaps more truly than philosophy or anthropology, an index to the human scene in its awareness of moral issues. There was Beowulf in the antecedents but *The Lord of the Rings* became a contemporary parallel in its own right. The long story there through three volumes depicted the steady courage of Frodo and his companions confronting the evil genius of Mordor and his minions.

There is something at least potentially Islamic in this confrontation, despite the elements of which most Muslims would disapprove. Tolkien's heroes are vulnerable in that there are odds against them in the wrongs of their world, but they are also vicarious in that they hold out against the odds and aim for final 'manifest victory', as the Qur'an would call it. They are engaged on the whole front against evil, aware of its machinations but undeterred. It could be seen as a sort of Meccan situation without the sharp sanction of what is there threatened with dire supernatural penalties.

---

[17] Even to the point of opining: 'What would Christianity now be if the Roman Church had in fact been destroyed?' Cited in ed. H Carpenter, *The Letters of J R R Tolkien*, London, 1981, p. 339. There was an index to his capacity for bigotry in his requiring that his bride enter the Roman Church despite her strong reluctance to do so. He was guilty too of gratuitous vilification of the Church of England as 'a pathetic and shadowy medley of half-remembered traditions and mutilated beliefs.' See H Carpenter, *Life of Tolkien*, London, 1977, p. 73. This Newmanian feature of his mind contributed to the tensions that arose with his erstwhile friend and fellow-mythologist, C S Lewis.

Tolkien, for all the pagan aura of his mythology, has a Christian— and Islamic—sense of the trust of the good earth. He evokes that attitude to the real cosmos which Christians call sacramental. The 'Middle Earth' of his legend is a realm of awe, where the deep 'soil of the Shire' is 'sacred', where in no wise did you 'break a thing in order to know what it was.' Such respect rides well with Quranic *khilafah*. It tells a kind of interfusion of the earth and the heart in the idiom of the poems of Dylan Thomas, where winds 'sigh' and the waves of the sea 'murmur' and a 'green fuse' runs through the limbs.

Islam would be unready to associate this quality of reverence with pagan lore. Tolkien, for his part, was careful to reject Frazer's theme of 'the dying god' who seasonally 'rose again.' For this was quite incompatible with the sheer happenedness of the Christian story. There the quality of 'God in Christ'—in birth and life and death and resurrection—had housed a total meaning as being also a historic drama on the stage of time. 'The place of the Name' of the Lord, to borrow a Hebraic phrase, had been planted on Galilean hills and had knelt in a garden called Gethsemane. Even so, in that entire historicity, it could consort with a saga drawn from one man's imagination, fed by an inspiration from pagan language. Islamic iconoclasm would need to disallow such borrowings as foreign to divine *Tawhid*, yet their reading of the human scene as the crisis between the good and the evil could entirely fit the Quranic *mise en scène*.

When Philip Larkin arrived in Oxford in 1940, Professor Tolkien was well entrenched and already celebrated. There is no evidence that their paths significantly crossed. Born in a modest home in Coventry, it was with the likes of John Wain and Kingsley Amis that Larkin consorted as an undergraduate. He was already adopting a mood of disillusion, of 'negative indicatives', and what might be called 'emotional economy'. In this he was symptomatic of much in his student generation and since. Spires dream only for themselves above the courts and quads where students—as Larkin had it—are 'the less deceived'.[18] He was a contemporary of the Americans, Norman Mailer and J D Salinger, who were liable to withdraw interest from anything significant, 'scorching

---

[18] The title of one of his collections. See Philip Larkin, *Collected Poems*, ed. Anthony Thwaites, London, 1988. For an appreciation of his poetic gifts, see Salem J Hassan, *Philip Larkin and his Contemporaries*, London, 1988, pp. 7-126.

their personal earth'[19] by gestures of subversive intent, as if how to live in this world could only be answered flippantly.

With his conscious literary talent and something of a destiny to achieve it, Larkin certainly transcended these 'advertisements for the self'. He was meticulous in his librarianship at the University of Hull and cared in an oddly ambiguous way about his literary image, but his letters reveal a strange self-caricature that both sought and eluded full recognition. His crowded diaries were destroyed days after he died.[20] His assured poetic gift was consecrated to a mood of 'not to be here, not to be anywhere and soon'.[21]

Larkin emerges from his verse as a sure craftsman of the art, with a subtle range of imagery and an eye for concrete instances that carry universal meaning. All is imbued with a brooding sense of time, the grief it brings, the mortality it remorselessly imposes. He laments like W B Yeats and breathes the pathos of Thomas Hardy—two of his early mentors. Obscure detail of mundane living serves to kindle a muse of melancholy which is more keenly mediated by the startling turns of phrase he employs—mostly in the interest of his gloom, lit as it can at times be with a wry suggestion of courage and reluctant joy.

Throughout, 'childhood [is] a forgotten boredom,' where 'always there is regret,' and 'featureless morning' going 'into fulfilment's desolate attic'. 'Nothing, like something, happens everywhere,' 'until—we begin dying' by 'eternal requirings'.[22] Thus Larkin's poetry is heavy with the transience of life, with journeys and trains as symbols of sadness and separation or 'progress' towards ultimate endings and hapless regrets. In 'Neurotics' he sees man's 'long defence against the non-existent'; in 'Wants' 'beneath all desire oblivion runs'; in 'Next Please' 'sparkling armadas of promises draw near' only to betray, when ('Triple Time') 'the present [is] a time unrecommended by event,' 'despite the artful tensions of the calendar'. For 'time is the echo of an axe within a wood.'[23]

---

[19] Quoting the title of one of Norman Mailer's self-indulgent yarns about mean-spiritedness as a disclosure of human despair. He seems to have seen stories as 'letters to the self' as denying anything significant.
[20] By Monica Jones obeying the dictum: 'Make sure those diaries ate destroyed.' Some ambiguity in his will(s) meant that letters survived and found publication in *Selected Letters: 1940-85*, ed Anthony Thwaite, London, 1992. On the destruction of the diaries, see ed. A Motion, *Philip Larkin: A Writer's Life*, London, 1993, p. 522.
[21] *Collected Poems*, 'Aubade', p. 208.
[22] *Ibid.*, 'Coming', p. 33; 'Love, we must part now', p. 260; 'Waiting for Breakfast', p. 20; 'The Less Deceived', p. 82; 'I remember', p. 82; 'Dry Point' p. 10; 'The Dedicated', p. 10.
[23] *Ibid.*, 'This is the First Thing', p. 295.

Urgent for loving and to be loved, he saw the yearning fraught with its own denial from within. There was a vulgar sordidness in his sexual reactions that squared oddly with the dignity of soul his verses could attain. A crippling dubiety harried all intimations of hope. Desire that could not be suppressed from within seemed doomed from without. There were notes of music in his words that queried by their quality as art the verdict they registered in the incidence of time and the certainty of death.

A strangely articulate Oxonian, he seems to have had only slight affection for his college.[24] His perception of 'the dreaming spires' might be caught in the lines elsewhere—'a touching dream by which we all are lulled but wake from separately.'[25] What, then, is the point of his presence here, what the bearing on Islam of his many ironies? The answer must be that he broached, by his very questing pathos, the whole business of religion. In 'Church Going' and elsewhere his engagement with the elements, liturgical and doctrinal, of Christian faith was elusive and querulous. But 'a serious house on serious earth' the sanctuary was, and 'a place fit to grow wise in.'[26] But was the 'wisdom' as from an old-time museum or from a living faith? His perceptions stayed deliberately ambiguous. Emotionally, if only from time to time, he yearned that some solace might be credible but effectively, like so many, his will lacked either the courage or the candour to 'let faith win.' Yet

Something will always be surprising him
To be more serious.[27]

'Let us love one another' is the final verdict and surely refining and excelling Matthew Arnold's 'only as we feel we know,'[28] with 'the heart in its own endless silence kneeling'.

How far, it will be well to ask, are Muslims involved in this contemporary distaste for the confidence of religions? Can this poetry of

[24] So we might conclude from 'Dockery and Son', p. 152, where Larkin is back at College with his old Dean who does not have the date of contemporaries clear in his mind and queries: 'Dockery was junior to you?' Larkin muses on the 'only end of age', with 'I catch my train ignored'.

[25] *Ibid.*, 'The Building', p. 192.

[26] *Ibid.*, 'Church Going', p. 98.

[27] *Ibid.*

[28] Matthew Arnold, *The Poems*, ed. Kenneth Allott, London, 1965, 'The New Sirius', p. 38, lines 81-84.

wistful distrust find place in the structured assurance of Islam or in the classic 'submission' of Muslims? How should 'Islam among the spires' reckon with so tentative a 'surprise' around things 'more serious'? Is it not essentially a structured 'seriousness' from which all tentativeness is banned?

vii

There is another noted Oxford figure to whom to defer before answering the question, namely Iris Murdoch (1919-98), of Somerville and St Anne's Colleges and a prolific novelist and probing philosopher. The implications of her point of view would seem to be devastating for Islam, insofar as its required scheme of things transgresses all that she holds dear, as crucial to what she finds to be intellectual honesty.

The point can be made via what she does with 'sincerity'—a crucial word for the Qur'an (the Arabic *ikhlas*). That we humans should be *mukhlisun lahu al-din*, 'sincere toward Him (Allah) in religion' is a repeated injunction.[29] So indeed we may be, thinks Murdoch but not—mistakenly—within an enclosed system of reference which has itself remained unexamined. As such it has been, unconsciously, self-immunised from criteria for which an open—as contrasted with a closed—framework would know itself liable.[30]

Thus religious 'sincerity'—like one implicitly believing his own propaganda—is guiltily self-centred. It 'deforms reality by a dream necessity,'[31] all the more beguiling when the 'dream' is via an absolute Scripture.

If thus 'for the hard idea of truth we have substituted a facile idea of sincerity,' we are improperly romantic about the human condition and about its capacity to be educable by religious means. Moreover, religious authority, in its instinctive absoluteness, connives with that other error of purporting to solace the soul in a world where no solace can be

---

[29] The accent on 'sincerity' belongs with the danger of dissembled conformity incidental to Islam's power structure. This *nifaq* or 'hypocrisy' on the part of *munafiqin* only made trustworthiness the more urgent. Also the Qur'an lays stress on purity of intention. Murdoch may be right in detecting in all religion a type of 'sincerity' that is 'entire' because it has never suspected its own parameters of faith-community to which the 'sincerity' is brought. But this idea of 'blinkered' loyalty is far from disqualifying all conviction as in that category.

[30] The point can be more explicit in two following chapters.

[31] Iris Murdoch in ed. M Bradbury, *The Novel Today*, London, 1990, p. 22.

honestly had. Here Murdoch's mood or mind (which ever it be) confronts the wistfulness for 'consolation', so ardent and so diffident in poetry like Arnold's and Larkin's. Hence, for her, the vital role of the novel as undertaking to divest us of false wistfulness by only presenting actual humans in their actual struggle to mean. 'Literature can arm us', she writes, 'against consolation,' the 'desire (for which) is a danger to our sense of reality.'[32]

The satisfied self-reference of religious dogma thus ignores or dismisses what alone can be duly transcendent, namely the moral 'sovereignty of good' registered by human moral sense and duly commanding us not, as with religion, because it is 'required' by dogma, but because it is understood from within. Murdoch's is thus a world in which we humans 'are on our own' a condition she 'merely asserts.'[33] She holds that 'we need to think in a non-metaphysical, non-totalitarian, non-religious sense the transcendence of reality.'[34] With those three 'nons' in place it is difficult to see how 'transcendence' survives.[35] And elsewhere Murdoch seems to have place for metaphysics.

For the main thrust of her charge against dogmatic faith is that it exonerates personhood from its genuine task of mind and will and entails on to it the guilt of staying innocent of reality, as only moral integrity can know it. The ultimate unselfishness can only be had without God, inasmuch as 'God' always ministers to pride, or sloth, or dubious 'sincerity'. We have to learn to step away from the ego-satisfaction to which assured religious allegiance always ministers. Not even a Buddhist discipline can relieve us of relentless egotism.[36] 'Approach to the good is a progressive discarding of relative false goods, of hypotheses, images and shadows eventually seen as such.'[37]

---

[32] *Ibid.*, pp. 22-3.

[33] Iris Murdoch, *The Sovereignty of Good*, London, 1970, p. 79. Cf. Chapter 9, note 6.

[34] In *The Novel Today*, (note 31) p. 22.

[35] One might question whether 'non-religious' is ever compatible with 'transcendent'. Cf. F R Leavis in *Thought, Words and Creativity*, London, 1976, p. 79: 'Lawrence we know is convinced that ... no belief ... can adequately sustain a civilization that is not at bottom essentially religious,' 'keeping unforgettably present for recognition the need to transcend all egoistic satisfactions and aims.' The last phrase is quite Murdochian.

[36] Cf. Iris Murdoch's novel *The Nice and the Good*, London, 1968, where a character thinks to find in Buddhist discipline 'an easy solution to the problem of relentless egoism', but was unable to escape from 'possessive self-fulfilling love', p. 358.

[37] *The Fire and the Sun*, London, 1977, p. 64.

The 'last enemy' of death is the final school of this realism in what Murdoch calls 'the range of the sufficiently serious heart'.[38] 'God has to be a task' and not an alibi or a pillow.[39]

Though Murdoch partly shares Larkin's 'Church Going' sense of something, i.e. religious, that has had its day, her disowning of religious faith is much more pointed and radical. 'Faith' indeed there needs to be, but only if and when rid of religious associations. As for doctrine, there is no intellectual way of protecting people from despair and to offer one is to be 'insincere'. Fictions of a theological nature only disguise this situation and feed the unwitting self with 'consolations' that do not truly belong, but which the ego will always lust to keep and trust.

Does it need much imagination to surmise what this radical Oxonian novelist would advise an Islamic Centre reading 'the siege in the soul' in these exacting terms? That, with the more poetic Larkins and Audens and Cloughs, she is part of the mental landscape is not in doubt. The egotism built-in to religious structures, and likely in the pride of allegiance, is not in doubt. Given a salutary readiness so to acknowledge, may not a religious structure of faith, value, ritual and community—these being inseparable from its viability—take on, and take up, the Murdoch rubric of 'God as a task'? Has not that not always been the core of Islam?

There would be one supreme condition, namely that the structure requires itself to heed its temptations, as Murdoch tells they are and so hold its authority as susceptible of the open reference that divests it of spiritual or intellectual tyranny. 'God as a task' would then be other than 'God as a taskmaster'. Religious authority needs to be ready to be provisional, until its content has been assessed. Only then can it become the kind of authority that deserves to be trusted. Only so is its mandate to be believed duly uncoercive, with an authenticity to which a free reckoning has positively contributed. It is feasible that an Islamic commitment could be of this order. To have it so must be the mission of any university membership and presence.

It is clear that the warrant in Iris Murdoch's case-making about religions, as consenting to egotism and its consolations, is itself a position claiming intrinsic validity. No philosophy is exempt from the will to be doctrinaire, in that it 'takes up' an 'angle on things' in order to determine

---

[38] *The Black Prince*, London, 1973, p. 299.
[39] *Under the Net*, London, 1954, p. 258.

'what goes.' Liberalism is no more free of *parti pris* than dogmatism. 'Truth' is 'a hard ideal' either way, provided that religious commitment—as we are arguing—does not exempt itself, by some sheer arbitrariness, from the business of having its authority exposed to any critique, intellectual, moral or social, which lively minds would bring against it. For then, what it holds and commends as an institutional loyalty has been freely susceptible to what patiently calls it to self-correction.

That Muslims might conceive of their Islam in this way is by no means un-Islamic. Themes proper to such a 'God-task' must await Chapters 8 and 9. In some respect its founding instincts of militant confrontation may seem to suggest otherwise. For there has to be more than iconoclasm. Yet even iconoclasm can idolise itself, unless the awareness of an incipient idolatry alerts it to the idol it may become. 'God as a task' cries, not *Islamu akbar*, but only *Allahu akbar.* In that sense Islam could be said to epitomise the supremely religious task of 'letting God be God', as being one which can never dispense with attention to the Iris Murdochs of its world, while not succumbing to their whole hostility. 'Can a conception of God', they ask, 'contain the certainty of its own reality?' in the light of the self-assertive movements of deluded self-will.' For 'introspection reveals only the deep tissue of ambivalent motive and fantasy.'[40]

The answer may be 'Yes!' provided that the 'certainty' marries with the 'introspection' and remembers that 'its own reality' is liable for a moral and intellectual integrity that is more than an enclosed, static and satisfied 'sincerity'.

viii

If these Oxford mentors of 'the siege in the soul', random as is the choice of them, are within the walls Muslims share, what is the evidence that their Islam is 'marching to the beat of the same drum'? It has sometimes been assumed that Islam is exempt from the secularism, the dubieties, here in view—given its capacity to be a self-sufficient, self-satisfying identity. There are ample signs to the contrary. To be sure, Islam monumentally shapes the culture of Muslims but the inroads of technology, of globalism and of pluralism are everywhere apparent. A part of its intellectual leadership is now firmly in the western world,

---

[40] Iris Murdoch, *Existentialists and Mystics*, London, 1994. p. 341.

where the issues of modernity are most acute or, as in India, where Muslim society is for ever out from under the comforting aegis of the Islamic state. And where, as in Pakistan, that crucial statehood has been sought, found and demarcated on the ground as the *sine qua non* of a right Islamicity, its half-century record leaves little room for pride. Sober Pakistanis might think to invoke Arnold's lines from a different world.

> Chief dreamer, own thy dream!
> Who with a monarch's hath no brother's part,
> Yet doth thine inmost soul with yearning teem ...
> I, too, but seem.'[41]

Pakistan, in Muhammad 'Ali Jinnah's vision, like Zion in Theodor Herzl's 'dream', leaves endless tragedy in its wake. For a monarch's power, whether under constitution or via coups, always finds elusive the 'brotherhood' of social justice and a compassionate peoplehood.

It was inevitable, in the aftermath of western imperialism in slow—or precipitate—retreat, that the Islamic mind would be pre-occupied with the painful politics of state-creation, whether in its Arab, its Asian or its African arenas. The political in any event has always been central to the genius of Islam. It is, therefore, natural that so much in contemporary writing, novels, poetry, drama should be engrossed in the frustrations of partisanship, the disappointments of pan-Arabism, the trauma of the Gulf War and the unrelieved tribulations of Palestinian hope.

Yet, inside these inescapable themes, Arab writing, for example, is replete with evidences of a 'siege in the soul' akin to all we find in the West. Indeed, a cross-fertilisation of literature is manifest on all hands with T S Eliot's *The Wasteland* finding echoes in sundry places[42] or Dostoevsky, Kafka, Sartre, Camus, Pavese, Beckett and Hemingway finding their counterparts in authors whether in Cairo, Damascus, Baghdad, Beirut, Lagos, Dakar or Khartoum. Writers across Islam brood on the same yearnings for faith as any in the West and apply the same techniques of symbol and irony to pose the questions that for ever

---

[41] Matthew Arnold, *The Poems*, *loc. cit.*, 'In Utrumque Paratus', p. 56, lines 37-40.
[42] Some data on T S Eliot in the Arab world was assembled in my *Troubled by Truth*, Edinburgh, 1992, in Chap. 9, pp. 166-86 on Salah 'Abd al-Sabur. See also ed. M M Badawi, *Modern Arabic Literature*, Cambridge, 1992, Chap. 4, S K Jayyusi, 'Modernist Poetry in Arabic'. Also Pierre Cachia, *An Overview of Modern Arabic Literature*, Edinburgh, 1990, pp. 192-3.

interrogate religious authority and the vested interests of doctrine and the doctrinaire. Any Oxford presence of 'Islam among the spires' has to set itself, and be seen to be set, in this ironisation of religious faith, conceding the sincerity of its impulse and alert to its agnostic mood. For its stance is not met either by a bland academicism that does not know its anguish, nor by a dogmatism that misses its subtlety.

The renowned Najib Mahfuz, for example, employs a symbolism as versatile as that of the Charles Dickens from whom he learned it. The role that prison plays in *Little Dorrit* or the Thames with its corpses in *Our Mutual Friend* is readily borrowed for the Cairo scene. Through a long and now famous sequence of novels and short stories, Mahfuz deploys a wide range of elusive imagery and fantasy to intimate and satirise the human condition. Thus a houseboat, moored in the Nile proves a telling setting for the listless boredom that converses there, relieved for the time being from the oppressiveness of meagre wage-earning.[43] His contemporary, Jamal al-Ghitani, follows Mahfuz' instinct to locate his scenarios in streets and alleys where neighbouring impulses are prey to subtle lights and shades of dignity and folly. Thus *Waqa'i' Harat al-Za'farani* ('What Befell in Zafarani Street') uses male impotence as symbolising much else. For, in a sort of epidemic of sexual limitations, the local men repair to a shaykh for advice. He exploits their anxieties callously and the satire embraces both the gullible and the mischievous, society and religion.[44]

Such contemporary writing in Arabic often sets its scenarios in ancient, medieval or Ottoman times, while barely disguising its current social relevance. The device has had many exponents, long before Boris Pasternak who found even translating *Hamlet* a means of inferring a critique of Stalinism. Circumventing political risks or doctrinaire suspicion in this way is eloquent of a realism alert to its vocation in rigorous commentary on life. It is, therefore, also clear measure of how keen a sense this literature has of the duty that belongs with official religion, not merely 'to soothe and sympathise', but to probe the mysteries.

Long taboos concerning what might be broached in writing have been notably ignored and defied, as in Al-Ghitani's handling of impotence 'in the alley', or, for example, Ihsan 'Abd al-Quddus's stories around the struggle of girls for personal liberation from family tyranny,

---

[43] *Tharthara fawq al-Nil*, Beirut, 1966.
[44] *Waqa'i' Harat al-Za'farani*, Cairo, 1976.

or the Dostoevskean probing of the inner springs of selfhood in the short stories of Yahya Haqqi.[45] For exploration of the predicament of the self in 'stream of consciousness' writing in the West searches the whole meaning of religious truth, as ever fully accessible when garnered into structured dogmatism, reinforced by 'scriptured' finality. Some measure of the instinct for agnosticism, tentative or burdened, is crucial for the integrity of faith and imaginative literature is the likeliest place in which to explore it.

Nor have the poets been lacking in such exploration in recent decades, far removed from the romantic lushness of a Khalil Jibran. The Palestinian tragedy, of course, has occupied them hugely[46] but not to the exclusion of the corollaries that century-old saga poses for the human quest of sanity and hope. Foremost among them noted earlier was Salah 'Abd al-Sabur with his verse-play celebrating the 'Passion' of Al-Hallaj modelled expressly on T S Eliot's *Murder in the Cathedral*.[47] Another, comparably eloquent, was Nizar Qabbani, a protagonist of women's rights and skilled in the poetry of social protest. After a long career as a diplomat his energies were turned, still more after the Arab futility of 1967, into the accusation of inept politics and its moral treacheries. His was the voice of an anger echoing widely through—it is reckoned—some million volumes.[48] Both Al-Sabur and Qabbani went far to rescue the Arabic language from long conventions of usage and vocabulary—a process of literary re-inventing that seconded their thematic ventures. In measure we might say, in Larkin's phrase, that they were 'unfencing existence', 'continuing to live' but less now as 'a habit formed'.[49]

If we apply that English poet's line—'for which was built this special shell'—to Ibn Qulun Mosque in Cairo, or Masjid-i Imam in Isfahan, or Sulamaniyyah in Istanbul, how might their present custodians

---

[45] Ihsan 'Abd al-Quddus (1919-90) among many practitioners of the short story. Yahya Haqqi (born 1905)a highly influential exponent of the genre and much esteemed.

[46] See data in my *Palestine: the Prize and Price of Zion*, London, 1997, Chap 10, pp. 168-85, and *The Arab Christian: A History in the Middle East*, London, 1992, Chap. 11, pp 257-78, with bibliography. More fully in Salma Khadra Jayyusi, *Anthology of Modern Palestinian Poetry*, New York, 1992.

[47] See note 13 above. One of his collections on the Palestinian grief carried the image of Christ crucified on its cover, to the chagrin of the *'ulama'* in Al-Azhar, with the title: *Aqulu lakum*, ('I Say unto You'), Beirut, 1969.

[48] Nizar Qabbani (1923-98), born in Damascus and dying in London, his early poetry was much influenced by the suicide of a sister after a thwarted hope of marriage. *Hayati fi-l-Shi'r*, ('My life with Poetry') was published in 1972.

[49] Larkin, *op. cit.*, p. 98 ('Church Going').

formulate the rationale behind the architecture, as 'serious house on serious earth'? The very eminence of the structures interrogates the enigmas the time they have survived into finds flowing around them.

Just as technology confronts all religions with the single issue of how it is to be controlled so it makes for a single test of what is in them of guidance, wisdom, courage and. integrity. This is partly why they must be attentive to the literature, to writers who explore 'the weight of all this weary world', where time is 'the echo of an axe within a wood',[50] and the puzzles and feats of technology are so far in the role of 'time's axe'.

Whether the random Oxonians we have noted, or the no less random literati from inside contemporary Islam, they together interrogate religious faith out of the pathos of their register of the world. The passions in the cinema are the precincts of the mosque. The cases in its courts are the people in the alleys. Religions have no final hiding-place in the hinterlands of scholarship from the crying in the streets. Novelists and poets, for the most part, will forebear to preach—the role they leave to men of faith. How ' faith' fulfils the role is the task of two following chapters.

---

[50] *Ibid.*, p. 295, 'This is the First Thing'.

Chapter 8

A VOCATIONAL STUDY

i

Oxford University long indulged an ingrained hostility to vocational courses. It saw them as displacing the intellectual disciplines that found their truest home in the rigours of 'Greats'. *Literae Humaniores*, as its Latin ran, purposefully took the mind away from vulgar professionalism into the issues of philosophy, history and statecraft, made the more authentic for scholarship by their very distance in time and temper. 'Plato's guardians'—as proconsuls and commissioners across the empire were once described[1]—could better fulfil that role by leave of Aristotle and Thucydides than by learning modern administration or the techniques of government.

The part that 'Greats' played in the dream of empire we saw in Chapter 4. Successfully resisting a proposal for a Diploma in Business in 1914, W A Spooner, Warden of New College, thought it 'a pity if too much of the brains and vigour of the country *[sic]* were attracted into a business career.' There were 'more ennobling careers'—at least for Oxonians.[2] That sense of things ignored the lesson—and the benefits—of the great Cecil Rhodes himself. Nor was Leopold Amery averse from extracting the funds for a Professor of the History of Empire and books to sustain his studies from a wealthy diamond prospector in the person of Alfred Beit.[3] Only slowly did language disciplines and contemporary themes penetrate the classicist dominance.

---

[1] See Philip Woodruff, *The Men who Ruled India*, London, Vol. 2, 1953, pp. 75-79. Cf. A Rumbold, *Watershed in India*, London, 1979, p. 55, 'Our duty, in the words of the *Te Deum*, is to govern them and lift them up for ever.'

[2] Cited from *The Oxford Magazine*, Vol. 32, Jan. 29, 1914, p. 162, by Richard Symonds, *Oxford and Empire*, London, 1986, p. 19, a useful manual on this whole topic.

[3] A South African entrepreneur happy to celebrate his name and prowess by founding a Professorship and Prize, H E Egerton was the first holder of the Chair, Reginald Coupland the second. St Antony's College, likewise, owes much to Antonin Besse, a financier who made his wealth largely in Aden.

It was a logic which plainly excluded the notion of 'vocation' from the due governance of the world even when for so many, via the classics, imperialism was almost a religious vision. 'Vocation' meant only specific training for and to a skill, a technical equipment that might dispense with the cult of intelligence for its own sake. Education was more than expertise. Pursuit of the latter could so readily displace the former. Yet, by a strange irony, 'vocation' on its own terms—as Lewis Carroll might have said—was 'one of the things in the dream'.[4]

A sense of vocation, ready to make itself expert while cherishing a scholarship that transcends all vested interest, is the aim of this chapter as being the *raison d'être* of any Centre for Islamic Studies operating amid the Oxford legacies we have reviewed. Given the welcome place of Islamic disciplines in the Oxford scene, what are its intellectual and spiritual tasks? What do western academics, Christian or agnostic or other, look for from Muslim scholars in their midst? What should we have from those in their mosques, their Azhars and Deobands, who—in Islamic terms—reciprocate the Arnolds, Newmans, Jowetts, Gibbs, Murdochs, Larkins we have had in retrospect in these chapters? In what terms do they handle the issues of authority, doctrine, secularity, intellectual freedom and spiritual anxiety that belong in universities by sheer warrant of their being such?

In beginning thus with persons—scholars, teachers, writers, culture-exponents—we begin in the right place. For it is with them, their attitudes, norms, prejudices as well as quality of talent, that so much belongs. All religions are in some measure prey to their pundits, at risk with their custodians, in fee to their clergy, those that speak for the heritage.[5] Theirs are always the hands on authority, so that there is always liable to be a 'hands off' cry about them on the part of those who—in the faith—beg to differ about it.

A university organ of religious study will be acutely involved in this issue of authority in faith and where its custody most truly lies. Some of its members, akin to the Canons of Christ Church, may be more

[4] Lewis Carroll, *Through the Looking Glass*, London, 1872, ed. of 1962, p. 51, substituting 'the' for 'his'.
[5] That authority and the status of its 'tellers' inter-depend is obvious enough. It was at the core of Newman's trauma about 'truth' and 'Church'. Even he was astute enough to see that the Church would look foolish without the laity but these should only be consulted by their Church as a doctor takes the pulse of a patient, not in any way as participating in the formulae of their faith.

evidently custodians than others carrying more 'lay' credentials in their scholarship.

It was said, by those like Taha Husain and Ahmad Amin who experienced it, that the shedding of the turban can be a very crucial piece of biography.[6] Certainly the turban takes a long time to wind and, so, a long time to unwind, and may thus be a symbol for a defensive mind.

Muslim history has long been familiar with the issue of 'professional' authority concerning 'true faith' and with the Newman-style necessity of prescribing for 'the laity' what the Schools best know from the texts they interpret. It has also known the *muhtasib*, the 'censor', adjudicating on matters of faith and conduct and frequently investigating or enforcing due conformity. To be sure, the motivation of habituation and the sanctions of solidarity so strongly availing from the Pillars of Religion have well served the disciplines of Muslim community, *muhtasibun* apart. Yet the *hudud*, the 'bounds' of conduct Islam ordains, have utilised them. A degree of social surveillance has its place in the intense privacy of Islamic obedience and piety.

The sharp debate through the Islamic centuries about the due custody of the credentials of faith and the criteria of law is familiar enough for present purposes. With the Qur'an as always supreme, its meaning, its *tafsir* and/or *ta'wil*, remain at issue, as between the broad rubric that 'the Qur'an means what Muslims find it means,'[7] and the claim that its exegesis requires an expertise which only duly accredited *'ulama'* or, in the Shi'ah tradition, only the Imams possess.[8] The famous distinction made in the Qur'an itself (3.7), between verses 'categorical' and verses 'allegorical', leaves the criteria between them unstated. Then there are esoteric meanings, likened to the underside of a Damascus brocade, and

---

[6] On the significance of first wearing the turban in 1889 and in 1926 doffing it, see Ahmad Amin, *Hayati*, Cairo, 1950, p. 50: 'I felt as if it had fettered me.' And see my 'Then and Now in Egypt: The Reflections of Ahmad Amin 1886-1954', in *The Middle East Journal*, Vol. 9, No. 1, 1955, Washington, DC. For Taha Husain, see *A Passage to France*, Leiden, 1976, (cf. Chap. 6, note 33), pp. 2 f. '... Not a place for turbaned students ...' he wrote of his access to 'the university'.

[7] See earlier discussion, Chap. 2, note 33. It is, intriguing to note how the issues between 'free, lay' right to a private readership belonged squarely in Christianity. How the Roman Church decried William Tyndale's assumption that even the 'plough-boy' could understand, once he had the English! Only Rome could tell him!

[8] Due reception of the Qur'an, along with the deep issue of suffering in non-success, is the central element in the Sunni/Shi'ah schism.

even an Ayatollah cannot be absolute about the exegesis he makes.[9] In any event, the Qur'an commends itself to *tadabbur* as the reflective readership it anticipates from all who come to it, whether Muslims or non-Muslims.[10]

Tradition is the second main source of guidance, on the condition of not being 'repugnant' to the Qur'an in the teaching it is held to yield. There follow, after the limited range of arguable analogy, the Sunni principle of 'consensus' across Islam. But how consensus is identified and who partakes in shaping it have long remained contentious. For what it may come to comprise needs to be pioneered by *Ijtihad*, or 'mental enterprise.' Who qualifies for this—the so-called 'gate of *Ijtihad*'—is precisely where mere 'lay' initiatives are suspected or excluded by those who hold their official skills as *'ulama'* and *fuqaha'*, duly schooled in the minutiae of grammar, law and commentary, to be indispensable. It is not clear whether a Muslim electorate, voting democratically, could underwrite a consensus for a Muslim legislature, without the role of a court of reference composed of learned ones to pass upon it.[11]

At best, the concept of *Ijma'* or 'convergence of thought' provides, a principle of development in Sunni Islam, in line with the familiar tradition of Muhammad that 'my community will never agree (converge) on an error.' It also fits Surah 42.38 which says of Muslims: 'their way of doing things is by counsel among themselves.' However, the vested interest of religious 'professionals' argues the retention of their powers of decision on matters of faith and doctrine, unless the pressures of 'lay' opinion and the rising claim of the issues 'lay' experience confronts contrive, against the odds, to make the case otherwise. It is in the day-to-day scene, with its rapid changes of attitude and perspective, that the problems present themselves. As for any religion, the mosque sermon

---

[9] He writes: 'The sense I am discussing is possible, not certain ... part of the possible meaning' (p. 375). Elsewhere: 'We can understand only a given aspect or dimension of the Qur'an: the interpretation of the rest depends upon Ahl-i-'Ismat, who received instruction from the Messenger of God.' (pp. 365-66). Again: 'The Qur'an is like a banquet from which everyone must partake in accordance with his capacity.' (p. 424) Ayatollah Khomeini, *Islam and Revolution: Essays and Declarations,* trans. Hamid Algar, Berkeley, 1981. Cf Chapter 6, note 28.

[10] Surahs 4.82 and 47.24, addressing non-Muslims. The noun *tadabbur* means deliberate thoughtfulness and reflection.

[11] As in the long process of Pakistani Constitution making with the 'Basic Principles Committee' as a necessary body appraising all laws proposed, though the non-elective status of such bodies could be said to infringe the whole democratic order, if over-riding an elected 'parliament'.

has to belong with the mosque audience. For all share in the *Ummah*. The audience, however, is only fully there as long as it brings—and is free to bring—all the queries and anxieties as to faith which the world arouses.

And then there is that more distant audience of Muslims that is less frequently—and perhaps less congenially—inside the mosque at all, for reasons emerging from Chapters 6 and 7. Such tentativeness is a present-day issue for all religions. Remitted from Chapter 3 was the subtle question of what 'apostacy' defines. If the definition is either ruthless or absolute, denouncing formal, verbal denial of the *Shahadah*, it surely loses the thread of all faith-allegiance. There has to be, in what claims to speak for religion, an awareness of multiple apostasies in life of mind and soul, through dubious, devious years. There has to be also a readiness to recognise the vicissitudes of clarity, of sincerity, of verity, within the heart. As George Herbert sang:

> Ah Lord! Do not withdraw,
>> Lest want of awe
>> Make sin appear
> And when Thou dost but shine less clear,
>> Say, that Thou art not here.[12]

It follows that faiths must concede a fluctuating, partial, struggling—because discerning—quality of faithful in its ranks.

This is likeliest in any converse of religions in a university setting. Oxford has nurtured many tentative agnostics, many hesitant believers. Such has been its métier, with readers of burdened novels about faith-loss or caught in Darwinian searchings of heart and reaching for an honesty of faith, with an urgency largely unknown to their heirs in the late 20th century. It was in measure, through them that the Church learned painfully, in the likes of William Temple of Balliol and Queen's, to know its entrusted meanings with a livelier cognisance of why others distrusted them. Can there be a kindred vocation inside Islam sharing the same world?

Faiths, to be sure, need orthodoxies they can identify, wherewith to be, in turn, identified. But has traditional, orthodox Islam been over sanguine and over simplistic in holding that verity with verification can rest on a *Shahadah* so brief, so readily uttered, so rarely expressly

---

[12] George Herbert, *The English Poems*, ed. C A Patrides, London, 1974, 'A Parodie', p. 187.

renounced, while so diversely given assent? For ambiguities present in allegiance have to be acknowledged worthily, if they are to be duly resolved. Hesitancies about belief, its forms and grounds, may fairly belong with the will for honesty and need respect for that very reason.

Is there, then, a vocation in contemporary Islam to de-absolutise its absolutism in the paradox of retaining it, a kind of unhardening of the heart, proper at least to the academic milieu and of potential warrant outside it? Vocational study, in those terms, means holding to faith while acknowledging open questions whose rigorous foreclosure would compromise sincerity of conviction or invite hidden 'apostasies' kept wistfully private. Or, in lines addressed to God, as Charles Williams wrote:

With terrible assessors
Thy seat is thronged about:
We too are Thy confessors,
Lord, hear us too who doubt.[13]

ii

Before moving to how this paradox of a faith duly confessional in its authority and duly open in its integrity might belong with Islam and for Muslims, it is well to realise how far it is complicated by relations with the West. In the will to be genuinely ecumenical—which is to have the paradox in practice—Muslims have found 'orientalism' too provocative, tedious and aggravating. Chapter 2 on 'The Place of Arabic' gave ample evidence of a phenomenon of western scholarship with which they were instinctively at odds. To many Muslims, it seemed an experience of unwelcome condescension and unseemly patronage that deserved only resentment. There were reasons for the negativism that merit some contrite sympathy from those they arraign. But the factors at work go much deeper than cultural resentment and the *amour propre* of a venerable tradition. They have to do with the postures of faith itself *vis-à-vis* credentials in a plural world.

Faiths cannot well be offered in the interior terms in which they are held. What justifies them to and for insiders cannot be justification to and for outsiders until mediated into who and where outsiders are. Thus

---

[13] Charles Williams, *Divorce and Other Poems*, Oxford, 1920, 'Office Hymn for the Feast of St Thomas Didymus, Apostle and Sceptic'.

scholarly, or other, interest of the West in Islam, somehow frequently provided an alibi by which to avoid or abandon this onus of interpretation. The West could be accused of a prejudice or a malice which had first to be renounced. For—on this view—it was only these that prevented Islam from being acknowledged true and final. It then had no onus to vindicate its meanings by patient explanation, since they were only out of focus for the West by wilful ignorance or perverse distortion. It was the West that had to come clean about Islam and, meanwhile, the business of Muslims was to stay aggrieved.

Or those from within Islam who sought to bridge the gulf and take up the intellectual tasks they recognised as theirs were reproached as 'liberals' who had succumbed to western blandishments and put their Muslim identity in doubt. Thus, for example, Taha Husain, four decades after his prime, was still being savaged as 'a manipulator of heathen, Hellenic ideas' and dubbed 'a *kafir*'.[14] Yet, erudite and assiduous in concern for social justice and Islamic meanings, he had striven, for example in *'Ala Hamish al-Sirah*, to educate his generation in the example of the Prophet.[15] He was a fine pioneer whose subsequent emulators duly received similar hostility, disputing their Islamic identity, and inspired by the same aversion for a perceived western factor at work. It is thanks to this psychology that Islam has been impeded in a more relaxed and objective encounter with issues, in no way inherently western but implicit in the very nature of religious faith. To reach for such encounter steadily and fruitfully is surely a vocation for an Oxford Islamics.

Moreover, it is much to be desired in the Muslim approach to Christianity, no less than in Islamic reaction to experience of orientalism. Beyond matters of bias, real or alleged, and all the stakes in controversy, there are often areas of perplexity about how 'being Christian' is seen. On Muslim count, the way convictions are held seems strangely personal or circumscribed. Some Muslim readers for example, found themselves

---

[14] Anwar al-Jundi, *Mahkamat Fikr Taha Husain*, ('The Thought of Taha Husain—on Trial'), Cairo, 1984. Taha Husain (1889-1973) was depicted on the book's cover standing in the dock. He had been Dean of Arts at Cairo University.

[15] The book—'In the Margin of the Life-Story (of Muhammad)' was published in 3 vols. in 1933 with the express intention of bringing Muhammad more fully into the ken of young Muslims. Many other writings pursued the same academic aim of lively education of Muslims into their faith and story. Perhaps it was his 1938 *Mustaqbal al-Thaqafah fi Misr* ('The Future of Culture in Egypt', Eng. trans. S Glazer, Washington, 1954), advocating a western kinship in Egyptian culture, that most offended his critics. See Pierre Cachia, *Taha Husain: His Place in the Egyptian Literary Renaissance*, London, 1956.

at odds with H A R Gibb's careful elucidation of what being Christian meant to him. Having first explained his desire 'to define precisely to himself and to his audience ... his point of view,' he continued:

> The metaphors in which Christian doctrine is traditionally enshrined satisfy me intellectually as expressing symbolically the highest range of spiritual truth which I can conceive, provided that they are interpreted not in terms of anthropomorphic dogma, but as general concepts related to our changing views of the nature of the universe.[16]

Commenting on this passage Ziya al-Hasan Faruqi concedes that Gibb can freely make what he will of his Christianity but claims that he has denied a similar 'entitlement to Muslims' in their Islam—precisely the very aim, not to say hope, of all Gibb's thinking on Islamic faith and story. His reviewer is pained that a scholar of Gibb's eminence has 'disregarded objectivity', failed to 'give due regard to the susceptibilities of Muslims,' and so 'neglected to observe the basic elements of scientific study.'[17]

The commentary sees a need to deplore as devious the very qualities of study Gibb believed himself to be pursuing and which he meant to stimulate in Muslim—and other—colleagues in the field. Thus there is a strange astigmatism here. There is puzzlement about Gibb's seemingly conditional acceptance of Christian faith and a charge of being 'unscientific' when he presumed to apply a similar mind-set when handling Islam. That Gibb's *confessio fidei* would be read by many Christians as being unduly subtle, even by their criteria minimal, is clear. The question, however, is whether or not that is the way a personal *confessio* has to be, seeing there needs to be an individual imprint on what sincerity requires and brings. Should it be arguably likewise with the individual Muslim? Is Islam minded to let it be so? The issue concerns any academic thinking but is much more than academic.

---

[16] H A R Gibb, *Modern Trends in Islam*, Chicago, 1945, p. xi. What he meant is not fully clear and was perhaps not meant to be. 'Changing views of the nature of the universe' meant he was not pre-Copernican! How the metaphorical belongs with the historical is left to silence. Muslims would have to approve of avoiding 'anthropomorphism', but might protest that Gibb's Christianity allows itself too much private liberty of interpretation.

[17] Ed. Asaf Hussain, Robert Olson and Jamil Qureshi, *Orientalism, Islam and Islamists*, Brattleboro, 1984, p. 185.

In a recent review, drawn at random, dealing with a book on 'Women in Islam', the reviewer regrets what he sees as 'a willing lack of ability ... to understand or fully appreciate equally the Islamic—rather than orientalist—terms of reference.'[18] Is a sensitivity about the latter asking, in effect, for exemption from examination of the former? What is definitively 'Islamic' in this and every field is the open question that has to be allowed. 'Orientalist' reading may contribute to it clumsily or with a prejudice fit for reproof, but that part of the equation cannot well exonerate what is due in the other.

Indispensable throughout is the will to 'good faith' given and received in genuine exchange, so that suspicion of *mal entendu* is not allowed to deflect issues or undermine confidence.[19] All practitioners have hills to climb in surmounting the obstacles of history and 'the adverse image of the other.' If 'religions' have reared them it is of the essence of 'religion' that they should be scaled only—as with mountaineers—for the reason that they are there and there massively.

iii

One critical area of mutual engagement between the Islamic and the Christian has to do with the nature of Scripture. Christian New Testament scholarship—or readership—has often seemed to Muslims to be oddly investigative, even cavalier, in the attitudes it brings, as if lacking in due veneration for a sacred text.[20] Their temper seems a far cry from the subdued awe with which Islam honours its Qur'an. Much misconception is involved here. For though the two Scriptures are equally central and supreme for each community, they proceed on contrasted concepts as to their divine provenance.

How incongruous, for example, to the Muslim mind must be the presence of 'Epistles' in the New Testament, purporting to be 'revelation'. For 'revelation' only comes down from heaven by *Tanzil* so that the Qur'an is uttered by the Prophet, word for word as the heavenly *Wahy* enables him in utterance, and that—according to the classic view—without the intervention or the discernment of conscious mental process of his own.

---

[18] *Dialogue*: Public Affairs Committee for Shi'ah Muslims, March, 2000, London, p. 8.
[19] *Op. cit.*, note 17, Chap. viii, 'Alongsidedness in Good Faith?', pp. 203-258.
[20] See, for example, Shabbir Akhtar, *A Faith for all Seasons*, London, 1990.

By that reckoning, Paul or Peter or James, writing as apostolic 'shepherds' of an expanding community in dispersion, urgent for education in the meaning of its identity and its ethical vocation as 'people of God', can only be a delusory Scripture.

Likewise the fourfoldness of the New Testament Gospels. If the *Injil* of Jesus was a 'heavenly text' mediated to him as teaching via a *Wahy* anticipatory of that by which Muhammad received the Qur'an, then manifestly it cannot be found in four variant, if mutually dependent, narratives. However, given that the person and event character of Jesus is where revelation has its dwelling,[21] again there is something arguably proper in that Christ-event finding its documentation in the same developing community of discipleship that welcomed its 'Epistles'.

The contrasts are familiar enough and have found exposition down the years. The radical way in which either's Scripture proves disconcerting to the other's assumptions, as to what might be 'holy writ' has too long confused or distorted the converse between Muslims and Christians. The issue has many facets, perhaps the most vexing of them the role of the human in the revelatory inspiration that is God's. The New Testament writers are understood as enabled in mind and spirit to articulate what Scripture comes to comprise by reflection on the Christ-event (where the prior revelation belongs) and by the application of its significance to life, conduct and community. It is proper for their own identities to be integral to this process, seeing that their inspiration is divinely theirs in the stream of daily life.

It seems to many readers that there must be something of this order also in the reception of the Qur'an by Muhammad, seeing that interaction between him and his hearers is so evidently present in the Qur'an.[22] Nevertheless, those who think it so have to honour, and defer to, the ruling Muslim perception of the Qur'an as wholly mediated to Muhammad, all mental processes or reaction to incidents apart. For it is seen as necessary to divine revelation that it be 'divine' in terms that exclude all human dimensions save that of 'word-recital'. For only in that way is the assurance complete that it is God's alone.

---

[21] Echoing the idiom of John 1.14, 'dwelt among us' derived from the 'tent' imagery of Hebrew Scripture, where 'the tent of meeting' was 'pitched' as the place of encounter.

[22] Witness the constant exchanges in the Meccan period: 'They are saying ... Say thou ...' Muhammad has to rebut a variety of disparaging and sceptical charges, such as; 'he is a wild poet,' 'he has it from strangers,' 'he disrupts our traditions.'

Even so, on the evidence of the Qur'an itself—'sent down upon the heart'[23]—that conclusion needs to reconsider. The point takes its place in a careful study of the entire dimension of the two halves of the *Shahadah*.[24] Meanwhile, in anticipation, there is the clear engagement of the Prophet with his audience, the Meccans. It is an engagement which, as his preaching mission develops, takes its place in the ensuing of the gathering Book. Can it be that he is abstracted from conscious thought while *Wahy* supervenes, returns to it to take resulting controversy in hand, and be once again abstracted to receive by *Tanzil* what has to be told in response? The 'they are saying, so say thou' sequences in the Meccan Surahs would seem to indicate that the text (that registers these so vividly) is contingent on them, not by abeyance of the personal equation, but by process of it. This need in no way mean that what the text arrives to say is any less such by *Wahy*—*Wahy* being understood as precisely the enablement of the human persona so strenuously undertaking the messengership. Nor need it mean that the personal human role either compromises or—still less—disserves the divine, or that what transpires *qua* text is less assuredly from God.

Similar conclusions would seem to be indicated also by the age-long clue to exegesis which Islam has found in 'the occasions of revelation'. Tradition was drawn into identifying what was 'situational'—this or that event, incident, or juncture—by which the text could be intelligently read. To be sure, these occasions, should be carefully distinguished from 'causes', since these lay inscrutably in the divine will to 'send down' that particular text. Even so, what 'situation' could hold in evidence for the exegete could hardly be absent for the exclusive recipient of the text itself. Should *Wahy* then not have room for mind, its whole content being so far plotted on to a biography?[25]

Moreover, as Muhammad's prophethood proceeded through the sequence of its engagement with controversy, it entailed a growing issue

---

[23] Surahs 2.97 and 26.194, the heart being the seat of the emotions, the place where the self feels and cherishes meaning.

[24] The whole purpose here is to concentrate on the *confessio* that acknowledges the status of Muhammad, deferring to Chap. 9 the *confessio* of divine unity. For some reflection on a 'theology of the juxtaposition' of the two clauses, see my *The Weight in the Word: Prophethood, Biblical and Quranic*, Brighton, 1999, Chap. viii. pp. 117-37.

[25] 'Plotted' in a mapping sense, in that Muhammad's *Sirah*, or story-in-life from 610 c. to 632, are the years of the Qur'an's *Tanzil*, so that text 'begins' with his call and ends with his death. It contains no 'biography' as such but all its 'occasions of revelation' belong in his life-career.

about his warrant, his status, his identity. The preaching elicited questioning about the preacher—queries that passed into scepticism, ridicule and calumny, all of which he had to counter by a vindication that rebutted them.[26] Thus, inevitably, what his message claimed about Allah and his being Allah's 'sent one', could—in no way—be isolated from the personal nexus this involved. 'Who' their bearer was became part of 'what' the words conveyed. It stayed so after his death in the enormous role Tradition assigned to his memory, the example of his daily life, as a source of guidance—firmly differentiated as these were from the text of the Qur'an he had received. They only carried forward, in a subordinate way for legal purposes, the whole revelatory role he personally filled for there to be any recipience of the Scripture.

It follows that there needs to be a prophetology that takes account of Muhammad's persona in larger and deeper terms than Muslim thinking generally has hitherto approved, to satisfy the whole phenomenon of the Qur'an and the second part of the *Shahadah*. The situation, theologically, is akin to that which required of nascent Christian faith the long and patient concern for a Christology, relating what was believed about Jesus as the Christ to the nature of God. The New Testament scene, with its confession of 'the Word made flesh', is in that sense sharply contrasted with the Quranic one. Yet the element of 'divine agency', as either Scripture believes it fulfils it, is present in each. In 'reciting the Qur'an'—however minimally Islam wants to understand that verbal role—Muhammad is the indispensable human 'party' in a divine transaction, namely *Tanzil* of the divine words. *Muhammadun Rasul-Ullah.*

What happens in *Tanzil*, on every classic premise of Islamic faith, confers entire exceptionality on the human instrument. What the divine employ signifies about the human 'employee' surely needs faithful formulation, avoiding what the fear of *shirk* would rightly exclude, but, nevertheless, realising the divine/human action in the Qur'an as 'the speech of God'. For the prophetic instrumentality remains 'associated' with Allah as the *Shahadah* categorically testifies—and, as such, deserves an adequate theological comprehension, so that the Qur'an's place in the economy of God duly incorporates the significance of Muhammad in that one economy.

---

[26] Note 22. The emphasis on his being *ummi* ('native') refutes the allegation about 'alien'—therefore suspect—sources. Similarly the vital distinction between mere 'poet-style' skills, which he abjures, and the matchless 'eloquence' of the Qur'an.

Thus far, concern for such a prophetology—relating *Tanzil* fully to God and relating Muhammad to prophethood—has stayed exclusively with bare recipience of the Quranic words. There are other issues which open out from that vital spokesmanship and to come later in this chapter. But why, in respect of how we understand *Tanzil*, does it matter? Why should outsiders want Muslims to think of their Muhammad as more consciously engaged in his experience of *Wahy*, his utterance of the Qur'an? What point is there in being concerned about the traditional idea of the Qur'an's being more convincingly divine, because it was had by divine dictation? Can it matter that Muhammad was more duly 'messenger' because his mental processes were rigorously excluded from the deliverances his hearers received from his lips?

If the answer is that exegesis could be more intelligible the other way, or that the whole transaction of *Wahy* would be retrieved from potential 'magic' or possible superstition, could thinking it so make any difference unless Muslims agreed? Do faiths need intrusions from intruders purporting to think 'better' about ancient mind-sets they do not understand or about those 'passionate commitments'—recalling Chapter 3 and Wittgenstein—they do not share? Should we not gladly live and let live?

The contrary reason, ultimately, is that faiths need urgently to forego aggressive confidence and 'gentle the condition' of their truths.[27] For the Semitic faiths, at least, beginning—unlike Buddhism—from the divine end, make such portentous claims. They cause such a wide vista to focus into such a specific image. The particularities they make so central and so pivotal incur such heavy historical odds and require such agnostic interrogation. Semites are such absolutists.

There is the mystery of how a single people so tenaciously read their history as an exclusive divine adoption of their destiny via exodus and land-implantedness. The conviction was so strong that Jewry was sustained by it over long centuries of diaspora, to renew its mandate on themselves in 20th century Zionism. Yet, historically, that whole self-image of Jewry is attended by sharply puzzling contingencies around tribal adventures and patriarchal migrations and mythicised personae,

---

[27] Shakespeare in *Henry V* has the King using the phrase in respect of yeomen, even peasants in the ranks. being 'ennobled' as equal to 'gentlemen' by their presence at Agincourt. But it lends itself well to the other sense of 'gentle' as opposed to aggression, pride and high-handedness.

which leave observers asking whether 'history' need matter seeing that faith and mystery take care of all.

It has often been alleged that Christian faith makes too much turn on too little. A maverick Jewish rabbi becomes 'the Saviour of the world'. That Cross on Calvary is 'grossly overloaded'.[28] A miscarriage of Roman justice became the focal point of a Christology that read 'very God of very God' in divine 'Word made flesh'. Could the resulting reading sustain what it purported to find? Christian critical scholarship has been busy ever since with what one practitioner phrased as 'Jesus—the Unanswered Questions'.[29] Can the perennially 'questionable' well be the abidingly 'eternal self-giving of God'?' Can transcendence be enfleshed in history, 'the Lord above' biographised?

Muslims might begin to think that their claims are more modest. They are no special people, nor do they tolerate divine Incarnation. Yet, in perspective, the assurance around Muhammad and the Qur'an is no less comprehensive, no less sedulous than the other monotheisms in the fashion of its confidence. Should Islam be, as it were, both judge and jury in respect of other religions, by the view that the Qur'an confirms and finalises all that was ever given in divine 'messages'? The specifics of Islam in its Arabian *manzil*, or first abode, in its focus on Mecca and Medina and in its inclusive finality, are as ambitious of total acceptance as those made elsewhere.

This is the more stringently the case, given the view of the Qur'an via Muhammad we have reviewed as so long the orthodoxy of Islam. To have to conclude so was the point of its exposition. For it is precisely the absolutely divine *Tanzil*, ensuring inerrancy, excluding a human party and bearing that sort of *imprimatur*, which contributes to a Muslim view of over-mastering omnipotence which then extends into other areas of religious life and politics. A religious text which its readers might more readily approach as having a human dimension—though no less on that ground revelatory—could teach a less magisterial exegesis.

---

[28] The point was often made, from the Jewish, side, about the 'over-loadedness' of the one Cross in the ten-year converse between a group of Rabbis and a similar number of Christian clergy, which published something of itself in *Dialogue with a Difference*, ed. Tony Bayfield and Marcus Braybrooke, London, 1992. The issue of 'sharp particularity' carrying universal relevances is present in all religions. Cf. *ibid.*, p. 23: 'The Jews—a people who made Him (God) a responsible party to history.' Indeed, but why they only—only their history?

[29] John Bowden, London, 1988—a book kindling my *What Decided Christianity: Event and Experience in the New Testament*, Worthing, 1989.

For a Qur'an, sacrosanct in the orthodox view of *Tanzil,* more readily underwrites a sense of theocracy in other realms as relating God in the same absolute order of things, whereby *Shari'ah* leaves no more place for conscience than *Tanzil* left participation for the Prophet. 'It is written'—reinforced by calligraphy and recitation—gives more overriding power to the *hudud,* the moral limits Allah has prescribed, than would be the case with a text less infallibly 'sent down' or, better expressed, in a 'sent-down-ness' more initially engaged with mind and conscious partnering.

Our study, then, of how Muhammad's role in the Qur'an might be truly affirmed more humanly matters inside the hope of making 'gentle the condition' of religious faith responsive to how the contemporary world is. To have religion less insistently absolute is the key to having its ambitions no longer yearning for a manner of theocracy over which it will preside. Theocracy, in any event, is surely ruled out by any perceptive understanding of the trusteeship vested in our human creaturehood. To pursue this theme duly it is necessary to study Muhammad's role as *Rasul-Ullah* in ways beyond those of the verbal incidence of the Quranic text so far in mind. For what we have called 'divine agency' goes further than this chapter has yet pondered. The wider dimension bears strongly on the temper Islam brings to its religious role in the world of today. How Muslims confess that second part of the one *Shahadah* will always be central to an Islamic ethics, an Islamic politics, an Islamic metaphysics and so, in turn, to an Islam as 'a mercy to the worlds'.[30]

iv

What thought on Islam has here to explore is all in that half of the *Shahadah: Muhammadun Rasul-Ullah*—'Muhammad the Apostle of Allah', directly conjoined with the divine unity confessed.[31] The sentence is 'nominal', 'is' being supplied in English, unnecessary in an Arabic nominal sentence. *Rasul-Ullah,* as grammarians would say is in

---

[30] For a prophetology (i.e. a thesis about how the singular figure belonged in the divine economy) will always be the crucial issue for theology in Islam. The juncture in the *Shahadah* makes it so. Likewise, in Christian faith, its Christology has always been inside its theology. In either case all else in life and society flows from how God is understood—to which understanding either 'the Prophet' or 'the Christ' are 'theological' clues.

[31] It is *not* saying: 'Muhammad is a prophet of God.' That would require a different grammatical use, since the 'possession', had 'in construct', is necessarily definite as '*the* Apostle ...'

'construct', making the first noun definitive, i.e. not 'a' but 'the'. There have, indeed, been many other *rusul* (pl.) as the Qur'an tells, but no others singularly in construct with 'Allah'.[32] The grammar is as exceptionalising as when Paul writes of 'the Christ of God'.

The point is index to much more in, but far beyond, the text issue earlier discussed. It is important reverently to study the intense implications of his experience in the Prophet's psyche, the stresses in a received vocation, the weight of a perceived identity. To be sure, he is only named as 'Muhammad' four times in the Book, but what of the private persona in the public task? 'O thou that art enmantled, rise and warn.' (74.1-2) and other passages brought these together. Consider how frequently is the second person singular pronoun in the Qur'an. Somehow 'saying, 'said' and 'say-er' belonged in one.

Moreover, as already noted, retort of hearers to the text passed into its further content with him as the theme. Then steadily as followers slowly emerged, or as hostility sharpened, that theme grew ever more crucial. Muhammad heard himself saying: 'Obey God and obey the messenger,' and. that, by sacred mandate.[33] What it was meant to mean in society involved what it must have meant in the psyche. Then came those provisions—doubtless an aspect of vigilance and security—concerning access to his physical presence or the privacy of his wives. A tradition from him runs: 'No other prophet was vexed as I have been.'[34] The Qur'an, we have to conclude, is not only the literary wonder Islam has always perceived it to be: it is also the document of a psychic experience as unparalleled in its world-wide sequel as it was numinous in the inner soul. But just how that 'numinous' has to be explored or explained is hard to know.

Perhaps, devout orthodoxy would think, it does not need to be. Can faith ever be in fee to history as historians and—in this case—psychologists might think to read it? What is from transcendence cannot be hostage to what they choose to find. Any prophetology for Islam must fall back on the 'witness' of the *Shahadah* and need no other lights. The whole theme is akin to the Christology of Christian faith, though in the contrasted Arabian context.

---

[32] 'Messengers'—in the plural, with never a people lacking one native to them, are a familiar theme in Islam. The plural of *rasul*, the highest category, i.e. *rusul*, occurs around a hundred times in the Qur'an.

[33] Surahs 3.32, 8.1, 8.20, 8.46, 58.13 and 64.12.

[34] Cited by Ayatollah Khomeini, *Islam and Revolution*, ed. and trans. Hamid Algar, Berkeley, 1981, p. 394.

Yet, in political terms, Islam has never—with rare exceptions—been content to leave Muhammad's prophethood as an article of theological faith. His centrality to the text and to the heavenly status of the text, in being its instrument in the grace of *Tanzil,* passed steadily into an activism of inter-city rivalry, into caravan routes and tribal preserves and finally into military trials of strength. These still further accentuated the personal role of Muhammad and brought his physical fortunes not only into the text of the Book but into the institutional shape of Islam. They also defined it as politico-religious in its integral character, still further accentuating within his persona the identity of means and end that had first been only verbal and prophetic. When it became also combative and jurisdictional, in the Medinan experience, it transpired that the preaching *Rasul* of a *balagh* only, passed into a political *Rasul* of a rising *din wa dawlah.*[35]

It is this sequence—which the *Shahadah* omits or only implies—that complicates the matter, earlier mooted, of Islam ever again after Mecca making 'gentle its condition'. For it was the Medinan Qur'an in the Medinan scene, which sanctioned the vision of an Islamic 'theocracy', establishing 'the régime of Allah' over human society. Islam assumes that the *Rasul* term in the Qur'an incorporates both the Muhammad of Mecca prior to the Hijrah and the Muhammad of Medina after it, though—as a term—*rasul* means only 'one who brings word.' It follows, therefore, that what is centrally at issue hangs on the extension of a purely preaching term into a 'power' content so that *rasuliyyah* (i.e. 'being a *rasul*') properly, and irreversibly, covers both. Certainly the text of the Qur'an, with its Meccan and Medinan Surahs, incorporates both, so that being 'the Apostle of God' included all the military actions that ensued after the Hijrah.

v

May it be that we have here identified, by help of the *Shahadah* itself, the crux of contemporary Islamic self-study, perhaps even the core of

---

[35] The explicit confining of Muhammad's mission to *balagh,* i.e. a verbal ministry, is found in Surahs 3.20, 5.99, 13.10, 24.54, 29.18, 36.17, 42,48 and 64.12, while 16.35 makes the same point about all 'apostles' (pl.): 'Have the messengers any other charge but transmitting the clear verbal meaning?' This was assumed changed into the power régime after the Hijrah by the logic of the unyielding resistance of most Meccans to the spoken word.

intellectual vocation? What, in effect, does 'being *Rasul-Ullah*' still mean? Was or was not its Medinan extension from religious 'message' alone, to a battling, armed cause legitimate? Is it *perpetually* Islamic?

How could it not be? one might ask. If 'the message' meant what it said, surely its success was vital and successful it surely became in the sequel—provided we are sure as to how, in what belongs with religion, success is identified.[36]

How it could not be legitimate would take us to the view that religious truth can only be always persuasive and never coercive. For the sake of all it purports to be, it can only wait on the free assent that is evermore the prime quality of sincere faith. It cannot compel and stay its due self, nor can it 'message' (turning noun into verb) the meaning of God or summon to worship in any violent terms. Its authority has to be one that seeks to deserve, and deserves to find, a free consent. For then alone is it worthy.

Given the actuality of the early Islamic history, we seem to have reached an impasse. But perhaps not. There is a ground on which Muslims might return to the original '*balagh* only' content of the word *Rasul* in the *Shahadah*. It is that the belligerence was inevitable in the given context of 'the island of the Arabs' and of the Meccan/Medinan world there and then in the 7th century. (Hence the word querying 'irreversible' some lines above.) The Medinan dimension in the Qur'an could be valid, but only in a context that no longer obtains. The Qur'an contains it: Islam experienced it. Both possess a finality that makes them abreast of all that the centuries develop in the transformations of history. For only so, like any other religion, is Islam not a museum piece.

There is then every ground for arguing that the 21st century scene, the perspectives of the 15th Islamic one, are no longer those that Muhammad, 'the Prophet armed', confronted—and confronted duly—in his immediate world. There is a clear case for an Islam of the *Rasul*, of serving the *balagh* in today's context and this would be the surest 'gentling of its condition,' foregoing the sundry aspects of belligerence that have

---

[36] For the term can be elusive. 'Manifest victory' was what Medinan Islam sought and it was clearly 'manifest' in the capitulation of Mecca. But Surah 49.15-17 makes clear that adherence was not always from the heart but only out of prudence. Then there was the *riddah* after Muhammad's death when some believed that his passing freed them from a submission that had only been to him in person. Then came political factions and the sects. Could the Shi'ah, before 'Ali's accession to the caliphate and after his murder, think in terms of 'success'? Indeed, what 'success' could mean became a theological and a political theme for seceders.

seemed explicit in the *Shari'ah* and customary for a traditional mentality. Islam would then be—in a phrase long uncongenial to its genius—'a religion only', the steady proponent of a disciplined God-awareness in face of the gathering secularity of an accentuating technology. There, it would seem, is the audience for the original *balagh* in the present meaning of detecting idolatries and 'letting God be God'. All that is implied here belongs with Chapter 9.

Meanwhile, this focus of *Al-Rasul* as 'messenger', this strict reading of the second clause in the *Shahadah*, are the intention behind the earlier emphasis in this chapter on their being a human element in Muhammad's reception of the Qur'an in its *Tanzil*.[37] The connection is clear. What is thought purely arbitrary in its incidence will likely be seen as purely arbitrary in the logic to which it points. If the Quranic text really admitted of no emotional or mental participation in its meanings on his part, it becomes the more absolute—as distinct from authentic—in its role for the faithful. What was not fused with lived history in its first incidence will hardly be fused with lived history in its readership. The sense of a dynamic role for Muhammad in the preached Qur'an also accords better—as we have noted—with the long tradition of exegesis by reference to 'occasions'.[38]

Thus having *balagh* central and having Muhammad as *Al-Rasul* intelligently appreciated in that role, will help to sustain and reinforce the case being made for an Islam more 'gentle' in its whole 'condition', both as constituted in its Scripture and fulfilled in its contemporary mind and structure. In recent decades this bold case for making the *balagh* the heart of a more 'gentle' Islam has been made in several quarters, though it has massive discouragement and veto to overcome from 'fundamentalist' style custodians. Even so, it can appeal to the precedent by which

---

[37] There was no occasion in the foregoing for discussion of how, in fact, the incidence of the Qur'an in Muhammad's experience might be explored. See, for example, Tor Andrae, *Muhammad: The Man and His Faith*, New York, 1936, and Fazlur Rahman, *Prophecy in Islam: Philosophy and Orthodoxy*, London, 1958. Fazlur Rahman became an exile from Pakistan in Chicago, partly because of his readiness to consider a certain 'authorship' to Muhammad in the Qur'an, without in any way meaning (as his accusers alleged) that Muhammad was its *author*. See his *Islam*, New York, 1966, pp. 31 f. Our concern has been with the relation between *balagh* and *rasul*, and its implications for the temper of Islam today.

[38] The link between text and reader is always crucial. The case being made for reading what was fitting then in Muhammad's *Sirah* as no longer fitting now could be seen as a larger application of *asbab al-nuzul* ('the occasions of the sending down')—but now *qua* centuries and cultures and not in events of the first locale and two decades.

abrogation of part by part can occur in the Qur'an. Such *naskh,* or 'abrogation', occurs there—subject to expertise—only in minor details, so that what is later 'abrogates' what is earlier if these do not tally. Time is, therefore, a conceded factor. The argument now is that the earlier *balagh*—for the sheer sake of which a degree of *ikraha,* or 'compulsion', once supervened—might now be the single sanction on which Islam relied as its sufficient commendation.[39]

It follows at once that such an 'Islamicity' would belong well with the civil pattern of contemporary statehood, where religions are free to worship and affirm themselves but concede a neutral governmental structure none dominates or controls, and in which all are free to participate in the democracy of equal citizens. Such a régime in no way 'secularises' society in any total sense, nor does it preclude an ongoing weight of historical faith-tradition, though being now of the *balagh* order exclusively.

That something like this is, in any event, the actual situation for Muslim minorities outside the political *Dar al-Islam* is clear enough. These are now perhaps one quarter of all the world's Muslims—in India, Europe and the Americas—a large community indeed. For them *balagh* is all and all is *balagh,* to be interpreted as the commended faith and applied to social norms and political action only by worth of its commendation and not by any sort of duress—in short, a Meccan rather than a Medinan Islam.

To ground essential Islam in the *balagh,* with the Medinan Islam a circumstantial one in that there-and-then, spells a radical Muslim decision but it is one that would do best justice to the second clause of the *Shahadah* and to the prime capacity of Muhammad as *Rasul-Ullah.*[40] The issue has finally to do with what religion is. In respect of Islam that can rest only with Muslims. It is right that the decision that resolves what religious faith is should be consciously taken by reference to how the world is and to how it reads and serves the human scene in that scene's

---

[39] The case for 'abrogation in reverse', with the earlier replacing the later, can be studied in, e.g., Abdullahi Ahmad An-Na'im, *Toward an Islamic Reformation,* Syracuse, 1990, expounding the ideas of Mahmud Taha of the Sudan (1914-85) and relating the theme to 'civil liberties, human rights and international law', each of which bears strongly on the concept and application of *Shari'ah* law. The author 'hopes to reconcile Muslim commitment to Islamic law with ... the benefits of secularism within a religious framework.' (p. 10). He warns, however, that 'the realistic prospects of the secular option are ... diminishing' (p. 44).

[40] One can truly say 'prime capacity' in that, as noted above, the Hijrah itself was on behalf of the 'message' and in no way an 'irreligious' venture pursuing power for power's sake. In that way Hijrah was an ancillary, supportive dimension in the larger whole which was 'the preaching'.

present tense. Was not such a perceptive reference to how the-then-world was, the very principle of the Medinan Hijrah—albeit in terms of power-quest opposite to those now obtaining? Could there, then, perhaps, be a sort of current Hijrah out of the long Medina-born tradition into the ecumenical venture of active co-existence in society and the spiritual Islamicity of 'message' from 'Messenger'?[41] If so, there can be no question about the deep relevance of the Muslim *balagh*, nor of vocation for an Islamic Centre.

vi

Its relevance is that it takes up, both for impulse and warrant, the heart-truth of Islam concerning our human *khilafah*, our entrustment with personhood, our having been set within an order of nature capable of responding to our 'dominion' and so yielding all culture and technology. This inherent human dignity, with its need for 'reminder' as to how rich it is, its need for 'guidance' towards due fulfilment,[42] has been with us in Chapters 3 and 6 and calls for fuller study in line with the first clause of the *Shahadah* in the chapter following. It is the sphere that necessitated prophethood—the clear corollary of the Creator's project with creaturehood in us humans.

The *islam* (the common noun without initial capital 'I') that humans are called to in Islam is, therefore, a submission from within an autonomy—a call to conformity that addresses a freedom. There is about it this 'asked-for-ness' from us, in line with the divine question in Surah 7.172: 'Am I not your Lord?' The context is of a sought-for and given cosmic acknowledgement about an *islam* at once voluntary and due. The word 'responsible' includes both, as when Marshall Hodgson in his *The Venture of Islam* offered the definition we noted in chapter 3, where he sought to contrast 'responsibility' (Islamic) with 'responsiveness' (Christian). The one emerged as a self-sufficient moral religion, the other as a 'cripple' with the 'crutch' of necessary grace.[43]

An effort was made earlier to study how there could have been

[41] On the historic Hijrah as a parable of many other 'ventures out of'—'on behalf of', see, for example, Mohamed A Lahbabi, *Le Personnalisme Musulman*, Paris, 1964.
[42] These two terms, *dhikr* and *huda*, are frequent in the Qur'an and almost become synonyms for the Book as a whole. Humans need 'reminding' because they are forgetful and 'guiding' as, being, otherwise, liable to 'err'.
[43] Marshall Hodgson, Chapter 3, note 31.

a responsiveness of his inside Muhammad's responsibility in receiving *Wahy* and the Qur'an it bestowed. What is not conjectural is that so much of the realm of faith—its content and structure—hinges on communal and personal responsibility exercised within the autonomy which *khilafah* hallows and allows. Readership, however theories see its role, is the presiding condition of the meaning of any and every writing. The Qur'an is in no way exempt. However awesome the calligraphy and rightly modulated the voice, the text yields itself into the comprehension exegesis affords it.

That vital role is partnered by the place of the human factor in the care of Tradition, its gathering, sifting and applying. Other factors in the shaping of *Shari'ah*, as we have seen, turn on the human involvement Muslims bring, resulting in 'Schools', (*madhahib*) whose contribution shares in what, while subordinate and collaborative, is alongside direct revelation *qua* the status it enjoys as *Shari'ah* also.

In these and other ways, the 'givens', the 'absolutes', the 'things decreed', of Islam are 'given' to the responsive care and essential participation of Muslims in the context of a *khilafah* where their 'submission'—far from being slavish or mechanical—recruits the discretions they must bring. That it has to be so, for religion and faith, is the first relevance of the original *balagh*.

Another is the anathema against idolatry, that cowering to pseudo-deities which it denounced. The resolute veto on *shirk* or false worships is timely in all vicissitudes of history, while it serves well to measure how radically times change and, therefore, perceptions with them. Few anywhere in Islam's 15th century are likely to be caught in the crudities of Arabian paganism in its first. Those Meccan goddess, Allat, Manat and al-'Uzza, have gone into limbo, with the tribal patrons and the daimons of local shrines. Such idolatries, such follies of misdirected wistfulness, do not mesmerise a sophisticated age.

Contemporary society has more blatant, more heinous idols in the form of false absolutes of state, or power, or pride, or of religion, to which we make the figurative prostration of adulation and allegiance. Society, the economic and political structures of culture and science, of trade and money, stay in urgent need of the indictment the *balagh* brought, the summons it served that 'only God is God.' That 'there is none but He' translates into 'letting God be God' and alone relativizes all our mistaken ultimates so that, duly subdued in the only right worship, their relative legitimacy can be safely possessed.

The sense of the Prophet's preaching that there are *hudud*, limits, bounds, within which our autonomy should move—not thereby malignly reduced but benignly endowed—is as urgently needed, now as then, but now against the arrogance of structures thought a law unto themselves. Moreover, the responsibility vested in us, both by the 'open question', of such crises in our conduct and our culture, and by the fact that religious directives turn on consent, argues that the *Shari'ah* may be in some measure a party to conscience.

It is clear that this happens all the time, even in rigorist circles, but more keenly in reformist ones. The most stringent injunctions of the *Shari'ah* as to beatings, amputations or other severities are hedged about, either in their Quranic context or by concerned casuistry, so that conscience finds some play in the rule of *Shari'ah*,[44] even to the point that penalties are not exacted where the guilty party does not willingly assent. To the outsider these things may seem like palliatives of what should be repudiated *in toto*. But that reaction hides an animosity it would be well to rethink, seeing that all situations are redeemable.

If it can be claimed that whenever society, through tolerance, avoids to apply the rigour of punishments decreed, it acts according to the spirit of Islam and the mind of the Prophet, it must mean that the very *Shari'ah* is malleable to that extent—and malleable by dint of Muslim conscience. It is only a step, if a large one, from that fact of things, to see conscience as a monitor of what *Shari'ah* intends. Changes so warranted could then be seen—and validated—not as any compromise or betrayal of *Shari'ah* but as its developing quality as final. In that event, the way is wide open to a livelier trusteeship of faith, in being the more closed to rigorist concepts of 'the letter' and the tyranny of bare decree.

Such vigorous centralising of *balagh* would tally with the measure of Quranic silence in the legal sphere,[45] how the book did not explicitly bind religion to any form of statehood or legislate the caliphate.[46] Such 'silence' does not mean that Allah is forgetful or remiss: it means

---

[44] For many examples, see M A S Abdel-Haleem, *Understanding the Qur'an*, London, 1998 and the review of them in Chapter 6 above.

[45] It is calculated that only some two hundred Qur'an verses are about legal matters, out of more than six thousand, though they are more lengthy verses.

[46] The only 'caliphate' in the Qur'an—apart from a bare mention of David (38.29)—the only *khalifah* is 'man', often in the plural of all humans as *khulafa'*, 'trustees' of Allah's creation in the meaning of Surah 2.30.

that He wills room for human participation—a perception about divine omnipotence which is in line with the generosity present in creation.[47]

Further, in this context, is the observation that the whole, when seen this way, is more consonant with the human scenario as we experience it today. To think of divine will as diminishing or precluding the human factor seems less and less to ring true to what we perceive of technological competence. It therefore prejudices many against all religious faith, as belittling the powers technology finds itself achieving and applying to society. A realism about those powers can then, in turn, seduce and betray those who wield them into the belief that they are left to themselves, alone in a godless world.

Such drift to total secularity will come in its own place in the next chapter. It is only halted or rescued from itself and its menace to sanity and modesty by a theology that calls it to gratitude and consecration, to an awareness of God consistent with its knowledge of human mastery as a summons to 'submission', not a mandate to arrogance. Such a theology Islam and its *balagh* fully and eloquently afford.

vii

Despite these compelling aspects of the case for a contemporary vocation of Islam in original Meccan terms, the quest proves long and hard. The hopes it enshrines face acute controversy. Their fulfilment may prove far to seek, despite the many actual situations in which they are the only feasible option. Syed Vahiuddin, a noted thinker in Indian Islam, writes:

> When we think of the future of Islam and of Muslims we do so predominantly in terms of power politics and the political future ... Politics and religion are linked in Islam and the concept of a Muslim state as a world state has dominated the imagination of Muslims. But it should not

---

[47] Is it not the inferior kind of power, jealous of its prerogatives, that fears to delegate anything or to risk any devolving of its authority? The point is well made by S Kierkegaard, the Danish thinker, 'Omnipotence constantly withholds itself ... is able to bring forth a being independent *vis-à-vis* itself ... It is a worldly notion of power that it (must) steadily augment itself to the extent that it can coerce and make dependent.' *Journals and Papers, A Selection*, ed. and trans. Alexander Dru, Oxford, 1938, No. 616, p. 180.

be forgotten that power has never enjoyed the first priority
and the state is never considered an end in itself.[48]

'The first priority' was, of course, the Meccan one. Insisting that he is a
Muslim 'seeking self-understanding', he lets Maulana Abul Hasan 'Ali
Nadwi expound 'priority' in his criticism of a celebrated leader of sharp
'Medinan' emphasis in the person of Maulana Abu-l-'Ala al-Mawdudi,
founder of the Jama'at-i-Islami.

> That the relation of God and man finds its most
> characteristic expression in the relationship of the sovereign
> to His subjects, or of command and obedience, does not
> give justice to the man-God relationship. However natural
> a corollary it might be of one's commitment to Islam, it is
> only a part—and that a limited one—of God's relationship
> with man, and not the whole of it. It is much more subtle,
> more comprehensive, deeper and delicate.[49]

Syed Vahiuddin goes on to note that 'while the political
dimension of life ... cannot be ignored,' ... 'it often happens that the
political quest for power ... can become aggressive and militant.' He cites
further how beset we modern humans are by threat of meaninglessness.
The terms are akin to those we explored in Chapter 7. To them Islam
does—and must—have relevance. For Islam, with all faiths, is 'affected
by the crisis of religious consciousness as a whole'. It is a crisis which

---

[48] *Islam in India: Studies and Commentaries*, ed. C W Troll, Vol. 3, 'Syed Valiuddin,' Delhi, 1986, pp. 70-71. Born in 1909, Syed Valiuddin studied in Osmania University, Hyderabad, before moving to Germany where he studied at Marburg and Berlin and had close contact with Rudolf Otto (1869-1937). He taught in Osmania and the University of Delhi. Abul-Hasan Ali Nadwi (1914-1999), a distinguished scholar in Lucknow, was the Founding Chairman of the Board of Trustees of the Oxford Centre, which he regularly visited. He died on the last day of the old millennium and is commemorated in the Centre's 'Special Issue' of January, 2000.

[49] *Ibid.*, p. 71. Al-Mawdudi (1903-79) was the most influential and charismatic of 'rigorist' figures in the sub-continent and author of *The Four Fundamental Concepts of the Qur'an*, and a Commentary. Ali Nadwi took him to task as unwarrantably narrowing the significance of Islam through (in Nadwi's view) a false centralising of divine dominion as designed for an earthly theocracy through exclusive power. Nadwi sought to displace the 'God and man' concept as that of sovereign power over subject-submission (and political agency) and to enthrone as prior the principle of Creator and creature. Mawdudi, he alleged, had 'reduced' the whole significance of worship in Islam, by diverting it from a true devotion-in-love to become, via the Five Pillars, merely a means to theocratic rule on earth—in Muslim hands.

'Muslim revivalist movements', having only 'their one-dimensional consciousness' fail to meet.

Such pleas, however, are strongly countered by those who are adamant that the true Islam is betrayed by them. It could well be that the adamant quality stems from fear lest the other case be true. Obduracy is often of that order. Thus doggedness that is afraid is not easily dissuaded. Rather it hardens for itself—in the words of another writer into:

> ... the certainty of the simple meaning of the Koranic verses and the absolute unilaterality of their message, form and structure, against all permeability, redefinition and innovative interpretation.[50]

The debate has been joined. It reaches back more than a century. For all who care about Islam, insiders and outsiders, its core theme— with all that modernity has now brought to it of complexity and anguish— has ever since been inherent in that prime Meccan/Medinan sequence. In what sense was the Hijrah, in being for the message, also a movement out of it? Yet that Hijrah never spelled an abandonment of Mecca and *balagh*. Indeed in the there and then it served to ensure that, at long range, the *balagh* spread world-wide. Success might forever seal its own logic. How will contemporary Islam, in loyal witness that 'Muhammad is the messenger of Allah,' resolve in present terms that deep founding issue in its destiny?

Away from the stress and tempers of statehoods and the world arena, an academy will be an evident place to seek an answer.

---

[50] Sadiq J al-'Azm, *South Asia.Bulletin/Comparative Studies of South Asia, Africa and the Middle East*, Vols. xiiii and xiv, 1993, 94, 'Islamic Fundamentalism Reconsidered: A Critical Outline of Problems, Ideas and Approaches,' off-printed text, p. 21.

Chapter 9

'ALLAHU AKBAR'

i

'Greater is God!'—the familiar cry with which Islam resounds around the world. Sufis in their *dhikr* will recite it rhythmically a hundred times and more. Friday congregations chant it in credal unison. We fellow humans know it as the theme of Islam. For some it arouses a will to understand what its recital signifies as the first clue to what the mosque intends all humans to learn by it.

That must turn or how it is said. Is it a celebratory cry as one might gleefully announce: 'Spring is here'? Does it have the feel of the hymn that sings: 'Morning has come, like the first morning'? In which case we must know it for a theology in doxology where theology should always begin and end. Or is it to be read as adversarial, even minatory, like the invocation of some 'Lord of hosts'? What posture have its five syllables, what temper tells its accents?

By a grammarian's measure, *akbar* is a comparative but does not act as one here. For Allah has 'none like unto Him' (Surah 112.4) and so may not enter into any comparison. The sense has to be superlative but not *al-akbar*, 'the greatest' if the superlative be read (as it may) as a sort of plural comparison, as one might say of three or more statesmen: 'X is the greatest.' For then, we are still comparing. Moreover, Allah is not a generic word. To have 'gods'—capable of being plural—we must have another word *alihat* (sing. *ilah*). Thus the only way is to let the English reverse the order, with the asset of being yet more emphatic, and elide all danger of even remotely implied comparison around the ineffable Lord: 'Greater is Allah.' or, in old Christian Latin: *Deus semper major*.

These necessary points of syntax are familiar enough to Arabs and Arabists. But for folk who pray and think and worship, and grammarians too, a further question presses, namely: Why does 'God is greater' need to be said? Who is, who can be, feasibly denying it? The cry is necessary, it will be explained, as serving notice on the atheists and the idolaters. Truly, there is day-to-day challenge to the indubitable sovereignty, so that what is, and has to be, essentially incontestable, needs an insistent iteration. 'Blessed be God,' as John Donne cried, 'only and divinely like Himself!'

For idolatry happens. Deities plural find credence and worship. Atheism is a human option. Hence the urgency of the imperative witness: *Allahu akbar*. It fulfils the whole genius of Islam as existing to ensure the due recognition of God—a paradox which houses the whole theme we have to explore. The Arabic words make a nominal sentence: an English 'is' is implicit. And there *is* our whole point, seeing that 'God is' (absolutely), yet 'God is not' (confessedly/empirically) inasmuch as His being God is denied. 'God is not in all his thoughts,' said the psalmist (Psalm 10.4) of 'the fool' who, on another occasion, might have God 'in his thoughts' just long enough to cancel them with: 'There is no God.' (Psalms 14.1, 53.1)

These fine points could seem tedious were they not the very heart of the matter. By the very urgency of affirming *Allahu akbar* we concede the truth that Allah has to be let be. There is a human cognisance, a recognition, which yields Him the being He indisputably possesses. Yet that inherent Reality He is, is inherently anticipatory towards, and intrinsically expectant of, our creaturely *islam*, our human submission. The very force of the words *Allahu akbar* comes from this paradox of their necessity on our lips. At the very heart of Islam is the truth of the God who, being, has to be let be, the Allah who transcends and condescends, both beyond and in our human confession.

Those two words *Allahu akbar* have no need, yet have every need, to be uttered—no need because no silence denies Him, every need in that our silence, or denial, would circumvent the sort of Allah He is. We stressed earlier how much wiser it is to speak of 'the God of existence' rather than abstractly of 'the existence of God'. That *Allah* is *akbar* indeed goes without saying in the reality 'as in heaven'. For that very reason it is to be imperatively said 'here on earth'. Truth does not turn, but waits, on recognition.

In this way, humankind outside Islam, for all their anxiety around the raucousness they register, have sound reason to salute and welcome the accents of *Allahu akbar*, the priority they assign, the burden they enjoin. The words can be taken as clarion cry against all false worships, the manifold idolatries in the oppressive structures that do not let man be man because they do not let God be God. These deifications of nation, or profit, or creed, or will, or power, or religion, only have the lie given to them by the demand of *Tawhid*. Only the right absolute duly subdues the false ones. Pagan superstition may have naively—perhaps in measure innocently—multiplied its worships, so exposed to chance and menace was their primitive pre-science. Far more heinous are the enthronements of the modern scene. The tasks we had in view in Chapter 8—and not least among them the usurpers of Allah in religion itself—reach back into the authority of the crowning principle enshrined in *Allahu akbar*.

ii

In the context of this final chapter there are two broad duties. One is to explore a divine sovereignty thus conditioning itself on human fellowship, the other is to know aright the moral realism that justifies the decision, in Christianity, for that meta-history of 'the Christ of God' studied in Chapter 5. The question, then left open, asked why the Gospel in the early Church made so much turn on what might thereby seem to have been over-valued and overloaded with significance, namely the Passion of Jesus.

These two belong together. For, in studying the absolute theism by which Islam is normally identified in the popular mind worldwide, we need the perspective Christianity affords on how perversely humankind at large has sinfully called it into question. It will be no bad things to conclude with honest realism while spires are still allowed to dream.

But first there is the question whether the absolute accents in which Islam is thought to speak of Allah, the imperious tones of *Allahu akbar*, were ever consistent with the humanism of the Qur'an and its perception of the real mandate to our creaturehood in clear trust with the world. We must beware of a zeal so absolute for divine unity that we fail to align that zeal with the magnanimity that is the clue to it. Affirming the divine unity in the setting of chronic paganism may have concealed from rightly zealous unitarians that there are other, more insidious denials to refute, if their theism is truly to bring an undivided worship learned in a comprehending theology.

What is at issue here may be clarified by ideas of divine suspicion, or even envy, towards humans current in the Graeco-Roman world. It was as if the gods felt umbrage at what humans could achieve in the mundane realm and became jealous of those mortal inferiors indulging the freedom of their voyages, the privilege of their deeds. Such deities, with their caprice and their jealousy, had to be placated and appeased or human affairs would be jeopardised by their unpredictable enmities.[1]

Far different the world of Biblical and Quranic divine generosity that had let out the good earth on a lease of trust to humankind to preside over its dependable and subduable resources and so become, in the modern term, entrepreneurs. 'Allah has caused you to be colonists (i.e. 'imperialists') in the earth,' says Surah 11.61.[2] The range of our competence, to be sure, is not infinite but it is generously wide and sure and—wondrously to realise—it is not withdrawn, despite the havoc and the ruin we perpetrate in our long story. We are back where we began in Chapter 1.

Humankind are not chained to barren rock and forbidden to draw power from the sun. That was the classic fate of Prometheus in the ancient legend, whereas man in the Semitic tradition is Promethean indeed in the achieved ambition to possess the earth and to master its secrets, which are of a sort to present their tokens to his steady search. Such is the 'dominion', the *khilafah*, humankind so evidently exercises and which contemporary developments in technology, far beyond the first wheel, the first plough, so unmistakably demonstrate.

The creation, then, and our creaturehood in and over it, have to be central to a right theology of the divine unity. To exclude them from the reckoning would be to distort all reckoning itself. There cannot be a confession of the divine unity which does not incorporate a recognition of the divine creativity in all the magnanimity of its human ends, its human programmatic.[3] The final and abiding sovereignty of God is not in question nor, under it, is the real entrustedness of humankind. *Deus semper major*, 'God is ever greater' with us humans ever lower. So to acknowledge is the meaning of our being and our learning.

---

[1] This notion of 'jealousy' among Graeco-Roman deities is not to be confused with the Mosaic address to Jewry: 'The Lord thy God is a jealous God,' where the meaning stands in the theme of 'covenant' and 'chosen-ness' and land destiny and connotes, rather, a 'zealousness' in their pursuit. At least in the early Biblical days, reflected in the Book of Judges, it would seem that similar patronage with tribal and territorial liabilities was coveted or enjoyed, e.g. Chemosh for Moab.

[2] This translation of *ista'marakum* is proper for the universal truth of the gift of habitat for inhabitants. Modern Arabic uses the same verbal root for the political thing when 'invaders' settle and take power who were never native. In the basic sense 'we are all imperialists' in our agronomy, our techniques and our economies.

[3] 'Progammatic'—not meaning here that God's creation is not verily committed into human hands to make fruitful, but that this tenure is set for human development and for the manifold cultures 'nature-under-man' is fitted to yield.

It is powerfully confirmed by the whole reality of prophethood which has at its heart the enjoining of creaturely submission as response to divine Lordship. Prophets sent to the human scene are the surest index to our human dignity as earthly managers under God, the urgent witness to the sole claim of the sovereignty that has it so. Prophets would be pointless if something intrinsic with God was not crucially at issue in a destiny of duty intrinsic to man. The *Shari'ah* they brought, the 'limits' they drew, the pleas they uttered, the warnings they gave—all these demanded to be received and understood as how the unity of Allah related to the human scene. The sending of the prophets made plain that the unity was no abstract proposition, no fond idea, but a dynamic sole authority obtaining imperatively over all things human in their quality as *amanah* and, therefore, asking in the haunting words of Surah 7.172: 'Am I not your Lord?' That an indubitable imperative was also a gentle interrogative captures the whole truth.

It was surely that inter-relation between the sovereign Oneness of Allah and the genuine vocation of humans that brought the *Shahadah* to its otherwise puzzling formula: *La ilaha illa-Allah: Muhammadun Rasul Allah*. How eloquent is this unembarrassed juxtaposition of the divine and the human, the Sender and the sent, the Lord of the messenger and the messenger of the Lord. There could be no more emphatic witness, for and to the Muslim faith, than its inclusive confession in seven words, those fifteen syllables, concerning how the unity of God has its counterpart in the human realm thus humanly summoned to *islam*. God has His purposes as we make them ours.

iii

Yet Islam in its historical shape and story has often seemed to teach and require a monotheism so solitary as to leave scant room for the whole reality of a created order and a human sub-creativity.[4] It no doubt did so unwittingly, though aspects of Islamic theology seem to have zealously wanted utmost severity in the concept of *Tawhid*. Such absolutists for Allah, ignoring the implications of their realized creaturehood and of their confession of Muhammad as *Al-Rasul*,

---

[4] Creative' but also 'sub', i.e. within limits—spacious as these are—but still both tributary and liberating This double truth of humankind in *khilafah* means being over things and under God.

yearned to relate all things to God as—for them—the properly inclusive confession of His sovereignty. Divine *qadr* and *qada'*, of 'will' and 'decree', were involved. It seemed necessary to believe that all the acts of humans, even of adulterers, murderers and unbelievers, were ordained to be by them committed, so that somehow guilt belonged to them in the action but not liberty in the doing. Or, in the difficult rescue of responsibility, theologians like the great Abu Hasan 'Ali al-Ash'ari (873-935) proposed the formula: 'Allah wills the action in the will of the doer.' If one were then seemingly invited to ask: 'Could the willer have helped willing it when Allah willed it in his will?' the question was held to be one 'not to be raised.' For the freedom still seemed to be excluded while, mysteriously the 'fate' had been reprieved. It was, of course, vital in some sense to retain human responsibility lest ethics be impossible. Yet responsibility needed to be conditioned—if not also forfeited—by absolute divine decree.

It has been a frequent habit of philosophers, in this and other realms, virtually to give back in an answer the very question on which they set out. But the real issue here, all theological subtlety apart, is to recover and hold the irreducible theology of divine creation, and human creaturehood under prophetic 'guidance' *(huda)*, as primary definitives in the divine unity. The Qur'an, no less than the Bible, is the conclusive witness to that theology. Our faiths—to speak crudely—cannot rightly 'unify' if they somehow 'de-create'. Or, positively, we confess that 'God is One' in owning Him 'maker and fashioner of the human world'. That 'there is none like to Him' (Surah 112) is a confession made in, and because of, creaturehood where alone it becomes at once, and Islamically, a responsive affirmation. The shape of human cognisance, which the 'God is One' witness draws gladly from us, is index to us of a seeking love beyond us which devised it so. If, as we noted earlier, we have 'been let be' in order 'to let God be' in our entrusted world, that must constrain our undiverted worship of His 'being', eternally 'underived and Self-complete'. (Surah 112)

Seeing that utterly rigorous perceptions of divine unity have prevailed in much of Muslim history,and given they so far dominate the popular distortions of the Islamic image in the West, and given further that they are so far at odds with the fundamentals of a Quranic theology of creation and humankind, it is vital that Islamicists, inside and outside the faith-community, should revise and correct the image and let *Allahu akbar* proclaim the fullest reach of magnanimity. Is not 'magnanimity' what *akbar* tells?

Allowing the ascription of praise to contain the whole generosity that creation and prophethood declare does not only fit a theology taking technology into its hallowing stride. It also pays grateful tribute to the witness in the human scene that first gave it currency in the Arab tongue. There must always be lively recognition of the sound initial motive then for Islam's radical emphasis on *Tawhid*, as strenuously countering the pagan factors in pluralisms in the there and then. These had powerful vested interests in the prestige and the commerce of pilgrimage which could only be defeated by the single-minded conviction that 'God is One' to which Muhammad's Meccan preaching insistently held.

Today's heirs, in their gratitude for what that heritage has made them, must sustain it in a different scene. The idolatries that now flout *Tawhid* are of a different order. They belong instead with the seeming irrelevance of God in a self-absorbed—if not self-betraying—culture of secular presumptions perversely drawn from the pride of a technology seen, not as enabled by a gracious divine bestowal in trust, but by human prowess alone. The forces that mould and decide the patterns of the world, via human surveillance and control, are read in secular idolatry as ours by right of skill, not by deed and gift of grace.

This situation is not to be brought back into the inclusion of a grateful celebration and a right worship, i.e. into the meaning of *Tawhid*, by the sort of bare assertion that has not taken account of how apparently plausible the secular version looks—and looks not only to technicians in their technique-inclosed laboratories but, more, to humans everywhere experiencing the massive efficiencies of science. That 'God is greater' has now to be said, not only with a new and different urgency, but with a new and intelligent awareness of its seeming pointlessness in a world calculated to have us think that we are on our own, so much left to us to do if it is ever to be done, to invent if it is ever to be had, to afford if it is ever to be afforded.

Have we not reached a point where, somehow, atheism does not need to be vociferous, the sense of God having become so rarefied, the will to worship so sluggish? The Lord who has 'let us be' in all our competences can be effortlessly 'let not be' in our unprecedented indulgence of the privilege. Where the impulse to gratitude has lost its vision, the drift to transcendent de-valuing begins. The Qur'an always saw *kufr* (God-negation) as antithetical to *shukr* (thankfulness).[5] The most grievous form of negation is not the laboured disproof of theology but rather the casual disregard. The God we ignore is the more excluded than the God we deny.

Somehow then the task of the intelligent theist is one of serving the recovery of attention. It is one that can only well be helped by those who are attentive themselves, attentive, that is, to the case and the logic of the heedless, which is that 'we are on our own,'[6] in technological control, or, contrariwise as we have glimpsed in Larkin's poetry, in forlorn absence from the boon of meaning.

Merely then to enjoin in loud conviction *Allahu akbar* without evidence of lively sympathy with either of these shapes of 'God-excludedness', is to risk playing into its hands.[7] These His witnesses, the reaction will say, have not looked into the void we sense, they have not seen the humans that we are, whether in our techniques or in our tensions, our conquests or our quarrels with the world. The assurances that prevailed in Mecca or availed in Galilee have further now to reach in the perplexities we know. To propose a Centre for Islamic Studies and locate it alongside the long heritage of Oxford Divinity in Christ Church and the Schools is a gesture of realism only if the mutuality it suggests is ready for the vocation all theology has now to register.

iv

'Grasping the nettle' or 'having the bull by the horns' are crude analogies but they have point here. The very factors secularity takes as duly shaping the God-vacancy we have reviewed are to be perceptively read as the tokens whereby *Deus semper major* is truly confessed. 'What have you

---

[5] There are many passages where the two terms engage each other so that 'knowing no gratitude' (a common human feature) is 'owning no Lord'. Thus Solomon (27.40) says: 'God is testing me whether I would be thankful or whether I would deny ...' 'Most of them (humans) give no thanks' is the report of Surah 10.7, while 'perhaps they may be thankful' comes very frequently.

[6] Cf. Iris Murdoch, *The Sovereignty of Good*, London, 1970, p. 79. 'I shall simply assert it. I see no evidence to suggest that human life is not something self-contained ... We are simply here ...' Any 'dream' of more 'must be sought within a human experience which has nothing outside it.'

[7] The term 'God-excludedness' exactly fits the constant refrain of the Qur'an about those who think and live 'to the exclusion of God', *min duni-Llahi*.

that you did not receive?' is the perennial question. Your very capacity for a God-excluded reading of the world comes from a scheme of things that argues an apprenticeship to wonder and joy, to authority and liability. Your God-neglect is a misreading of the God-relation into which you are invited. It is the option left patiently available as alone consistent with the trust you have received and the sovereignty beyond it.

Great effort of mind is necessary for the Muslim instincts lodged in the cry *Allahu akbar* to steal away from the overwhelming, traditional, awareness of divine power and terrifying competence. All theisms, to be sure, register this temptation in their respective idioms of 'election', 'grace' and 'revelation'. But it is undoubtedly most intense in the Islamic sphere. The reasons are built into origins as Mecca and Medina knew them. They became implacable as Islamic theology grew more scholastic and articulate in obedience to what, in the discoursings of philosophy, seemed imperative. How could the omnicompetence of Allah be couched in less that entirely arbitrary terms? So it seemed for the Creed of Al-Nasafi (died 1142).

The vocation now is to realise, not that Allah is somehow less great than we used to hold, but differently greater. The notion of a sublime, spectator God is entirely excluded by the meaning of creation, of creaturehood within it and of prophet-sending for guidance. For these are obviously relational both ways. What they affirm humanly to be—as current secularity itself ever more extensively discovers *qua* the human imperium—they affirm divinely to be. The Architect is known by the architecture. What that presents, as humankind possesses it, is a magnanimous conferment of power and self-direction which—though they can be read as merely 'happening'—are more intelligently understood as a dignity received.

If on every human count, we do not 'have to do' with any spectator God, nor do we 'have to do' with some 'tyrant crowned'. Insofar as Islam has thought, or has been perceived to think, in such terms, the repudiation properly comes from Quranic norms themselves. To have them do so is the urgent current task of Islamic studies. In no way is it a matter of 'Christianizing' Islam with a mind to how Christian faith, via faith in the Incarnation and Passion of Jesus, has a more 'gentle' omnipotence. The charge of 'Christianizing' has often mistakenly been made.[8] The case for Allah differently *akbar* being pleaded here is had on exclusively Islamic grounds.

---

[8] For example, most recently in Ziauddin Sardar, *Orientalism*, Milton Keynes, 1999, pp. 80-81.

The fact is that the more implacably we 'tyrannize' our measure of divine greatness, the more dangerously we incline people to atheism. For we call in question—all theological subtleties apart—the index of our own human-ness. We disesteem the sacraments we discover in our personhood, our sexuality, our wonder at ourselves. To make a tyrant of the divine is to tyrannise the human—the arbitrariness of the One in the subjugation of the other. A sphere of tyranny either way could never be a realm meant for prophets, needed or heeded. Nor could it be reconciled with 'the God of justice' repeatedly so known in the Qur'an.[9]

Quizzically Christian as he was, it was still on fully Islamic ground that Robert Browning cried:

Pure faith indeed—you know not what you ask!
Naked belief in God the Omnipotent,
The Omniscient, Omnipresent, sears too much
The sense of conscious creatures to be borne.[10]

The poet does not deny those attributes: he tempers their meaning by the 'naked' word. They are not a law unto themselves so that they cease to be the law of the divine nature. Allah is not One for whom the sheer exercise of untrammelled sovereignty, as distinct from its truly sovereign ends—and the human terms of these—is a crude indulgence for which to have means relentlessly to wield. Just as hypocrisy in worship can never be a true worship so bare tyranny in God can never be a divine Lordship.[11]

For it obviates the necessary role of the human spirit in the implementation of the divine will, embodied in the text of the Qur'an and the laws of the *Shari'ah*. Time shapes that necessity for 'us in line with God' and does so unremittingly. Just thirty years ago, Fazlur Rahman thought that, in about a decade (1980) Muslim thinkers 'would come to see that the only way of genuinely implementing the purposes of the Qur'an' would be to bring *fiqh* 'under strictly historical study'. Otherwise Islam would be reduced to a set of rites with diminishing emotional attachment.[12] Three decades have now passed.

---

[9] See Muhammad Daud Rahbar, *God of Justice: Ethical Doctrine of the Qur'an*, Leiden, 1960.

[10] *Poetical Works*, Oxford. 1940, p. 444 ('Bishop Blougram's Apology').

[11] It belongs with the concept of *shirk:* all worship of God that has ulterior motives or is not an end in itself commits the sin of the *mushrik* who is never a true monotheist.

[12] Fazlur Rahman in ed. E J Jurji, *Religious Pluralism and World Community*, Leiden, 1969, p. 261-2.

Back in 1954, the historian, Ahmad Amin, referring to abrogation in the Qur'an, observed:

> If the Prophet were alive today and had to deal with the circumstances with which we are today confronted, then some verses of repeal would certainly be revealed to him.[13]

But which verses and 'repealed' in what sense? And who is to say, seeing that 'repeal' within the Qur'an ceased when it was closed— as, indeed, all prophethood was held to be after Muhammad? Who then is to say, and say now? Such surmisings about 'adaptation' under the exigencies of ongoing time have been widely current since Ahmad Amin's day. Their significance here, in a random citing, is simply the fact that 'the things of God' in holy writ and divine law are cast back upon the human mind in their reception, the human will conditioning their authority.

It follows that we can only 'be absolute for Allah' by the reverent lights of our mortal trustedness with His sacred will. It is clear that, in literal terms, no theocracy is ever possible, if we understand the term as the immediate incidence of the divine will upon the earthly scene, unpartnered by humankind. If we want to use the term, theocracy finds agency in human minds and means and these must inevitably situate its working. Such was the reality in prophethood itself as duly recruited for divine purposes, not because of some divine inadequacy but as the crucial form of adequacy in the givens of time and place. The same holds true of what Christian faith understands about 'God in Christ', namely the omnipotence of God as being where creation, revelation, redemption, tell it as it is. The words of F H Bradley that 'when the concept of God passes into that of the Absolute, God is lost and religion with Him,'[14] are true for Islam as for any and every theism.

If here is the central task of Islamic studies inside the worldwide Muslim community, any Oxford location underlines the immediate corollary. It is that any fellowship, or only adjacency, on the part of Christians, creates sharp psychic problems discouraging even the recognition, still more the undertaking, of the issues. To think Allah 'differently greater' than long tradition held is seen as subtle propaganda

---

[13] In Muhammad Yusuf Musa, *Jurisprudence in the Book and the Sunnah*, Cairo, 1954, p. 15 *(Fiqh al-Kitab wa-l-Sunnah)*.

[14] Cited in F Copleston, *Religion and the One*, London, 1982, p. 91.

or wilful subversion, and not as a genuine interior theme. Wisely read, secularity bred of technology might be asking both our theisms to have our awareness of God tuned aright to our awareness of human autonomy. For only then will our worship be no idle fantasy, no lust for solace, no device for moral evasion, but, instead, a context for the due discipline and consecration of all our techniques. These are full of menace. *Allah akbar*, rightly meant and fully cried, is their only final safety.

From power that meant to be, and stay, absolute, no creation could derive. Divine omnipotence pertains to our creaturely autonomy in the meaning of grace, not in that duress which would be a sort of 'unbecoming' of the human. There is no doubt that this belongs inside Islamic theology as the clear mandate of its entire source in Scripture and the Prophet. As exegesis and Tradition possess these, they only recapitulate this truth. We need to see the thrust of secularity reinforcing it, a thrust that only becomes a threat if it is not taken as a summons to surer vocation with our theology.

V

If in this way, our theologies send us—for their own integrity—to a right perspective on humanity, on the human factor in the divine economy as called into the purposes of the One sovereign Lord, then 'Islam among the spires' must be firmly sited there. The human dimension in custodial creaturehood becomes, as we have seen, the setting of the rule of God. That total secularity finds it the setting for the entire elision of Allah only makes a theological humanism the more crucial. When Philip Larkin in his awkward way in 'Church Going' thought the place 'a serious house on serious earth', the sentiment—for less ambiguous reasons—would be apt on Muslim lips about the mosque as 'proper also to grow wise in'.[15]

Things human, then, in both the Quranic and the Biblical revelations are plainly, unequivocally crucial to the things of God—a cosmic situation willed into being by the divine will to have it so. The

---

[15] *Loc. cit.*, p. 98. 'Ambiguous' in that he is not 'going' to church for worship but 'dropping in' there while cycling. His mood is detached and ironic, even laconic ('... up at the holy end ...') It deepens, however, and grows serious, from the sense of time and the sacred rites in which folk through long years have registered the cycle of their mortality—all a familiar Larkin theme now movingly 'housed' in a church.

pivotal passage in Surah 2.30—as we have seen already—makes it clear that the human role of trustee over the natural order was decisively taken on the part of Allah in over-ruling all angelic demur about its evident risk, even its sorry folly. Creaturehood, in that intriguing play on words, *khaliqah/khalifah* (creature/custodian) left the world prey to the 'corruption' certain to flow from law-ignoring, fractious, volatile beings such as humans are.[16] Such the deferential view of the angels in heavenly counsel, their view still more trenchantly urged by *Al-Shaitan,* the arch-accuser. They were over-ruled. The Lord knew His own purpose. Humankind should know that they had behind them the explicit mandate from God to undertake the *amanah*, the trust of history, with the assurance of its warrant beyond all counter dispute around the risks it harboured.

Biblical 'dominion' is no less real a dignity. Both Scriptures have Adam conversant with the names of things[17]—such nomenclature being the first necessity, the primary instinct, of the will to mastery and the rudiment of science. History in the space and time of God's creation is realised as the due *imperium* of man, a sub-sovereignty where this human stature is the index to divine wisdom commissioning creaturely agency.

All else follows. Prophethood, for guidance and tuition, is doubly the divine tribute to the instrumentality, the divine concern for the frailty, of the human governance of the created order. Prophets are supremely the monitors from heaven as mentors of the earthbound. Their summons and their cares are plainly the corollary of the human liability for history, the human liability to err and stray. There would be no point in prophets in a universe of innocent spectators, every point in a scene of incipient perversity with vital stakes that are both God's and man's.

'A serious earth', indeed. It is one the Qur'an interprets with entire corroboration. With the grounding of acknowledged creaturehood, humankind is encompassed with the holy law, the limits of conduct, the directives for society. The pre-Islamic 'ignorance' is eliminated in and by the inclusive, final Scripture where all dubiety is at an end. The truth

---

[16] Given that the earliest scribes of the Qur'an used few diacritical points, it has been conjectured that *khalifah* might be read as *khaliqah*, there being just one 'dot' different between *fa'* which has one and *qaf* which has two. In that event the play on words further makes the meaning clear. The 'creature' is the 'custodian'. The context is about the one in the capacity of the other. The angels, thinking themselves far more apt custodians, want to dissuade Allah from taking so hazardous a step.

[17] In Genesis he names them, in the Qur'an their names are told him. Either way there is no 'dominion' over nature that cannot first identify 'things' it contains. The steady advance of science has multiplied more and more the names it must employ.

of divine law thus mediated to a creaturehood whom it perfectly fits[18] is enshrined in a structure of 'Pillars' fitted to enable and discipline a humanity broadly amenable to their authority and their discipline. Islam, as both faith and form in religion, has ideally and realistically afforded to our creaturehood the meaning and the means of its fulfilment.

'The serious earth' and its serious faith-and-life system have been brought together with a convincing finality both credal and legal, definitive and practical. A revelatory finality has issued into a *Shari'ah* where community reads its proper destiny. That community, in the fast and the pilgrimage, possesses powerful organs of solidarity. They are corroborated by the factor of habituation supremely learned in the discipline of five daily prayers. These, on the one axis to Mecca, converge like the spokes of a cycle wheel drawing the far reaches of concentric circles of their world's *maharib* (s. *mihrab*—the niche direction to Mecca)—spokes which become caravan routes and airline skyways in the pilgrim season. Together these reinforce, in a way unique to Islam, the awareness of identity as incentive to the loyalty they transact.

That solidarity via habituation has its social expression in the duty of *zakat*, of almsgiving to educate property and wealth towards public liability. The pattern of prostration in *Salat*, bringing the erect posture that is the symbol of the human 'kingdom' in the external world by stages of deliberateness to the ground, can be seen as—in a Christian term— the 'sacrament' of God-awareness subduing all the aspects of what that 'kingdom' holds in trust. The brow that comes to earth in an act of humility is the very organ of the wisdom that obeys.

Over all, ever since the outcome of the Hijrah to the second city of Islam in 622, there has been, and ideally needs to be, the aegis of the Islamic state. The centuries-long caliphate by which Muhammad's personal rule (though not his inalienable prophethood) was passed to successors, ended in 1924 but the sundry nation states in Islam sustain the strong tradition of a political religion in that Muslims are only truly ruled by Muslims, the faith and the authority being one. The presiding warrant of the Islamic state is the guarantor of Muslim society.

These several dimensions and factors of Muslim fulfilment of Islam, of the Islamic shaping of Muslims, incorporate a deep *gravitas* of individual responsibility. The Qur'an's theme of 'forwarding' whereby

---

[18] Surah 30.30 has the word *fitrah* for (human) 'nature' that may also indicate 'religion'. The verse, with others, yields the conviction that Islam is the religion ideally matching what human nature needs.

deeds of daily life are garnered into celestial record, their worth or unworth ledgered, lays a rigorous onus on personal conformity. The 'scales' of a 'just balance' are awaiting the reckoning of the last assize. Negligence nullifies a heedless prayer just as carelessness distorts a recital of the Qur'an. Focusing a right 'intention' needs to precede all the rites of the believer.

This intense personalism in Islam obscures the inherent vicariousness of human life, as we studied it in a preceding chapter. All accounts *qua* guilt, if not *qua* incidence, are severely individual and there is no mutual burden-bearing. 'No man may deliver his brother,' nor do the solidarities of guilt, so apparent in the cumulative wrongs of systems and societies, come squarely into the private onus of the private self in Islam. Yet institutions, too, have guilt. Divine vigilance, the awe of truth's finality, the framework of a comprehensive structure and the onus of a last reckoning—all these mean that the being of the loyal Muslim is a soul-theocracy of deeply reverential order and concerted meaning.

It is this very privateness which underwrites its other crowning feature, namely a confidence in the amenability of humans to divine law, The two belong together. Because the faith has so comprehensively received the necessities for its due achievement, it need contemplate no radical despair nor question the viability of its sober expectations. This does not mean that it can lapse into sanguine ease—a temptation its own disciplines exclude. The Qur'an makes ample reference to the ruination of ancient tribes, the calamities they brought upon themselves by their heedlessness when prophets came. It knows well that men and societies are capable of *zulm al-nafs*—'It was their own selves they wronged.'[19] Indeed, alongside all the foregoing as to human law-conforming, it would be readily possible to draw from the Qur'an a portrait of humankind as dark as by any Isaiah or Paul.[20] The honesty of the Qur'an can be as impressive as its confidence in due submission—if we can forget the collective guilt of institutions.

---

[19] One might compare Hosea: 'O Israel, thou hast destroyed thyself.' (13.9) *Zulm* utmost wrong, is very frequently found in the Qur'an in its several derivations. Self-violation as a reality in life makes clear that the Qur'an has a radical measure of the human crisis.

[20] Note, for example, as well as *zulm*, the use of *marad*, 'sickness', to describe evildoers. Also the dark panorama it frequently draws of tribal history and past calamities visited on the obdurate. Surah 50.37 on one such occasion, adds: 'Truly there is much thoughtfully to ponder for whoever has a heart or heeds with alert perception.'

Given the criteria as they are, such deeper realism must be held a minor key. Both measures anyway come under the awesome writ of the last judgement, the tribunal so vividly drawn in the Qur'an with its contrasted destinies of Heaven and Hell. They may be read as requital, either way, of Islam's enabled attainers and the miscreants who would not take its admirably 'straight path'.

vi

Such, then, is the seriousness of Islam. How readily Muslims could fit themselves into Oxford University's *Dominus Illuminatio Mea*, 'the Lord my light'. The pronoun 'my' is at the heart of Islamic personalism, and Allah is 'the light' whose revelation, with its sequel in *Shari'ah* and communal structures, as we have reviewed them, illuminates the patterns proper to human life.[21] In these terms 'Islamic studies' could well present themselves amid the spires.

If we think these studies associates of a Christian architecture—architecture only being Christian by dint of faith and worship truly underwriting it—then we must reckon with how our common humanism leads us into a radical contrast. There is a clear kinship in all the foregoing in Islam with the central theme of Paul in his Letter to the Roman Christians—a document which we can regard as the inaugurating treatise of Christian theology. It has the identical theme of the crisis of a creation made subject to human *khilafah*. The human factor is the crux both in the Qur'an and in Romans of a created order whose destiny turns on the quality of the human custody in which it lies.

There is, however, a radical difference. Paul sees that creation waiting for these humans to be genuine sons of God.' (8.19f.) Its subjection runs into deeper reaches of travail described as *hupetage*, translated as 'subjection,' 'vanity', 'frustratedness', even 'futility', akin to the Qur'an's 'corruption' *(fasad)*. This is the 'calamitous thing' (Paul's Greek says *mataioteti*) the angels had grimly foreseen and feared when Allah proposed the human trust. Romans has the same *hupotasso* (Greek verb) 'prospective hope' (where risk is present). But the entire theme of man's jurisdiction, over nature under God, is read in more sombre, tragic terms.

---

[21] 'Proper' in the sense of their suiting what human nature requires. (See note 18) Other faiths are sometimes reckoned by Muslims as too ascetic, too idealistic, impractical, so that we are ill-served by them.

Nature shares man's destiny but his 'jurisaction' (should we name it rather than 'jurisdiction'?) holds a darker menace. It has some echo of the *al-masir* of the Qur'an, the cumulative tally of ill-doing that hardens into fate. Humans are read as subverting the dignity a generous Lord bestowed on them, so that the created order they were meant to handle with due God-fearing sincerity, 'groans and travails' neath their hand.

So Paul—in a sense more sombre than the lines of that Victorian Oxonian, Gerard Manley Hopkins (1844-89):

> And all is seared with trade: bleared, smeared with toil;
> And wears man's smudge and shares man's smell ...
> And for all this, nature is never spent ...[22]

being 'charged with the grandeur of God'. Those marks of human hands, by the full measure of what Paul is telling in his high lyricism in Romans 8, leave no room for being sanguine about the human crisis nor as to its correction by the light of tuition and Scriptural education only. The human predicament, as he feels he fathoms its deepest reach, tells a perversity that is not halted by reproach nor 'de-perverted' by counsel and warning. For it possesses a capacity to acknowledge law and, doing so, defy it, to appreciate the good and turn toward the false. It has a proneness to wrong in what the Qur'an, too, knows as *al-nafs al-ammaratu bi-l-su'*, and *lawwamah*, 'the soul with a bias to wrong' and 'self-blaming'.[23] Like the young Isaiah realising, through the Temple vision, his own and his people's wrongness, Christian perception of the self finds it can only first relate to divine sovereignty in self-accusation and a will to penitence.

Gerard Manley Hopkins' 'seared, bleared, smeared' line had in poetic view the peril of the landscape from the tenancy of man, the resilience of nature hardly surviving our vulgar utility, our artifices of exploitation. A poet could be even less confident now when 'the ooze of oil' spills from the *Exxon Valdez*, and nature is 'spent' more callously. Such thoughts are only half a story.[24] The human custody he ponders has for Paul in Romans—and elsewhere—a sterner indictment that reaches beyond what wistfully or savagely we do with things. It has in mind what

---

[22] Gerard Manley Hopkins, *The Poems*, Oxford. 1970. p. 66, 'God's Grandeur'.

[23] Surah 12.53—on the lips of Joseph in his hour of great temptation and 75.2.

[24] One of many catastrophic oil-pollutions which occurred in Alaska on 24 March 1989 when eleven million gallons of oil polluted the shore. Hopkins' poem thought on 'the ooze of oil crushed', doubtless in some fruit garden or an olive-press.

we *are* in soul. The New Testament probes beyond doing to being. 'Wretched man that I am,' Paul cries, 'the good I would I do not;' 'the evil I would not is what I do!' His dilemma is beyond the writ of good advice, beyond the reach of moral education, since—given the set of his will—it is precisely the valid ethic that accuses him.

'Light *and* salvation' was what the old psalmist said (27.1) when Oxford University took its briefer motto from him. Is it not here that we come to the very core of inter-religious studies in any place of higher education? Is 'light' itself 'salvation' so that 'illumination' takes the will also in hand? Why did the psalmist add the second noun and, adding it, what did he intend it to mean? Maybe such illumination as we are led by our faiths to think the Lord has granted is itself all the 'salvation' His mercy offers and all our situation requires.

The secular mind, opting out of theism altogether, would be likely so to think. For it is common with them to hold that the Christian appeal for 'the saviour', being totally unfounded, is no more than a lust for solace, a quest to be consoled. And consolation, if we are honest, is not to be had. The yearning for it is simply an extravagant indulgence in proud self-importance which it would be braver to deny ourselves.[25] Singing of 'a second Adam (who) to the rescue came' is a coward's music.

Many in Sunni Islam would certainly agree.[26] The ground of given law suffices. We do not go to the Qur'an for 'rescue' but for 'submission', not for initiation into God's grace but for directive into His will. That might well seem the more fitting posture, given an absolute reading of divine command.

Yet may not a will for 'salvation' re-assert itself and be authentic on the very ground of law itself? We have seen how we cannot omit from divine authority the reality of our custodial dignity. The precious *khilafah/ amanah* is never withdrawn. Indeed it is the very necessary realm of law itself and precedes it, so that without our human autonomy divine claim itself would have no territory.

It must follow that law itself argues something existential at the heart of all obedience. Because we are trustees/agents for Allah—by His own wise ordaining—His directives are not bare scripts for puppetry:

---

[25] This 'anti-consolation' stance and the firm exclusion of 'traditional' notions of God, characterise the work of Iris Murdoch, *The Sovereignty of Good*, London. 1970. Cf. note 6 above.
[26] 'Sunni' here because many in Shi'ah Islam cherish faith in one who is to appear, the now 'hidden' Imam, and in the redeeming virtues of the Martyrs.

they are His will's purposes enlisting servants' fulfilment. The point was finely made in the Jewish context by Claude Montefiori: 'In law, God's sanctifying presence is felt within the heart.'[27] When divine law comes into the human affections ('Lord, how I love your law!' Psalm 119.97)— an element that inter-relates divine and human—then much more than a taskmaster is present and law itself might let its ends take it beyond its legal means into something like 'salvation'. 'Am I not your Lord?' of 7.172 is hardly the kind of question which is set to fail of an answer when a sin-defeated humanity lacks the goodness that should bring one. The French Islamicist, Louis Massignon, thought of all the prophets as Allah's visitors calling us back to ourselves. Seen that way, their mission has to do with our 'self-wronging' *(zulm al-nafs)* as more than merely broken law. It follows that 'calling us back to ourselves' must take 'law-giving' into some 'saving word' of forgiveness and grace.

> God, stooping, shows sufficient of His light
> For us in the dark to rise by—and I rise ...[28]

So Robert Browning, never a student by 'the dreaming spires'. What he meant by 'stooping' Islam can not abide. For he meant Christ's Incarnation. Otherwise, he captures the whole 'light/salvation' theme. Perhaps he tells us where to leave it. Earlier chapters have sufficiently reviewed what unites and what divides two communities of faith, each with their bewildering inner diversities. The Christian requires a greater realism about humankind and so, in turn, a more radical expectation from God—an expectation seen as answered in the dimensions of Christology within theology. These, in the Incarnation and the Cross, stay to make Christianity at painful odds with their disavowal round the mosque.

Yet they are the Christian corollary about our entrusted humankind, as also the basic humanism of Islam. Either may find the other's 'light from God' 'insufficient' or perhaps 'luminous' in ways we cannot take. But 'light divine' is 'for us in the dark to rise by'. Only faiths read faithfully and fulfilled from within can fruitfully relate. We

---

[27] Claude Montefiore, *Lectures on the Origin and Growth of Religion*, etc. London, 1897, p. 548. A comparable accent on the 'heart' of both the Prophet and believers is clear in the Qur'an. Divine law has to be always more than legalism.

[28] Robert Browning, *The Ring and the Book*, London, ed. 1971, Book vii, 'Pompilia', p. 375, lines 1845-46.

have seen throughout how treacherous it is to academicise religion, to have it merely discursive when its essence is to demand allegiance. Islam in its Qur'an does not exist to be debated, nor does the Christian commission read: 'Go ye into all the world and discuss the Gospel.' That might argue a mutual intransigence of the sort a university must disavow. Oxford's precept to itself, *Dominus illuminatio mea*, came via a Hebrew Psalmist through a Latin Christian psalter and the New Testament tradition of faith. That corporate *mea* is much attenuated today with the secular hospitalities it concedes in the modern idiom of universities in the western world.[29]

'Our limping metaphor translate,' C S Lewis wrote, maybe referring to Chapel Prayer in Magdalen. In so far as 'Lord be our light' is of that order beneath all the sundry spires, his words could well be the university's at large. For their translation turns finally on the addressee. The first Apostles from Jerusalem knew well that *Illuminatio Domini* meant 'the light of the knowledge of the glory of God as in a face—the face of Christ.' (2 Corinthians 4. 6)[30] Paul was borrowing Aaron's theme of 'face as light'. The face of one crucified, surpassing all otherwise scripted text, is the Christian 'light' upon a crucifying world to tell the truth of its history's Lord.

Dominus illuminatio est is in the Arabic of Surah 24.35. Whether 'striding' or 'limping', 'partisan' or 'patient', the light metaphor is the Lord's to translate into our minds, ours to translate into where it takes us in the world. A university should carefully serve both necessities.

---

[29] Cf. how Iris Murdoch sees it: 'We do not have to believe in God to make sense of the motto of Oxford University, displayed upon an open book, *Dominus illuminatio mea. The Fire and the Sun: Why Plato Banished the Artists*, Oxford, 1977, p. 45

[30] He links it very firmly with the light of creation, seeing that 'the Word made flesh' is one with 'the Word that let us be.'

REFERENCES TO THE QUR'AN

INDEX OF NAMES AND TERMS

Other titles by Melisende

PATTERNS OF THE PAST, PROSPECTS FOR THE FUTURE:
THE CHRISTIAN HERITAGE IN THE HOLY LAND
eds.Thomas Hummel, Kevork Hintlian and Ulf Carmesund £15.00 ppr,
330 pages, 1999

PATTERNS OF THE SACRED, ENGLISH PROTESTANT AND RUSSIAN
ORTHODOX PILGRIMS OF THE NINETEENTH CENTURY
Thomas and Ruth Hummel £10.00 ppr, 96 pages, 1995

THE CHRISTIAN HERITAGE IN THE HOLY LAND
eds. A O'Mahony with G Gunner and K Hintlian £15.95 ppr, 320 pages, 1995

THE NOBLE HERITAGE, A PORTRAIT OF THE CHURCH OF THE
RESURRECTION
Alistair Duncan £15.00 hbk, 80 pages, 1986

MAMLUK JERUSALEM: AN ARCHITECTURAL STUDY
Michael Burgoyne £125.00 hbk, 622 pages, 1987
(World of Islam Festival Trust)

LIFE AT THE CROSSROADS. A HISTORY OF GAZA
Gerald Butt £16.95 hbk, 208 pages, 1995
(Rimal)

JERUSALEM: WHAT MAKES FOR PEACE!
A PALESTINIAN CHRISTIAN CONTRIBUTION TO PEACEMAKING
eds. Naim Ateek, Cedar Duaybis and Marla Schrader £12.50 ppr, 372 pages, 1997

WESTERN SCHOLARSHIP AND THE HISTORY OF PALESTINE
ed. Michael Prior CM £8.50 ppr, 128 pages, 1998

CHRISTIANS IN THE HOLY LAND
eds. Michael Prior and William Taylor £12.50 ppr, 254 pages, 1995
(World of Islam Festival Trust)

HOLY LAND–HOLLOW JUBILEE: GOD, JUSTICE AND THE
PALESTINIANS
eds. Naim Ateek and Michael Prior. £12.50 ppr, 334 pages, 1999

PALESTINIAN CHRISTIANS: RELIGION, POLITICS AND SOCIETY IN THE
HOLY LAND
A. O'Mahony £12.50 ppr, 224 pages, 1999

A THIRD MILLENNIUM GUIDE TO PILGRIMAGE TO
THE HOLY LAND
ed. Duncan Macpherson £7.95 ppr, 2000

FORTHCOMING

OTTOMAN JERUSALEM: THE LIVING CITY 1517-1917
eds. Sylvia Auld and Robert Hillenbrand
architectural survey by Yusuf Natsheh £145.00 hbk 2000
(Altajir World of Islam Trust)

DYING IN THE LAND OF PROMISE:
PALESTINE AND PALESTINIAN CHRISTIANITY
FROM PENTECOST TO 2000
Donald E Wagner £12.50 ppr, 2000

THE GIFT HALF UNDERSTOOD:
ESSAYS ON EUROPEAN THEMES
Alastair Hulbert £12.50, ppr 2000

FUSTAT GLASS OF THE EARLY ISLAMIC PERIOD:
FINDS EXCAVATED BY THE AMERICAN RESEARCH CENTER IN EGYPT
George T Scanlon and Ralph Pinder-Wilson £18.00, ppr 2000
(Altajir World of Islam Trust)

All available
from

Melisende
39 Chelmsford Road
London E18 2PW England
tel. +44 (0)20 8498 9768
fax +44 (0)20 8504 2558
e-mail: melisende@cwcom.net
www.melisende.cwc.net